PENGUIN BOOKS

Collected Poems

Tony Harrison was born in Leeds in 1937. His poetry includes *The Loiners*, which won the Geoffrey Faber Memorial Prize; *v.*, which became a cause célèbre when broadcast on Channel 4 in 1987 and was broadcast again in full on BBC Radio 4 in 2013; and *The Gaze of the Gorgon*, which won the Whitbread Prize for Poetry. He has written extensively for film, theatre and opera, producing work for the National Theatre, the Metropolitan Opera, the RSC, the BBC and Channel 4. He has received numerous awards, including the inaugural PEN Pinter Prize in 2009, the European Prize for Literature in 2011 and, most recently, the David Cohen Prize for Literature in 2015. He lives in Newcastle.

Collected Poems

TONY HARRISON

PENGUIN BOOKS

PENGUIN BOOKS

UK | USA | Canada | Ireland | Australia
India | New Zealand | South Africa

Penguin Books is part of the Penguin Random House group of companies
whose addresses can be found at global.penguinrandomhouse.com.

First published by Viking 2007
Published in Penguin Books 2016
001

Copyright © Tony Harrison, 2007

The moral right of the author has been asserted

Typeset by Rowland Phototypesetting Ltd, Bury St Edmunds, Suffolk
Printed in Great Britain by Clays Ltd, St Ives plc
A CIP catalogue record for this book is available from the British Library

ISBN: 978-0-241-97435-3

www.greenpenguin.co.uk

MIX
Paper from
responsible sources
FSC® C018179

Penguin Random House is committed to a
sustainable future for our business, our readers
and our planet. This book is made from Forest
Stewardship Council® certified paper.

CONTENTS

ACKNOWLEDGEMENTS

Some of these poems first appeared in the following collections, magazines and newspapers:

Earthworks (Northern House, Leeds, 1964)
Newcastle is Peru (Eagle Press, Newcastle, 1969)
The Loiners (London Magazine Editions, 1970)
Palladas: Poems (Anvil Press Poetry, 1975)
from The School of Eloquence (Rex Collings, 1978)
Continuous: 50 Sonnets from The School of Eloquence (Rex Collings, 1981)
A Kumquat for John Keats (Bloodaxe Books, 1981)
U.S. Martial (Bloodaxe Books, 1981)
Selected Poems (Penguin Books, 1984)
v. (Bloodaxe Books, 1985)
The Fire-Gap (Bloodaxe Books, 1985)
Selected Poems (Penguin Books, 1987)
Anno 42 (Scargill Press, 1987)
Ten Sonnets from The School of Eloquence (Anvil Press Poetry, 1987)
v. and Other Poems (Farrar, Straus and Giroux, New York, 1990)
A Cold Coming (Bloodaxe Books, 1991)
The Gaze of the Gorgon (Bloodaxe Books, 1992)
Laureate's Block (Penguin Books, 2000)
Under the Clock (Penguin Books, 2005)

Arion (Boston, USA); *The Guardian*; *The Independent*; *The Independent on Sunday*; *In Coda per Caronte* (Einaudi, Italy); *London Magazine*; *London Review of Books*; *Marxist Quarterly*; *Poesia* (Italy); *Poetry Review*; *Stand*; *Times Literary Supplement*

My Migratory Bird and the Divine

Once I let him go, since through Thy loving hand
Broken wings expand, so Thou couldst count my swallow
Fleeing my cold snow for fertile golden land.
When I command, my crippled bird must follow
His restless band out of Thine El Dorado,
Dropping wet guano in Thine old and loving hand.

The Hybrid Growth

Her roses were her life.

Her roses were the life death could not spare.
As gardener and growth she played her part.
For private use death grows a woman's heart.
They cultivated each with equal care.

With choicest heads her people fill her room.
They draw the blinds to hide the autumn light
She loved through trees at fealties with air.
These roses intercede with growing night
The live believe. They stifle death in bloom.

In time her heart will open out, the rose
Invested with new flags will strike its own.
The flowers' fallen horns are raised and blown
By night conspiring cautiously with sound.

They do not hear or know who have not found
A garden to ordain their ordered world.
She knew the way the rose's leaves unfurled
To dying out or dawn, that growing fails
The hybrid growth of time. And now she knows

Death warms his hands around her sprawling rose.
Lighter than life the fumes which he inhales
Afford him easy motion through the world.

The Flat Dweller's Revolt

Dogs in mangers feel, he thought, like this;
He cast bread on the pavement for the birds.
Their claustrophobic voices, hers and his,
Their guarded actions louder than their words,

The booming, morning wind brought back tenfold;
Time after time their suffocated talk
Filled and left, like rats a sodden hold,
His keeling mind: he had to go and walk,

To think of all he still had chance to save
And claim the open spaces of the park,
The earth that held his birthright and his grave,
And strictly meditate the fruitless dark.

He kicked the fuzzy stalks of London Pride,
Unfettered hairy seeds on tended plots:
That fallow night he hoped the wind had died
And, like unwanted children in cheap cots,

Between proud dahlias and hollyhocks,
On half-built sites the length and breadth of Leeds,
Neat crematorium, demolished blocks,
Like risen men, would stand the purple weeds;

And most profusely spread where common earth
Combined more spacious parents than his own,
Where such as he thought grimly on one birth
And ageing sons laid flowers on one stone.

That night he learnt himself by heart, his prayers
Unsaid for safety, summoned flesh and bone,
His ripe autumnal love and climbed the stairs
And in the bathroom, washing, begged the moon,

The queen of female courses and of tides,
To shine on insured love in rented rooms
And break the dykes of all protected brides
And flood the little land of fertile wombs.

The New Earth

Time may spur but will not bridle birth;
Death bore down together with the wife;
Two thirds the revolution of the earth
Brought a mortality as small as life.

Earth's from the start that clod of birth
Brushed from sheer life by such waves the moon
Recalls and hurls against the old cooled earth
That turns round slowly and is never soon.

The Promised Land

'I will allure her, and bring her into the wilderness, and speak
comfortably unto her.'

(Hosea ii.14)

Outside the storm drew tide and land,
And with the land, the promised seed.
The house she had, but not the need
   Her house would keep without
      where winds impede

The struggling winds and strangle trees.
(Outside there may be storm and flood;
Within, this wind should blow us good;
   There should be light and calm
      Upon the blood.)

Her carpet grew the perfect rose.
Her steady eyes absorbed the floor
And mine her face; night always tore
   My eyes away to put them back
      Outside her door.

(Let there be flood enough to make
This flower bloom around her toes,
And I would point and say, 'A rose,'
   And swiftly plucking it,
      'A dying rose.'

Again. 'Was that a shot I heard?')
Love is no luxury in war.
Love must be made like houses, or
   Like her contented cat
      Be shown the door,

To find outside the reason why
It has no right to purr like that.
The cat, indulged with cushions, sat
   Disdainful of its curdled cream
      And will grow fat.

On her devotion and replenished bowls.
Grow fat, immobile, tired, and die.
Her pet deflated, she might cry
   And want my soothing words,
      My soothing lie.

(Let there be flood enough to drown
This cat and make the desert green
For her, just brought ashore, to glean
   Us love.) And even then
      Things come between!

(And through the straits dividing us
As we stand and look across and wait
Until these endless seas abate,
   And I impatient so,
      For I am late,

Slow-melting, glacial dead
Dislodge and roll the yet to be
Into this old deterrent sea
   That shall make buoyant
      You and me;

And even at the water's edge
I am afraid.) I start, to see
At last a hand outstretched to me.
   I took it all for love.
      The offered tea

Was spilled, a dark stain disappeared,
Absorbed into that perfect rose,
Her life manures, and carpet grows
    For her to wear out daily
        As she goes.

The Pit of Perception

Upended roots, the bare November trees
Seemed growing upside down into the earth.
Broken twigs were strewn to burn or freeze,
The scattered leavings of inverted birth.

Behind, but barely glimpsed, the only signs
Of life were people, neither young nor old,
Transfigured forms, inhabitants of mines,
Earth-coloured, crumbling, drowned in gold.

Then sprinkled petrol leaped as startled flames.
Behind the heat the half-built houses shook,
Sinuous jambs and glassless window frames,
The forms dissolved and lost their human look.

Carved and polished trees and dinner ware
Of hardened clay. *O Fiat Lux!* There rise
The mountains, water falls, the land is there
And surfaced creatures see with human eyes

Dense undergrowth, ravines, denuded plains,
Corrugated, pitted ground, twin peaks
Above the chosen site of crystal brains,
The hall of perfect forms and shapeless freaks;

Microbial traffic, full canals, lithe sperms
Evolving generations of the blind,
Militant corpuscules combating germs,
The glutton cells that gorge upon their kind;

Cannibal or social, war or peace,
To make one tenant die or two unite
That out of huddled bondage they release
A third from hibernations into light.

Next summer when the earth turned up again,
With riddled wood and worn foundation stones,
A world of vegetation stripped of men,
The branches of the flesh stretched out their bones.

The Pathetic Fallacy

Antlers clean or charred, half-raised to gore
Some chancred mammoth with six crumpled horns,
Shattered bodies on a churned sea floor,
Trees with wet seal's muscles and bull's brawn.

The ocean just cleared off and left them there;
The hoarse asthmatic struggles of the strong
Beached creatures thrashing round for air;
The wind came like a passion one night long.

A strange man and a strange pale girl lay
Together on a hired bed. As if Christ could
(O Christ!) have risen with three days' decay,
Spring came like an infestation on the wood,

The crushed flung branches fattened their small lice;
Such lengthening shades of Eden as were thrown
That first wet April out of Paradise,
The dark seed leaping from pale groin to groin.

The Hands

All his hopes were hands, his ventures hands,
All hands; hands no less crucial, no less lithe
Than a desperate climber's or a drowning man's,
On swollen silks and bulging velveteens
Ran sideways on, stopped, slithered off, gained ground
Again, then flopped like frogs into a pond
And surfaced white and weightless like dead frogs.

And all the wine they hurried back and forth
For warmth into his mouth was but a drop
In all the coastless oceans that they pushed
Or scooped or drifted on, until they caught
An instant on a breast or thigh, or skulked
From hostility in some rank hair and scuttled off,
Sensing injury if they but stopped for breath.

Left to themselves again while others paired
Or nested gently on sweet hair, his crept away,
Albino things abandoned of their kind;
Crouched quivering on his face. He flung them down.
They bunched in terror from this savage beast.

They say that afterwards the pair of them
Were huddled on the parapet and he
Gazed at them hard, half lovingly, half cold,
Like a man at kittens he is going to drown.

He dropped them twitching in the cold canal.

Heavily weighted, they struggled well,
Kicking up the water, then went down.

A Part of the Mainland: Bardsey Island

Twenty thousand saints (all Welsh)
Are buried on the island, are its earth,
Each friable crumb of it, and every worm
Conceals some sanctity beneath its skin,
Each mashed morsel of tomorrow's fish,
Hauled over holy moonlight into Wales.

Wild holiness has risen in west Wales;
God wallows in the pigsties and is whirled
Beyond the snowblown Beacons in black gulls,
Crashes with clods between his toes onto the shires,
Slithers a little, dives into the sea off Hull
And strikes for Europe like a savaged whale;

And someone notes tonight the sea is rough,
And under it might note twenty thousand demons
(Foreign every one and certainly not Welsh)
Crawling on red claws across the sand.

Thomas Campey and the Copernican System

The other day all thirty shillings' worth
Of painfully collected waste was blown
Off the heavy handcart high above the earth,
And scattered paper whirled around the town.

The earth turns round to face the sun in March,
He said, resigned, *it's bound to cause a breeze.*
Familiar last straws. His back's strained arch
Questioned the stiff balance of his knees.

Thomas Campey, who, in each demolished home,
Cherished a Gibbon with a gilt-worked spine,
Spengler and Mommsen, and a huge, black tome
With Latin titles for his own decline:

Tabes dorsalis; veins like flex, like fused
And knotted flex, with a cart on the cobbled road,
He drags for life old clothing, used
Lectern bibles and cracked Copeland Spode,

Marie Corelli, Ouida and Hall Caine
And texts from Patience Strong in tortoise frames.
And every pound of this dead weight is pain
To Thomas Campey (Books) who often dreams

Of angels in white crinolines all dressed
To kill, of God as Queen Victoria who grabs
Him by the scruff and shoves his body pressed
Quite straight again under St Anne's slabs.

And round Victoria Regina the Most High
Swathed in luminous smokes like factories,
These angels serried in a dark, Leeds sky
Chanting *Angina –a, Angina Pectoris.*

Keen winter is the worst time for his back,
Squeezed lungs and damaged heart; just one
More sharp turn of the earth, those knees will crack
And he will turn his warped spine on the sun.

Leeds! Offer thanks to that Imperial Host,
Squat on its thrones of Ormus and of Ind,
For bringing Thomas from his world of dust
To dust, and leisure of the simplest kind.

Ginger's Friday

Strawberries being bubbled in great vats
At *Sunny Sunglow*'s wafted down the aisle.
He heard the scuffled vestments through the slats
And could not see but felt a kindly smile.
Grateful, anonymous, he catalogued his sin,
The stolen postcards and allotment peas;
How from his attic bedroom he'd looked in
On Mrs Daley, all-bare on her knees,
Before her husband straddled in his shirt,
And how he'd been worked up by what he saw;
How he'd fiddled with his thing until it hurt
And spurted sticky stuff onto the floor.
And last his dad's mauve packet of balloons
He'd blown up, filled with water, and tried on;
And then relief. The hidden priest intones:
Remember me to Mrs Kelly, John.

He loitered, playing taws until the dark
Of bad men with their luring spice and shell-
shocked feelers edged onto the empty park,
And everything that moved was off to tell.
His gaslamp shadows clutched him as he ran
Shouting his *Aves. Paternosters* stuck
At *peccata*, and the devil with his huge jam pan
Would change his boiled-up body back to muck.
And no Hail Marys saved him from that Hell
Where Daley's and his father's broad, black belts
Cracked in the kitchen, and, blubbering, he smelt
That burning rubber and burnt bacon smell.

The Pocket Wars of Peanuts Joe

'Poor old sport,
he got caught
right in the mangle.'

The -*nuts* bit really -*nis*. They didn't guess
Till after he was dead, then his sad name
Was bandied as a dirty backstreet Hess,
A masturbator they made bear the blame
For all daubed swastikas, all filthy scrawl
In Gents *and* Ladies, YANK GO HOME
Scratched with a chisel on the churchyard wall;
The vicar's bogey against wankers' doom.

We knew those adult rumours just weren't true.
We did it often but our minds stayed strong.
Our palms weren't cold and tacky and they never grew
Those tell-tale matted tangles like King Kong.
We knew that what was complicated joy
In coupled love, and for lonely men relief,
For Joe was fluted rifling, no kid's toy
He fired and loaded in his handkerchief.
Some said that it was shell-shock. They were wrong.
His only service was to sing *The Boers*
Have Got My Daddy and *The Veteran's Song*
And window-gazing in the Surplus Stores.
In allotment dugouts, nervous of attack,
Ambushing love-shadows in the park,
His wishes shrapnel, Joe's ack-ack *ejac-*
ulatio shot through the dark
Strewn, churned-up trenches in his head.
Our comes were colourless but Joe's froze,
In wooshed cascadoes of ebullient blood-red,
Each flushed, bare woman to a glairy pose.

'VD Day' jellies, trestle tables, cheers
For Ruskis, Yanks and Desert Rats with guns
And braces dangling, drunk; heaped souvenirs:
Swastikas, Jap tin hats and Rising Suns.
The Victory bonfire settled as white ash.
The accordion stopped Tipperarying.
It was something solemn made Joe flash
His mitred bishop as they played *The King*.
Happy and Glorious . . . faded away. *Swine!*
The disabled veteran with the medals cried.
The ARP tobacconist rang 999.
The Desert Rats stood guard on either side.
Two coppers came, half-Nelsoned, frog-
marched poor Penis off to a cold clink.
He goosestepped backwards and crowds saw the cock
That could gush Hiroshimas start to shrink.

A sergeant found him gutted like a fish
On army issue blades, the gormless one,
No good for cannon fodder. His last wish
Bequeathed his gonads to the Pentagon.

Allotments

Choked, reverted *Dig for Victory* plots
Helped put more bastards into Waif Home cots
Than anywhere, but long before my teens
The Veterans got them for their bowling greens.
In Leeds it was never *Who* or *When* but *Where.*
The bridges of the slimy River Aire,
Where Jabez Tunnicliffe, for love of God,
Founded the *Band of Hope* in eighteen-odd,
The cold canal that ran to Liverpool,
Made hot trickles in the knickers cool
As soon as flow. The graveyards of Leeds 2
Were hardly love-nests but they had to do –
Through clammy mackintosh and winter vest
And rumpled jumper for a touch of breast.
Stroked nylon crackled over groin and bum
Like granny's wireless stuck on Hilversum.
And after love we'd find some epitaph
Embossed backwards on your arse and laugh.
And young, we cuddled by the abattoir,
Faffing with fastenings, never getting far.
Through sooty shutters the odd glimpsed spark
From hooves on concrete stalls scratched at the dark
And glittered in green eyes. Cowclap smacked
Onto the pavings where the beasts were packed.
And offal furnaces with clouds of stench
Choked other couples off the lychgate bench.

The Pole who caught us at it once had smelt
Far worse at Auschwitz and at Buchenwald,
He said, and, pointing to the chimneys, *Meat!*
Zat is vere zey murder vat you eat.
And jogging beside us, *As Man devours*
Ze flesh of animals, so vorms devour ours.

It's like your anthem, Ilkla Moor Baht 'at.
Nearly midnight and that gabbling, foreign nut
Had stalled my coming, spoilt my appetite
For supper, and gave me a sleepless night
In which I rolled frustrated and I smelt
Lust on myself, then smoke, and then I felt
Street bonfires blazing for the end of war
VE and J burn us like lights, but saw
Lush prairies for a tumble, wide corrals,
A Loiner's Elysium, and I cried
For the family still pent up in my balls,
For my corned-beef sandwich, and for genocide.

Doodlebugs

Even the Vicar teaching Classics knows
how the doodled prepuce finishes as man,
a lop-eared dachshund with a pubis nose,
Caspar the friendly ghost or Ku-Klux-Klan,
and sees stiff phalluses in lynched negroes,
the obvious banana, those extra twirls
that make an umbilicus brave mustachios
clustered round cavities no longer girls'.

Though breasts become sombreros, groins goatees,
the beard of Conrad, or the King of Spain,
bosoms bikes or spectacles, vaginas psis,
they make some fannies Africa, and here it's plain,
though I wonder if the Vicar ever sees,
those landmass doodles show a boy's true bent
for adult exploration, the slow discovery
of cunt as coastline, then as continent.

The White Queen

1. *Satyrae*

I

Professor! Poet! Provincial Dadaist!
Pathic, pathetic, half-blind and half-pissed
Most of these tours in Africa. A Corydon
Past fifty, fat, those suave looks gone,
That sallow cheek, that young Novello sheen
Gone matt and puffed. A radiant white queen
In sub-Saharan scrub, I hold my court
On expat pay, my courtiers all bought.

Dear Mother, with your hennaed hair and eyes
Of aquamarine, I made this compromise
With commodities and cash for you, and walk
These hot-house groves of Academe and talk
Nonsense and nothing, bored with almost all
The issues but the point of love. Nightfall
Comes early all year round. I am alone,
And early all year round I go to town
And grub about for love. I sometimes cruise
For boys the blackness of a two-day bruise,
Bolt upright in the backseat of the *Volks*,
Or, when the moon's up full, take breathless walks
Past leprosarium and polo grounds
Hedged with hibiscus, and go my rounds
Of downtown dance and bar. Where once they used
To castrate eunuchs to be shipped off East,
I hang about *The Moonshine* and *West End*,
Begging for pure sex, one unembarrassed friend
To share my boredom and my bed – *one masta want
One boy – one boy for bed* . . . and like an elephant
That bungles with its trunk about its cage,
I make my half-sloshed entrances and rage

Like any 'normal' lover when I come
Before I've managed it. Then his thin bum
That did seem beautiful will seem obscene;
I'm conscious of the void, the *Vaseline*,
Pour shillings in his hands and send him back
With the driver, ugly, frightened, black,
Black, black. What's the use? I can't escape
Our foul conditioning that makes a rape
Seem natural, if wrong, and love unclean
Between some ill-fed blackboy and fat queen.

Things can be so much better. Once at least
A million per cent. Policeman! Priest!
You'll call it filthy, but to me it's love,
And to him it was. It *was*. O he could move
Like an oiled (slow-motion) racehorse at its peak,
Outrageous, and not gentle, tame, or meek –
O magnificently shameless in his gear,
He sauntered the flunkied restaurant, queer
As a clockwork orange and not scared.
God, I was grateful for the nights we shared.
My boredom melted like small cubes of ice
In warm sundowner whiskies. Call it vice;
Call it obscenity; it's love; so there;
Call it what you want. *I just don't care.*

Two figures in grey uniforms and shorts,
Their eyes on quick promotion and the tarts,
Took down the number of my backing car.
I come back raddled to the campus bar
And shout out how I laid a big, brute
Negro in a tight, white cowboy suit.

II

Advanced psychology (of 1910)
Bristled from thin lips the harmattan
Had cracked and shrivelled like a piece of bark.
She egged me on to kiss her in the scented dark,
Eyes bottled under contact lenses, bright
And boggling, as if for half the night
She'd puffed cheap hashish to console
Her for the absences, that great, black hole
Pascal had with him once, *l'abîme ouvert*
He thought was special but is everywhere.
He cackles from Heaven at the desperate Earth.

We permit ourselves too much satiric mirth
At their expense, and blame the climate, so
I touched her bosom gently just to show
I *could* acknowledge gestures, but couldn't stroke
Her leathery, dry skin and cracked a joke
Against myself about my taste in little boys.
Then the party drowned us in its noise
And carried us apart, I, to my jests,
She, to her gesturing with other guests.

I've seen her scrawny, listless husband still
Such rowdy booze-ups with a madrigal,
His tonic water serving for rare wine
Toasting the ladies with *O Mistress Mine*;
Sort of impressive. I confess such prick
Songs make me absolutely bloody sick,
But he can sing them straight at his *third* wife.
Changey-changey! But they can't change life,
Though they meditate together with joined hands,
Though his psyche flutters when he thinks he's kissed,
Cuddled and copulated with New Zealand's
Greatest, unpublished, *woman* novelist.

All night a badly driven armoured truck
With grinding gears crunched on the gravel, shook
The loose louvres and the damp mosquito mesh,
And glaring headlights swept across my flesh.
Back to loneliness, pulling myself off,
After a whole *White Horse*, with photograph
And drag, a Livingstone with coloured plates,
That good old stand-by for expatriates
Hooked on the blacks; again have to withdraw
Into myself, backwards down a corridor,
Where in one of many cold, white cells
They play cold water on my testicles,
When I should be breaking out . . . must . . . must
Matchet the creeper from my strangled lust.

The sticky morning comes and some loud gun
Fires short-distance shells into the sun.
Patrols and shots; the same trilingual drone
Goes on about curfews through a megaphone.
A new anthem: *tiddly-om-pom-pom*
Blares the new world like a Blackpool prom
And promises corruption's dead and lies
Riddled with bullets in three mortuaries.
An American's got it all on tape.
The proclamation: murder, looting, rape,
Homosexuality, all in the same breath,
And the same punishment for each – death, *death!*
He plays it back to half-seas-over, hushed
Circles in the bar. I flush with defiant lust.

Now life's as dizzy as the Book of Kells.
Thank God for London and Beaux/Belles.
I must get back again. I must, but must
Never again be locked away or trussed

Like a squealing piglet because my mind
Shut out all meaning like a blackout blind.

Next door, erotomaniacs. Here, queers,
And butch nurses with stiff hoses mock
As we grow limp, *Roundheads* and *Cavaliers*,
Like King Charles bowing to the chopping block.

IV
Insects strike the clapper. The school bell
Clangs for nothing. Nothing; and her little hell
Begins when darkness falls. Her garden moves
With mambas, leafage like damp leather gloves,
Cobras, rats and mice, and bandicoots,
The drunk *maigardai* and their prostitutes
Who help them pass their watch. Time drags
For such lonely, unlovable old bags.
There's too much spawning. Men! Beasts! Ticks!
Spawn in their swarmfuls like good Catholics.

She wanted children but she gets instead
Black houseboys leaving notes beside her bed:
Madam your man is me. Where is the yes?
Putting pressed frangipani in her dress.
She's not as desperate for a go as that.
She has her gaudy parrot and her spayed, grey cat
For company. *Babar*'s a champion impressionist
Of whisky noises when his owner's pissed.
She pretends he's learnt it when he's heard her wash
And offers visitors a choice of squash.

Darkness. The swoosh of soda and the glug
Of Scotch come from *Babar* as that drunken thug
She hired as a watchman and *must* fire, treads
Down her phlox and pees on her arctotis beds.

She knows what he's up to. Brute! The garage door
Swings on its hinges for the watchman's whore.
And now they're rocking. One cracked heel
Scrapes after purchase on her *Peugeot* wheel.
Rustle and gasp, black creatures claw
At one another in her packing straw.
You never know in these hot climates; *coups*
Can throw the whole white quarter on the booze.
Whisky and danger. Ah who knows? Who knows?
Some drunken Public Works might still propose.
But she wouldn't have him. No, not her. Boy!
She'll give you the sack for those grunts of joy.

v

Northwards two hundred miles, an emptiness
As big as Europe; *Sah'ra*; Nothingness.
South six hundred, miles of churning sea
Make of the strongest swimmer a nonentity,
Bleaching the blackest flesh as white as spray.
The sea makes no demands but gets its way.

The campus wants its pep- and sleeping pills.
It's not diseases, but the void that kills,
The space, the gaps, the darkness, that same void
He hears vibrating in clogged adenoid
And vocal cords. Through his cool stethoscope
He hears despair pulsate and withered hope
Flutter the failing heart a little, death
Of real feeling in a laboured breath.
He knows with his firm finger on a pulse
It is this Nothingness and nothing else
Throbs in the blood. Nothing is no little part
Of time's huge effort in the human heart.
There's love. There's courage. And that's all.
And the *itus et reditus* of Pascal.

He's not asked out to drinks or dinner much.
He knows how the slightest sweatrash on the crutch
Scares some and with good reason, whose child's whose,
Whose marriage depends on sjamboks, and who screws
In *Posts & Telegraphs*, and reads instead
His damp-stained *Pensées* on their double bed.
The Nothingness! Lisa – she couldn't stand
The boredom and packed off for Switzerland.
She sends him a postcard of a snowblown slope:
Boris, ich bin frei . . . und friere. He can't cope
Here alone. There's nothing for a sick MO
Sick of savannah, sick of inselberg,
Sick of black Africa, who cannot go
Ever again to white St Petersburg.

2. *The Railroad Heroides*

I

A lake like lead. A bar. The crowding, nude
Slack-breasted, tattooed girls made lewd,
Lascivious gestures, their bald groins
Studded with wet francs, for my loose coins.
I'm surrounded by canoes. *Cadeau! Cadeau!*
I fling out all my change, but they won't go.
One paddles underneath and pokes a straw
At my bare ankles through the gaping floor.
I'm on my fifth warm beer. I need my cash.
I crunch her knuckles hard, and yell out;: *Vache!*
Then as she pulls my sandals: *Tu, vache noire!*
They rock the rotten stilts that prop the bar.
My boatman saves me, and for ten francs more
Canoes me blushing to the nearest shore.
I lie back like a corpse Valhalla bound
And sleep. Only a wet, withdrawal sound
Sucks at my ear. I dream. I dream the sun
Blackens my bare balls to bitumen.

II

Again I feel my school belt with the snake-
Hook, silver buckle tauten and then break
From the banisters I swung off. Suicide –
The noose's love-bites and a bruised backside.
I laughed a long time and was glad I fell.
The white wake swabbing at the woundless swell,
The swashing, greasy pool, the spindrift fine
As *Shelltox* seasoning my lips with brine
Makes sadness shoreless and shakes sullen grief
Apart like gobs of spittle. Off Tenerife
French soldiers from Gabon dressed up as sheikhs
Waltzed amidships and blackamoors cut cakes

Iced thick with tricolours. The *Marseillaise*
Boomed from the tannoy and the easy lays
Beamed at the officers. I flung your zig-zag
Tuareg ring and the red, goat-leather bag
I'd bought for our swimming things into the sea
Placating nothing. A little lighter, free
To saunter in fancy dress the festooned decks,
In the midst of plenty, hungry for good sex,
I found a lonely woman. I got you off my chest,
But had to have my hand held and I lay
All night with my confessor, fully dressed,
Afraid of my terror, longing for the day.

III

Bordeaux – Paris – London – Leeds; I get
Cold and tachycardia in my couchette.
With weeks of travel thudding in my brain,
Bilges, ship's engine, and the English train,
Too much black coffee and cold lager beer
I find sleep impossible. My throbbing ear
Bangs on the pillow with an angry thud –
It's you, it's you, with a sound like blood,
After the bloodshed, if your tribe survives,
Pounding a big man's yams among young wives.

IV

Leeds City Station, and a black man sweeps
Cartons and papers into tidy heaps.

3. *Travesties*

'. . . the vanity of translation; it were as wise to cast a pansy into a crucible that you might discover the formal principle of its colour and odour, as seek to transfuse from one language into another the creations of a poet.'

(Shelley, *A Defence of Poetry*)

Distant Ophir

(after Hieronymi Fracastorii, *Syphilis, sive Morbus Gallicus*, Veronae, MDXXX)

'Westerners, who laid the Sun's fowl low,
the flocks of Apollo, now stand and hear
the dreadful sufferings you must undergo.

This land, where you are now, is that Ophir
your flashy maps show off like jewellery
but not yet yours to own, nor domineer

its quiet peoples until now quite free;
cities and new sacraments you won't impose
until you've suffered much by land and sea.

Self-lumbered pilgrims of San Lazaro's,
brothels and gold bars bring you no joy,
porphyry and rape bring no repose!

You'll war with strangers, bloodily, destroy
or be destroyed, your discoveries will cost
destructions greater than the siege of Troy,

worse wanderings after with more thousands lost,
comrades you fitted out search parties for
hutches of bleached ribs on our bare coast.

You'll go on looking, losing more and more
to the sea, the climate, weapons, ours *and* yours,
your crimes abroad brought home as civil war.

And also *Syphilis*: sores, foul sores
will drive you back through storm and calenture
crawling like lepers to our peaceful shores.

The malaise of the West will lure
the scapegoats of its ills, you and your crew,
back to our jungles looking for a cure. –

You'll only find the Old World in the New,
and you'll rue your *discubrimiento*, rue
it, rue Africa, rue Cuba, rue Peru!'

And away behind the crags the dark bird flew.

And everything it prophesied came true.

Note. Hieronymus Fracastorius (1483–1553), the author of *Syphilis*, was
born, as perhaps befits a true poet, without a mouth. The fact is
celebrated in the well-known epigram of Julius Caesar Scaliger (1484–
1558). Fracastorius died, after an apoplexy, speechless.

4. Manica

'An experienced doctor has said that he has never seen tropical neurasthenia develop in a man with a sound philosophy of life.'
(*Notes on the Preservation of Personal Health in Warm Climates*, London, The Ross Institute of Tropical Hygiene, 3rd edn, 1960)

1. *The Origin of the Beery Way*

The Coast, the Coast, a hundred years ago!
Poisonous mangroves and funereal palms,
Victorian hearse-plumes nodding victims in
To bouts of wifeless boredom and *El Vomito*,
Shacking with natives, lovely Sodom's sin,
Boozers with riff-raff in their *British* arms,
Reports put down 'futility & worthlessness' –
I'm just a big *colon*: kick, kick, caress,
Administer, then murmur *beau, beau, beau*
Like some daft baby at your Mandingo.
From *dashi, dashi* to *cadeau, cadeau,*
Armed with my *Dettol*, my *Od-o-ro-no*,
My *African Personality*, I go
For a bit of the old Français finesse,
Not work at your bollocks like a kid's yo-yo,
Then buck you off them like a rodeo.
With prudish pansies I am passionless.
My sex-life's manic like a bad rondeau.
I need to forage among Francophones.
A real beaubarian and buckaneer, that's me, Yo Ho,
Bottles of *Black & White* do me for rum.
I soft-shoe shuffle on the white man's bones,
Windborne or brittle as a popadum.

Omar, not Khayam, the Gambia's mad Marabout
Changed the Commissioners' bullets into water;
Into water being Moslem. I, being atheist,
Am full of more potent potions when I'm pissed.

A century later, full of *Guinnesses* and *Stars*,
I'm God's own Heaven, and as I slash I shout:
The white man's water turns back into fire!
Braving castration at their scimitars,
And single-handed put Islam to rout,
And vanquish the missions with my bent desire,
Spouting a semen capable of slaughter.

Flat on my back, beneath the Galaxy, I fear
This burning in my groin is gonorrhoea.

II. *The Elephant & the Kangaroo*
The first rains slap the leaves like slow applause.
My nerves are soothed by it.
The insects' constant grind has been put down.
It means a night indoors;
nothing doing in the town;
power failure; all the dives unlit.

The imported apples begin to look like shit.
The *Star* beer's warmish, the cut fruit brown.
Chops will be rotting in the Lebanese Cold Stores.
The rainmaker wraps away his amulet
and hugs his gods to see the great downpours.

So the world comes back into its own
and all the houses through a stage-scene gauze
of wavering, driven rain and drunkenness. *It*
goes on spinning and will not run down.
In cool bush-shirt and shorts I sit
feeling the world spinning, the spinning floors
between the brandy and verandah. Laterite.
Bush, like effigies of bush, is washed of it.
A clean green everywhere and it still pours.
This is Noah's weather. All will drown –

But I'll escape by crawling on all fours.

III. *The Foreign Body*

Each blue horizontal thrust
into the red, rain-spattered dust
brings my tachycardia back.
My heart's a thing caught in a sack.
Lashes of tall grass whip
at my genitals, the thick ears flip
hard insects from sprung stalks
and the fraying lightning forks.
Boom! The flame trees blaze
out the ancientest of days.
All the dead in running shoes!
A bootless marchpast of dead Jews!
Boom! Bad blood cells boom
in unison for *Lebensraum*.
Burst corpuscles and blood cells spray
the dark with fire and die away.
The brief glares strewed
flamboyants in my face like blood.
Boom! Boom! And at each wrist
a worm as blue as amethyst
burrows its blunt head in my palm
to keep its bloodless body warm.

And in my bed I hear the whine
of soliciting anopheline,
and diptera diseases zoom
round and round my foetid room,
and randiness, my life's disease,
in bottle-green Cantharides,
and the bloody tampan, that posh louse
plushy like an Opera House,
red as an Empire or lipstick,
insect vampire, soft-backed tick –
all females, the female womb
is stuffed with blind trypanosome.

Which of your probosces made
my heart fire off this cannonade,
or is its billion-gun salute
for lover or for prostitute?
Boom! Boom! And now here comes
the endless roll of danger drums,
and the death-defying leap
jerks me panicking from sleep.
Boom! Boom! Bonhomie!
America's backslapping me.
Starchy Baptist cherubim
give me tests at the SIM,
and swallowed US tracers trace
my body's Cuban missile base.
Boom! Boom! World War 3's
waging in my arteries.

Desperately I call these app-
rehensions Africa but the map
churns like wet acres in these rains
and thunder tugging at my veins.
That Empire flush diluted is
pink as a lover's orifice,
then *Physical, Political* run
first into marblings and then one
mud colour, the dirty, grey,
flat reaches of infinity.

The one red thing, I squat and grab
at myself like a one-clawed crab.

5. *from* The Zeg-Zeg Postcards

I

Africa – London – Africa –
to get it away.

II

My white shorts tighten
in the market crowds.
I don't know
if a lean Fulani boy
or girl give me this stand
trailing his/her knuckles
on my thigh.

III

Knowing my sense of ceremonial
my native tailor
still puts
buttons on my flies.

IV

I bought three *Players* tins
of groundnuts with green mould
just to touch your hand
counting the coppers into mine.

V

My Easter weekend Shangri-la, Pankshin.
I watch you pour the pure
well water, balanced up the mountain,
in blinding kerosene cans,
each lovely morning, convict,
your release date, nineteen years from now,
daubed in brown ink on your rotting shirt.

VI

My *White Horse* plastic horses carousel
whirls round an empty and my hell,
when the last neat whisky passes my cracked lips,
is a riderless Apocalypse.

VII *Water Babies*

She hauls at his member like a crude *shaduf*
to give her dry loins life, and calls it love.

She's back in England pregnant. Now he can
flood the damned valley of his African.

VIII

Sex beefs at belled virginity. The wives
nag back at sex. Ding, Dong! Ding, Dong!
rings no changes on their married lives
clapping out *Love's Old Sweet Song*.

What's that to me? I can get a stand
even from maps of the Holy Land.

IX

Je suis le ténébreux . . . le veuf . . .
always the *soixante* and never the *neuf*.

X

It's time for tea and biscuits. No one comes.
I hear the flap of Dunlop sandals, drums,
terrifying cries. My clap still bothers me.
Siestas make me dizzy. I stagger up and see
through mesh and acacia sharp metal flash,
my steward, still in white uniform and sash,
waving a sharpened piece of Chevie, ride
his old *Raleigh* to the genocide.

XI

The shower streams over him
and the water turns instantly
to cool *Coca-Cola*.

XII

We shake baby powder over each other
like men salting a spitroast,
laughing like kids in a sandpit,
childish ghosts of ourselves,
me, puffy marshmallow, he,
sherbert dusted liquorice
licked back bright
and leading into *Turkish Delight*.

XIII

Buttocks. Buttocks.
You pronounce it as though
the syllables rhymed: *loo; cocks.*
I murmur over and over:
buttocks ... buttocks ... BUTOX,
marketable essence of beef –
négritude – dilute to taste!

XIV

I'd like to
sukuru
you.

XV

Mon égal!
Let me be the Gambia
in your Senegal.

Note (no. xiv). *Sukuru* (Hausa) = screw, as in *sukurudireba*, screwdriver.
A useful portmanteau word.

The Heart of Darkness

Disjointed like a baobab,
gigantic first, then noonday blob,
my shadow staggers, lurches, reels,
elasticated at my heels,
then stretches out with its blind reach
way beyond the gasp of speech.
The wind's up and our last weak light
dithers and lets in the night.

Shadowless, one dark hand flits
spiderwise for crusted bits
of Christmas candle, German *art-
creation* wax with plastic Chartres
Cathedral windows, coloured light
evoking Europe till Twelfth Night
and aspirations from our dust
with no repository but lust.

Earthed so, lust like radar beams
bleeps for realities from dreams
out of darkness for the new, rich life,
the unmistakable pulsation – wife,
my blurred light in the blind
concentric circles of blank mind,
this blackout makes our flesh and bone
an Africa, a Livingstone.

Like galoshes going *vitch* . . .
vitch . . . an Easter birch switch
going *vitch* . . . the fan slows
down and stops, dense mangoes
rustle and a Congo band sings
indigenous and Western things.
The crowds flock in, agog to feel
new *frissons* out of Brazzaville.

Novelties! Good drummers come
miles to hear a different drum
as men go to adulteries. Sounds!
Women! It's the same. Our ground's
stamped and rutted, so we choose
either to hog it in squelched ooze,
or get resurrection and find sties
most radiant with novelties.

My shadow's back as if it could
smell lust steaming off my blood:
Fee, Fi, Fo, Fum,
this is my *Praeconium*.
Paging angels set down this
fastidious and human kiss;
and this; and this; and this; and set
down this, my *Exultet*:

Everything in this rich dark
craves my exclamation mark.
Wife! Mouth! Breasts! Thigh!
certe necessarium Adae
peccatum . . . felix culpa . . . O felix
dark continent of fallen sex.
Harrowing Christ! O Superlamb,
grown lupine, luminous – *Shazam!*

Not so bravado now, but bare
cold, and sober on a camel-hair
Saharan blanket. Tuareg guards
patrolling with their rusty swords
swing up a lamp and weldmesh
thief-bars check our flesh
gleaming: breasts; thigh; bum;
out of our aquarium.

Our fruitless guava quincunx
curvets on its supple trunks.
The candles in the empties flare
sideways in the stirring air
and then go out. The curtains soar
horizontal with the floor.
It seems a whole sea must pour through
our all-glass house at Samaru.

And now all's dark and the first rains
splatter at the window panes,
flattening down ten rows of beans,
a bed of radishes. This means
no news from England, no new war
to heighten the familiar:
Nigeria's Niger is not yet
harnessed to our wireless set.

The Songs of the PWD Man

'We were not born to survive, alas,
But to step on the gas.'
                    (Andrei Voznesensky)

I

I'll bet you're bloody jealous, you codgers in UK,
Waiting for your hearses while I'm having it away
With girls like black Bathshebas who sell their milky curds
At kerbside markets out of done-up-fancy gourds,
Black as tar-macadam, skin shining when it's wet
From washing or from kissing like polished Whitby jet.
They're lovely, these young lasses. Those colonial DO's
Knew what they were up to when they upped and chose
These slender, tall Fulanis like Rowntrees coffee creams
To keep in wifeless villas. No Boy Scout's fleapit dreams
Of bedding Brigitte Bardot could ever better these.
One shy kiss from this lot has me shaking at the knees.
It's not that they're casual, they're just glad of the lifts
I give them between markets and in gratitude give gifts
Like sips of fresh cow-juice off a calabash spoon.
But I'm subject to diarrhoea, so I'd just as soon
Have a feel of those titties that hang down just below
That sort of beaded bolero of deep indigo blue;
And to the woven wrapper worn exactly navel high,
All's bare but for ju-jus and, where it parts, a thigh
Sidles through the opening with a bloom like purple grapes.
So it's not all that surprising that some lecherous apes
Take rather rough advantage, mostly blacks and Lebanese,
Though I'd heard it tell as well that it were one of these
That *white* Police Inspector fancied and forced down
At the back of barracks in the sleazy part of town.
Well, of course, she hollered and her wiry brothers ran
And set rabid packs of bushdogs on the desperate man.
He perished black all over and foaming at the mouth.
They're nomadic, these Fulanis, driving to the South

That special hump-backed cow they have, and when they're on trek,
They leave wigwamloads of women, and by blooming heck,
I drive in their direction, my right foot pressed right down
Laying roads and ladies up as far as Kano town.
Though I'm not your socialistic, go-native-ite type chap
With his flapping, nig-nog dresses and his dose of clap,
I have my finer feelings and I'd like to make it clear
I'm not just itchy fingers and a senile lecher's leer.
I have my qualms of conscience and shower *silver*, if you please,
To their lepers and blind beggars kipping under trees.
They're agile enough, those cripples, scrabbling for the coins.
But not half so bloody agile as those furry little groins
I grope for through strange garments smelling of dye-pits
As I graze my grizzly whiskers on those black, blancmangy tits.
I don't do bad for sixty. You can stuff your Welfare State.
You can't get girls on National Health and I won't masturbate.
They're pleased with my performance. I'm satisfied with theirs.
No! I think they're very beautiful, although their hair's
A bit off-putting, being rough like panscrub wires,
But bums like melons, matey, lips like lorry tyres.
They all know old Roller Coaster. And, oh dear, ugh!
To think I ever nuzzled on a poor white woman's dug,
Pale, collapsed and shrivelled like a week-old mushroom swept
Up at Kirkgate City Markets. Jesus bleeding wept!
Back to sporting, smoky Yorkshire! I dread retirement age
And the talking drum send-off at the Lagos landing stage.

Out here I'm as sprightly as old George Formby's uke.
I think of Old Folk's England and, honest, I could puke.
Here I'm getting younger and I don't need monkey glands,
Just a bit of money and a pair of young, black hands.
I used to cackle at that spraycart trying to put down
That grass and them tansies that grew all over town.
Death's like the Corporation for old men back in Leeds,
Shooting out its poisons and choking off the weeds.

But I'm like them tansies or a stick cut in the bush
And shoved in for a beanpole that suddenly grows lush
With new leafage before the garden lad's got round
To plucking the beans off and digging up the ground.
Yes, better to put the foot down, go fast, accelerate,
Than shrivel on your arses, mope and squawk and wait
For Death to drop the darkness over twittering age
Like a bit of old blanket on a parrot's cage.

II

Life's movement and life's danger and not a sit-down post.
There's skeleton cars and lorries from Kano to the coast;
Skeletons but not wasted, those flashy Chevie fins
Honed up for knife blades or curled for muezzins
To megaphone the *Koran* from their mud mosques and call
The sun down from its shining with their caterwaul.
But it's not just native say-so; it's stark, realistic fact;
The road's a royal python's dark digestive tract.
And I expect that it'll get me one rainy season night,
That sudden, skating backwheel skid across the laterite,
Or a lorry without headlights, GOD IS LOVE up on the cab,
Might impale me on my pistons like a raw *kebab*.
Smash turned into landscape, ambulance, that's that,
A white corpse starkers like a suddenly skinned cat.

As kids when we came croppers, there were always some old dears
Who'd come and pick us up and wipe off blood and tears,
And who'd always use the same daft words, as they tried to console,
Pointing to cobble, path or flagstone: *Look at the hole
You've made falling.* I want a voice with that soft tone,
Disembodied Yorkshire like my mother's on the phone,
As the cook puts down some flowers and the smallboy scrapes the spade,
To speak as my epitaph: *Look at the hole he's made.*

The Death of the PWD Man

'Chivo que rompe tambor con su pellejo paga.'
(Abakuá proverb)

I

Earth-brown Garden Bulbuls in the Bathurst graveyard trees
Sing, they say, 'quick-doctor-quick' or 'fifty-nine degrees'.
God knows, but I'm drawn to graves like brides to baby-wear
Spending an afternoon ashore to see who's buried there.
Ozanne, DO Blackwater Fever. FAITHFUL UNTO DEATH.
A commissioner, they say, who mustered his last breath
And went on chanting till he croaked the same damn thing:
A coffle of fourteen asses bound for Sansanding!
Then *Leeds* medic Rothery Adgie, dead at twenty-six,
His barely legible wooden cross a bundle of split sticks.
Though mostly nineteen-hundreds half the graves have gone
Succumbing like the men below to rains and harmattan.
But fine windborne sand and downpours can't obliterate
BLAKEBOROUGH'S (BRIGHOUSE) from the iron hydrant grate
Outside the Residence, and I've a sense of dismal pride
Seeing Yorkshire linger where ten Governors have died.
The same as in Nigeria, though the weather rots the cross,
There's HUNSLET (LEEDS) in iron on an engine up at Jos.

Wintering house-martins flutter round MacCarthy Square
And bats from Mauritanian shops get tangled in your hair.
Sunset; six; the muezzin starts calling; church bells clang,
Swung iron against iron versus amplified *Koran*.
It's bottoms up at sundown at the praying ground and bar,
Though I prefer the bottle to the Crescent and the Star,
The bottle to the Christians' Cross, and, if I may be frank,
Living to all your Heavens like a woman to a wank.
And it's a bottle that I'm needing as I get back to the boat
With a lump like coal or iron sticking in my throat.
Though I take several bottles, though I hawk like hell and cough,
It stays fixed like a lodestone Northwards as the boat casts off.

Sunday Scotsman Northwards, autumn trees all rusting up;
My fifth *Light Ale* is swashing in its BR plastic cup.
Coming back to England; there's no worse way than this
Railroad North from London up to *Worstedopolis*.
Britannia, Old Mother Riley, bending down to pray,
The railway line's the X-Ray of her twisted vertebrae.
I'm watching England rolling by; here a startled grouse
Shoots out from a siding, and there Sabbath-idle ploughs
Clogged in soggy furrows are seizing up with rain.
Life's either still or scurrying away from the train.

Anxious, anxious, anxious, anxious, perhaps the train'll crash.
Anxious, anxious, anxious, Doctor Adgie, there's a rash
The shape of bloody Britain and it's starting to spread.
My belly's like a blow-up globe all blotched with Empire red.
Chancres, chancres, Shetlands, spots, boils, Hebrides,
Atlasitis, Atlasitis, British Isles Disease!

The rot sets in at Retford and the stations beyond;
Coffles of coupled, rusty coaltrucks chalkmarked COND.
But at each abandoned station shunned like a suicide
There's that loveliest of flourishers, the purple *London Pride*.
Though why the 'proud' metropolis should monopolize weeds
Beats me, when we've got millions more all over mucky Leeds,
Springing up wherever life is teetering on the brink
Like pensioned-off yours truly's pickled in his drink.
With a bit of help off Bitter, I can do it on my own.
They can stuff their pink *Somalgins* and their *Phenobarbitone*,
O those lovely bubs that almost touched black chin and shiny knees,
Leaping up and down to drumming like hoop-jumping Pekinese!
Ay, it's a pity all that's over. From now on every night
It's *Whatsoever Thy Hand Findeth To Do, Do It With Thy Might.*

Anxious, anxious, anxious, anxious, perhaps the train'll crash.
Anxious, anxious, anxious, Doctor Adgie, there's a rash

The shape of bloody Britain and it's starting to spread.
My belly's like a blow-up globe all blotched with Empire red.
Chancres, chancres, Shetlands, spots, boils, Hebrides,
Atlasitis, Atlasitis, British Isle Disease.

Veni, vidi, vici, Death's cackling in my ear.
And there he is a Caesar with an earth-caked Roman spear.
Queer sorts of dozes these are, where I'm nodding off to dream
Of being chased by Caesars and I wake up with a scream.
Must be that pork-pie I've eaten or the British Railways Ale.
Night behind the window. My coaster's tan gone deathly pale.
It's me! It's me the fauna's fleeing. Nothing'll keep still.
My adrenalin moves Nature now and not God's heavenly will.
Lean closer as the darkness grows. My vision's fogged by breath
Clouding up the window as life's clouded up by death.

Anxious, anxious, anxious, anxious, perhaps the train'll crash
Anxious, anxious, anxious, Doctor Adgie, there's a rash
The shape of bloody Britain and it's starting to spread.
My belly's like a blow-up globe all blotched with Empire red.
Chancres, chancres, Shetlands, spots, boils, Hebrides,
Atlasitis, Atlasitis, British Isles Disease.

Death's chuntered in my ear-hole since I was thirty-five,
And I've guffawed at his stories but I've kept myself alive
Long enough to get fed up of the same old, worn-out joke.
Death, piss off, you shaggy dog, you proper natterpoke!
Nay! Come on, Julius Seizure, you black, buck bastard come.
I can hear those muffled heartbeats like a Yoruba drum.
And see the curving shadow of the sinister drumstick,
A bit of whittling that depicts an old man's drooping prick,
Poised above the tautened heart, on the point of being played,
Just once, just once, and then I join the goners' masquerade.

Anxious, anxious, anxious, anxious, perhaps the train'll crash.
Anxious, anxious, anxious, Doctor Adgie, there's a rash

The shape of bloody Britain and it's starting to spread.
My belly's like a blow-up globe all blotched with Empire red.
Chancres, chancres, Shetlands, spots, boils, Hebrides,
Atlasitis, Atlasitis, British Isles Disease.

My transparent head and shoulders ringed with reading lights
Goes sliding over hillsides, graveyards, demolition sites.
I'm a sort of setting sun, all my light drawn in to shed
Only darkness on the living, only darkness on the dead.
Life the bright compartment between dark cattle trucks
Concertinaed in the crush like a bug between two books.
Night and silence, and the Scotsman rushing, second
Coupled to anxious, anxious SE*cond* . . . COND . . . COND . . .
    COND . . .

Schwiegermutterlieder

I

Mother and daughter German refugees
were not much wanted in nineteen
forty-five. She had to skivvy for rich Jews
in Manchester's posh 'Palestine'.

I never really could believe
her story of your being thrown out
by some, one *snowy* Christmas Eve,
for having real wax candles on your conifer,
their children shouting: *Kraut! Kraut!*
until she brought the tea-chests out of store.

Then I saw the hotel towels, the stolen
London café spoons,
bits of half-eaten *Stollen*,
casserole and cooking pans
packed hot from the oven.

Kleptomaniac,
dear *Schwiegermutter*,
did you have to pack
a ½lb Kosher butter?

I've seen her waltz
off with rare, bright plants she's pinched
from Kew, but the good bed-linen
was her own, brought bunched
up in bundles from Berlin,
embroidered: *Mein Heim ist Mein Stolz.*

After thirteen years she fished
out her treasures; none any use.
She gave us a perished
red-rubber douche.

II

After the wedding she insisted on
a head-and-shoulders photograph that just
got her *real* violets on your breast
but not your belly in.

She sang and spun round in a raven
black, hook-buttoned waitress dress.
She was in some sort of heaven,
Viennese with happiness,
her arms round everybody's neck,
warbling from pre-war musicals,
and *Rů-, Rů-, Růženka Maria*, your name in Czech,
with cracked ecstatic trills. –

But dying uncle Bertolt
made his '14–18 amputation tender
by stamping his tin foot, when he was told
you'd married an *Engländer*.

III

Else Crossfield, Dietzsch,
née Schubert – *British* bitch!

The Curtain Catullus

'Frontiers oppress me . . . I want to wander as much as I like . . . to talk, even in a broken language, with everybody.'

(Yevtushenko, 1958)

Your fat, failed ballet dancer's calves
Bulge left, right, left. I'm out of breath and stop
To get a peep in at the skirted halves,
Those pale four inches past the stocking top.
That sight's more in my line. I'm not so sold
On all this Gothic and this old Baroque.
My fur hat tickles and I'm freezing cold.
I need a drink, a sit-down and a smoke.
I speak my one word of your language: *thanks!*
Let's kiss. You laugh and pivot on one toe
To point out Hus still preaching, Russian tanks,
And Kafka's ball-less eyes caked up with snow.

I glance round for my tail. We met head-on
In one blind alley, face to face. We grinned
And nodded and went on. I hope he's gone.
He'd shop us if he saw my bourgeois hand
Slide down the zip-line of your dress and pass
The vertebrae, your parted Party lips
Against my lips. Relax! No cause or class
Can take the pleasure from between your hips.

Astraea! Stalin's chocolate-Santa-Claus-
like statue's made piecemeal. Descend! Descend!
We're human, young, and lustful, sick of wars.
I want this gorgeous red bird for my friend.
Descend like a snow maiden from the air.
Fill Chrysostom's or Basil's empty niche,
Crumple stiff Nelson in Trafalgar Square.
Hear masses shouting: *Goddess!* bosses: *Bitch!*
We know you foreign Mata Hari whores.

I'm tired of stone bodies. I want yours.

Security's embarrassing, bored noise
Booms in these cracked cupolas: *Avoid,*
Avoid glad eyes, come-hithers, girl's or boy's.
Beware Caucasian and Mongoloid . . .
Above all, please remember Gerald Brooke.
O I could see the flags, red, white and blue,
And Red struck to half-mast for a fuck
Between a caught-out couple like us two.

Your body plumped by bread and dumplings strains
Against your imitation bearskin as you peer
Upwards at huge saints, your peach neck cranes
At some Church soldier launching a gold spear
Against the Turk. One lurking Infidel
Is herded by Christ's army into Hell.
I'm tired. Natasha! Olga! Masha! Come
To my bugged bedroom. Leave mausoleum,
Church, museum be. Leave your clothes there – Cold War
Bashing its dead torches on our door.

The Bedbug

Comrade, with your finger on the playback switch,
Listen carefully to each love-moan,
And enter in the file which cry is real, and which
A mere performance for your microphone.

Curtain Sonnets

1. *Guava Libre*

for Jane Fonda,
Leningrad, 1975

Pickled Gold Coast clitoridectomies?
Labia minora in formaldehyde?
A rose pink death mask of a screen cult kiss,
Marilyn's mouth or vulva mummified?

Lips cropped off a poet. That's more like.
That's almost the sort of poet I think I am.
The lips of Orpheus fished up by a dyke
singing 'Women of Cuba Libre and Vietnam!'

The taste, though, taste! Ah, that could only be

('Women! Women! O *abajo* men,
the thought of it's enough to make you come!')

the honeyed yoni of Eurydice

and I am Orpheus going down again –

Thanks for the guavas soaked in Cuban rum.

2. *The Viewless Wings*

(Monkwood, Grimley)

The hungry generations' new decree
turns Worcester orchards into fields of sage.

Tipsy, courtesy cheap wine and EEC,
I hear, as unaware of ours as Keats's age,
the same blithe bird but its old magic fails
and my longing for you now is just as bad
at England's northern edge for nightingales
as those White Nights last year in Leningrad,
where, packed for my flight back, thick curtains drawn
but night too like full day to get much kip,
I wanted you to watch with me from bed
that seamless merger of half dusk and dawn,
AURORA, rosy-fingered kind, and battleship
whose sudden salvo turned the East half red.

3. *Summer Garden*

Winter false dawns woke me: *thud! thud! thud!*
Lorries loaded with chipped ice and not quite four!
Felt-swathed babushkas stooping to chip more –
Leningrad's vast pool of widowhood,
who also guard the Rembrandts and rank Gents,
who stand all day with stern unbending gaze
haloed with Tsars' crowns and Fabergés,
their menfolk melted down to monuments.

It's their eyes make me shy I've fallen for
a woman who they'd chorus at *nyet! nyet!*
and make me edgy walking here with you
between the statues VERITAS, HONOR,
and PSYCHE whom strong passion made forget
conditions of darkness and the gods' taboo.

4. The People's Palace

Shuffling in felt goloshes saves the floor
from the unexpected guests of history
who queue all day to see what once was for
the fruits of just one bonsai family tree.

IUSTITIA and POMONA in their crates.
Come winter and the art, all cordoned off,
's wired to a US import anti-theft device
and opened only for researching prof.
and *patineur* from Academe who skates
those ballrooms patterned like cracked Baikal ice
buffing the princely parquets for the few
who'll see them reproduced in some review.

Watch that elegant glissade as he yahoos
into the soundproof pile of overshoes.

5. *Prague Spring*

on my birthday, 30 April

A silent scream? The madrigal's top note?
Puking his wassail on the listening throng?
Mouthfuls of cumulus, then cobalt throat.
Medusa must have hexed him in mid-song.

The finest vantage point in all of Prague's
this gagging gargoyle's with the stone-locked lute,
leaning over cherries, blow-ups of Karl Marx
the pioneers 'll march past and salute.

Tomorrow's May but still a North wind scuffs
the plated surface like a maced cuirass,
lays on, lays off, gets purchase on and roughs
up the Vltava, then makes it glass.

The last snow of this year's late slow thaw
dribbles as spring saliva down his jaw.

The Nuptial Torches

'These human victims, chained and burning at the stake, were the blazing torches which lighted the monarch to his nuptial couch.'
(J. L. Motley, *The Rise of the Dutch Republic*)

Fish gnaw the Flushing capons, hauled from fleeced
Lutheran Holland, for tomorrow's feast.
The Netherlandish lengths, the Dutch heirlooms,
That might have graced my movements and my groom's
Fade on the fat sea's bellies where they hung
Like cover-sluts. Flesh, wet linen wrung
Bone dry in a washerwoman's raw, red,
Twisting hands, bed-clothes off a lovers' bed,
Falls off the chains. At Valladolid
It fell, flesh crumpled like a coverlid.

Young Carlos de Sessa stripped was good
For a girl to look at and he spat like wood
Green from the orchards for the cooking pots.
Flames ravelled up his flesh into dry knots
And he cried at the King: *How can you stare
On such agonies and not turn a hair?*
The King was cool: *My friend, I'd drag the logs
Out to the stake for my own son, let dogs
Get at his testes for his sins; auto-da-fés
Owe no paternity to evil ways.*
Cabrera leans against the throne, guffaws
And jots down to the Court's applause
Yet another of the King's *bon mots*.

O yellow piddle in fresh fallen snow –
Dogs on the Guadarramas . . . dogs. Their souls
Splut through their pores like porridge holes.
They wear their skins like cast-offs. Their skin grows
Puckered round the knees like rumpled hose.

Doctor Ponce de la Fuente, you,
Whose gaudy, straw-stuffed effigy in lieu
Of members hacked up in the prison, burns
Here now, one sacking arm drops off, one turns
A stubble finger and your skull still croons
Lascivious catches and indecent tunes;
And croaks: *Ashes to ashes, dust to dust.*
Pray God be with you in your lust.
And God immediately is, but such a one
Whose skin stinks like a herring in the sun,
Huge from confinement in a filthy gaol,
Crushing the hooping on my farthingale.

O Holy Mother, Holy Mother, Ho-
ly Mother Church, whose melodious, low
Labour-moans go through me as you bear
These pitch-stained children to the upper air,
Let them lie still tonight, no crowding smoke
Condensing back to men float in and poke
Their charcoaled fingers at our bed, and let
Me be his pleasure, though Philip sweat
At his rhythms and use those hateful tricks
They say he feels like after heretics.

O let the King be gentle and not loom
Like Torquemada in the torture room,
Those wiry Spanish hairs, these nuptial nights,
Crackling like lit tapers in his tights,
His seed like water spluttered off hot stone.
Maria, whose dark eyes very like my own
Shine on such consummations, Maria bless
My Philip just this once with gentleness.

The King's cool knuckles on my smoky hair!

Mare Mediterraneum, la mer, la mer
That almost got him in your gorge with sides
Of feastmeats, you must flush this scared bride's
Uterus with scouring salt. O cure and cool
The scorching birthmarks of his branding-tool.

Sweat chills my small breasts and limp hands.

They curled like foetuses, *maman*, and cried.

His crusted tunics crumple as he stands:

Come, Isabella. God *is satisfied.*

Newcastle is Peru

'Correct your maps: Newcastle is Peru!'
(John Cleveland)

'Venient annis saecula seris,
Quibus Oceanus vincula rerum
Laxet & ingens pateat tellus,
Tethysque novos detegat orbes,
Nec sit terris ultima Thule.'
(Seneca, *Medea*, 375–9)

For defending in our Civil Wars
the King's against the better cause,
Newcastle got its motto: FORTIT-
ER TRIUMPHANS DEFENDIT.
After Nigeria and Prague I come
back near to where I started from,
all my defences broken down
on nine or ten *Newcastle Brown*.

A sudden, stiff September breeze
blows off the sea along the quays
and chills us; autumn and I need
your shoulder with a desperate need.
A clumsy effort at control,
I faff with paper chips and coal,
and rake out with elaborate fuss
one whole summer's detritus.

A good draught and the fire roars
like muted Disney dinosaurs,
and last week's Sunday paper glows
yellowish, its urgent prose,
like flies across a carcass, spreads
and fattens on the voiceless dead.

A picture shows lobbed mortar bombs
smashing down Onitsha homes.

The fire sucks in the first cold air
under the coverage of massacre.
The fire chatters, almost flies,
a full-fledged bird of paradise.
I lay down, dizzy, drunk, alone,
life circling life like the Eddystone
dark sea, but lighting nothing; sense
nor centre, nor circumference.

A life-long, sick sixpennyworth
of appalling motion round the Earth;
scared, moonrocketing till Pop-
eye and blurred planets stop;
Switchback; *Helter Skelter*; *Reel*;
the Blackpool Pleasure Beach Big Wheel,
its million coloured lightbulbs one
red halo like an empty sun.

The *Caterpillar*; Hunslet Feast;
one hand on my first woman's breast;
darkness; acceleration so
we're desperate with vertigo;
then chained in solitary *Chair-
o-planes* through whistling air
as all the known Leeds landmarks blur
to something dark and circular.

Venus, Vulcan, Cupid stare
out vacantly on City Square,
and *Deus iuvat impigros*
above the bank where God helps those
who help themselves, declares
Leeds purposeful in its affairs.

Mercator; *miles*, school chapel glass
transparencies to blood and brass.

And *Self Help* Samuel Smiles was said
to have waltzed round our first bed
in our partitioned ballroom flat
with hardly room to swing a cat.
Worthies! Loiners! O King Dick
Oastler and his rhetoric,
and William Hey, the first to show
syphilis *in utero*.

O highlife crocodiles that went
round one palm tree in the bare cement!
The dizziness! That spiral stair
up St Vitus's Cathedral; there
the golden cockerel and great Prague
before us like a catalogue;
slides. Bloodless mementos, all
Time-Life International.

And now with vistas like Earl Grey's
I look out over life and praise
from my unsteady, sea-view plinth
each dark turn of the labyrinth
that might like a river suddenly
wind its widening banks into the sea
and Newcastle is Newcastle is New-
castle *is* Peru!

Swirled detritus and driftwood pass
in state the 1880 *Sas-
inena Cold Storage Co.*,
and Neptune gazes at the Tyne's flow
seawards, where the sea-winds 'boast
and bluster' at the North East coast,

the sluggish Tyne meandering through
the staithes and shipyards of Peru.

Shadow girders faced with sun
shimmer like heaped bullion.
Commerce and contraceptive glide
and circle on the turning tide;
Plain, *Gossamer* and *Fetherlite*
and US *Trojan*, knotted tight,
ferry their unborn semen, free
for ever from discovery.

Discovery! Slaves, now trains,
like *spirochetes* through dark brains,
tunnel the Andes, spiralling for zinc
and silver, gold and lead; drink
still makes me giddy; my mind whirls
through all my wanderings and girls
to one last city, whose black crest
shows all the universe at rest.

At rest! That last red flash
as life's last ember turns to ash
and riddled dusts drop through the grate
around the heart. O celebrate,
as panic screws up each charged nerve
to cornering the next sharp swerve,
Earth, people, planets as they move
with all the gravity of love.

First this Victorian terrace, where
small scars of the last World War –
those wrought-iron railings made
into shrapnel and grenade,
acanthus leaf and fleur-de-lys,
victorious artillery –

are enough reminder that we brave
harsh opposition when we love.

This cluttered room, its chandelier
still spinning from the evening's beer,
this poor, embattled fortress, this strong-
hold of love, that can't last long
against the world's bold cannonade
of loveless warfare and cold trade,
this bed, this fire, and lastly us,
naked, bold, adventurous.

Discovery! wart, mole, spot,
like outcrops on a snowfield, dot
these slopes of flesh my fingers ski
with circular dexterity.
This moment when my hand strays
your body like an endless maze,
returning and returning, you,
O you; you also are Peru.

And just as distant. Flashing stars
drop to the ashpit through the bars.
I'm back in Africa, at ease
under the splashed shade of four trees,
watching a muscled woman heave
huge headloads of dead wood; one bare leaf
for covering wilts in the heat,
curls, then flutters to her flat, cracked feet.

And round each complex of thatched huts
is a man-high cactus hedge that shuts
out intruders and the mortars thud
like a migraine in the compound mud.
Night comes, and as drunk as hell
I watch the heavens and fireflies, and can't tell,

here at my Shangri-la, Pankshin,
where insects end and stars begin.

My fingerprints still lined with coal
send cold shudders through my soul.
Each whorl, my love-, my long life-line,
mine, inalienably mine,
lead off my body as they press
onwards into nothingness.
I see my grimy fingers smudge
everything they feel or touch.

The fire I laid and lit to draw
you downstairs to the second floor,
flickers and struts upon my bed.
And I'm left gazing at a full-page spread
of aggressively fine bosoms, nude
and tanned almost to *négritude*,
in the Colour Supplement's *Test
Yourself for Cancer of the Breast.*

Durham

'St Cuthbert's shrine,
founded 999'
      (mnemonic)

ANARCHY and GROW YOUR OWN
whitewashed on to crumbling stone
fade in the drizzle. There's a man
handcuffed to warders in a black sedan.
A butcher dumps a sodden sack
of sheep pelts off his bloodied back,
then hangs the morning's killings out,
cup-cum-muzzle on each snout.

I've watched where this 'distinguished see'
takes off into infinity,
among transistor antennae,
and student smokers getting high,
and visiting Norwegian choirs
in raptures over Durham's spires,
lifers, rapists, thieves, ant-size
circle and circle at their exercise.

And Quasimodo's bird's-eye view
of big wigs and their retinue,
a five-car Rolls-Royce motorcade
of judgement draped in Town Hall braid,
I've watched the golden maces sweep
from courtrooms to the Castle keep
through winding Durham, the elect
before whom ids must genuflect.

But some stay standing and at one
God's irritating carrillon
brings you to me; I feel like the hunch-
back taking you for lunch;

then bed. All afternoon two church-
high prison helicopters search
for escapees down by the Wear
and seem as though they're coming here.

Listen! Their choppers guillotine
all the enemies there've ever been
of Church and State, including me
for taking this small liberty.
Liberal, lover, communist,
Czechoslovakia, Cuba, grist,
grist for the power-driven mill
weltering in overkill.

And England? Quiet Durham? Threat
smokes off our lives like steam off wet
subsidences when summer rain
drenches the workings. You complain
that the machinery of sudden death,
Fascism, the hot bad breath
of Power down small countries' necks
shouldn't interfere with sex.

They *are* sex, love, we must include
all these in love's beatitude.
Bad weather and the public mess
drive us to private tenderness,
though I wonder if together we,
alone two hours, can ever be
love's antibodies in the sick,
sick body politic.

At best we're medieval masons, skilled
but anonymous within our guild,
at worst defendants hooded in a car
charged with something sinister.

On the *status quo*'s huge edifice
we're just excrescences that kiss,
cathedral gargoyles that obtrude
their acts of 'moral turpitude'.

But turpitude still keeps me warm
in foul weather as I head for home
down New Elvet, through the town,
past the butcher closing down,
hearing the belfry jumble time
out over Durham. As I climb
rain blankets the pithills, mist
the chalkings of the anarchist.

I wait for the six-five Plymouth train
glowering at Durham. First rain,
then hail, like teeth spit from a skull,
then fog obliterate it. As we pull
out of the station through the dusk and fog,
there, lighting up, is Durham, dog
chasing its own cropped tail,
University, Cathedral, Gaol.

Ghosts: Some Words before Breakfast

for Jane

'These rooms have been furnished by the League of Friends
For your comfort and rest while illness portends.
Take care of the things which from us you borrow
For others are certain to need them tomorrow.'
> (Inscribed in the League of Friends rest room, Royal
> Victoria Infirmary, Newcastle-upon-Tyne)

'C'est mon unique soutien au monde, à présent!'
> (Arthur Rimbaud, 2 July 1891, *Oeuvres*, p. 528)

A *Scottish & Newcastle* clops
past the RVI and traffic stops
to let the anachronistic dray
turn right into the brewery.
Victoria, now that daylight's gone,
whitens, and a Park lake swan
loops its pliant neck to scoff
the bits of sandwich floating off
the boathouse jetty. Empress, Queen,
here slender, beddable, your clean-
living family image drove
my mother venomously anti-love,
and made her think the stillbirth just
retribution for our filthy lust;
our first (the one we married for)
red splashes on a LADIES floor . . .
inter urinam et faeces nasc-
imur . . . issues of blood. You ask,
as brought to bed you blench and bleed,
then scream, insisting that I read,
as blood comes out in spurts like piss,
a bit of *Pride & Prejudice*

I will her breaths. Again! Again!
my daughter heaves in oxygen
and lives, each heaved breath
another lurch away from death,
each exhalation like death throes,
a posser squelched down on wet clothes,
and the only sign of life I see
is a spitting tracheotomy.
When you're conscious, Jane, we'll read
how that caparisoned, white steed
helped the younger son get past
leafage clinging like *Elastoplast*
and win through to bestow the kiss
that works the metamorphosis.
But frogs stay frogs, the briar grows
thicker and thicker round the rose.
I stoop to kiss away your pain
through stuff like florist's cellophane,
but my kiss can't make you less
the helpless prey of Nothingness –
ring-a-ring-a-roses . . . love
goes gravewards but does move.
Love's not something you can hoard
against the geriatric ward.
Mother, all, *all*, of us in this
brave trophallaxis of a kiss
that short-circuits generations scent
mortality's rich nutriment.

The waiting room's an airless place
littered with comics: *Spectre*; *Space*;
Adventure; love and hate
in AD 3068:
interplanetary affairs
policed by *Superlegionaires*:

74

STONE BOY of the planet Zwen
who turns to stone and back again,
and BRAINIAC, space-genius,
who finds Earth's labs ridiculous,
and MATTER-EATER-LAD resist
the mad, moon-exiled scientist –
Dr MANTIS MORLO! Will he smash
our heroes into lunar ash?
Air! Air! There's not enough
air in this small world. I'll suf-
focate. Air! Air! – In each black
PVC disposal sack,
I see two of my dimensions gone
into a flat oblivion.
Weightless, like a stranger caught
loosely flapping on my mother's grate,
down corridors, a shadow man,
I almost sleepwalk, float past *An-
aesthesia, X-Ray, Speech
Therapy* and, come full circle, reach
again the apparatus where you lie
between the armless and the eyeless boy.
I sicken. Jane! I could cut off
your breathing with a last wet cough,
break the connections, save you from
almost a lifetime's crippledom,
legs splayed outwards, the crushed bones
like the godfish Olokun's.

The black spot crossing; on both sides
a blank male silhouette still strides
off the caution and just keeps
on striding, while Newcastle sleeps,
between the Deaf School and the Park,
into his element, the dark.

The Scottish drivers have begun
the last stretch of the homeward run;
another hundred and they'll pull
into the brightening capital,
each lashed, tarpaulined hulk
groaning borderwards: *Blue Circle Bulk
Cement*; *Bulk Earthmoving*; *Bulk Grain*;
Edinburgh and back again.
And up the Great North Road in twos
great tankers of Newcastle booze,
returning empty, leaving full,
swashing with comfort for John Bull
and John Bull's bouncing babes who slug
their English anguish at the bottle's dug.
O caravanserais! I too could drown
this newest sorrow in *Newcastle Brown*.
I thrash round desperately. I flail
my arms at sharks in seas of ale.
Organs. Head/-lights/-lines. Black. White.
The on/off sirening blue light;
heart/lungs like a grappled squid;
BLIND PARAPLEGIC'S CHANNEL BID.
Blood; piss; oceans; taste of salt.
Halt! Halt! Halt! Halt!

I surface and the Tynemouth Queen,
that death's door study streaked with green,
is sitting dwarfish, slumped, alone
on her seawind-eroded throne,
scowling at a glimpse of sea
and wrecked, Dane-harried priory.
Above the grounded RVI
a few wind-driven seagulls cry
like grizzling kids. Out there; out there
where everything is sea and air,

at Tynemouth and at Seaton Sluice,
the sea works bits of England loose,
and redeposits on the land
the concrete tanktraps as blown sand.
Blood transfusion, saline drip,
'this fiddle' and 'stiff upper lip'
have seen us so far.

                    You'll live,
like your father, a contemplative.

Daylight, but a pale *Blue Star*
still just glimmers on the nearest bar.
An orderly brings tea and toast.
Mother, wife and daughter, ghost –
I've laid, laid, laid, laid
you, but I'm still afraid,
though now Newcastle's washed with light,
about the next descent of night.

PALLADAS: POEMS

1

Think of your conception, you'll soon forget
what Plato puffs you up with, all that
'immortality' and 'divine life' stuff.

Man, why dost thou think of Heaven? Nay
consider thine origins in common clay

's one way of putting it but not blunt enough.

Think of your father, sweating, drooling, drunk,
you, his spark of lust, his spurt of spunk.

2

Ignorant of all logic and all law
Fortune follows her own blind course,
kind to the criminal, trampling on the just,
flaunting her irrational, brute force.

3

Life's a performance. Either join in
lightheartedly, or thole the pain.

4

Born naked. Buried naked. So why fuss?
All life leads to that first nakedness.

5

Born crying, and after crying, die.
It seems the life of man's just one long cry.
Pitiful and weak and full of tears,
Man shows his face on earth and disappears.

6

Our nostrils snuffle life from delicate air.
We turn our faces to the sun's bright glare,
organs that get their life out of a breeze.
Give our windpipes just one stiffish squeeze,
life's gone, we're brought down low to death.

We're puff and bluster cut off with one press,
utter nothings, sustained by nothingness
browsing the thin air for our life-breath.

7

Why this desperation to move heaven and earth
to try to change what's doled out at your birth,
the lot you're made a slave to by the gods?

Learn to love tranquillity, and against all odds
coax your glum spirit to its share of mirth.

8

Man's clay, and such a measly bit
and measuring the Infinite!

Leave geography alone, you can't survey
the paltry area of that poor clay.

Forget the spheres and first assess
not space but your own littleness.

9

Agony comes from brooding about death.
    Once dead, a man's spared all that pain.

Weeping for the dead's a waste of breath –
    they're lucky, *they* can't die again.

10

If gale-force Fortune sweeps you off your feet,
    let it; ride it; and admit defeat.

There's no point in resisting; it's too strong –
    willy-nilly, you'll get swept along.

11

Death's a debt that everybody owes,
and if you'll last the night out no one knows.

Learn your lesson then, and thank your stars
for wine and company and all-night bars.

Life careers gravewards at a breakneck rate,
so drink and love, and leave the rest to Fate.

12

Don't fash yourself, man! Don't complain.
Compared with those dark vastnesses before
and after, life's too brief to be a bore
and you'll never pass this way again.

So until the day you're in your grave
and inevitably you become an incubator
for the new-born worms, don't you behave
as though damned here and now, as well as later.

13

Each new daybreak we are born again.

All our life till now has flown away.

What we did yesterday's already gone.

All we have left of life begins today.

Old men, don't complain of all your years.
Those that have vanished are no longer yours!

14
Life's an ocean-crossing where winds howl
and the wild sea comes at us wave after wave.

With Fortune our pilot, weather fair or foul,
all alike drop anchor in the grave.

15
God's philosophical and so can wait
for the blasphemer and the reprobate –

He calmly chalks their crimes up on His slate.

16
God rot the guts and the guts' indulgences.
It's their fault that sobriety lets go.

17
Observe decorum in your grief. First drink and eat.
Remember Homer's:
                    Guts grieve for nothing but more food.
Remember his Niobe, burying her butchered brood,
all twelve children, with her mind on meat.

18
Death feeds us up, keeps an eye on our weight
and herds us like pigs through the abattoir gate.

19
Loving the rituals that keep men close,
Nature created means for friends apart:

pen, paper, ink, the alphabet,
signs for the distant and disconsolate heart.

20

Hope! Fortune! *Je m'en fous!*
Both cheats, but I've come through.

Penniless but free, I can ignore
wealth that looks down on the poor.

21

Shun the rich, they're shameless sods
strutting about like little gods,

loathing poverty, the soul
of temperance and self-control.

22

When you start sneering it's not me
you're sneering at, it's poverty.

If he'd been poor and human, Zeus
'd've suffered from the same abuse.

23

Yes, I'm poor. What's wrong with that?
What is it that I've done to earn your hate?

It's not my character you're sneering at,
only the usual senselessness of Fate.

24

Just look at them, the shameless well-to-do
and stop feeling sorry you're without a sou.

25

It's no great step for a poor man to the grave.
    He's lived his life out only half-alive.

But when the man of plenty nears the end of his,
   Death yawns beneath him like a precipice.

26

So, Mister Moneybags, you're loaded? So?
You'll never take it with you when you go.

You've made your pile, but squandered time. Grown old
you can't gloat over age like hoarded gold.

27

Totting up the takings, quick Death can
reckon much faster than the businessman,

who, balancing, blacks out for ever, still
with the total ringing on the till.

28

Racing, reckoning fingers flick
at the abacus. Death's double-quick
comptometer works out the sums.

The stiffening digits, the rigid thumbs
still the clicking. Each bead slides
like a soul passing over, to the debit side.

29

Poor devil that I am, being so attacked
by wrath in fiction, wrath in fact.

Victim of wrath in literature and life:

1. The *Iliad* and 2. the wife!

30

Grammar commences with a 5-line curse:
Wrath's first and *fatal*'s second verse;

then *sufferings*. The third verse sends
many men to various and violent ends,
and then the fourth and fifth expose
men to Zeus's anger, dogs and crows.

Sad study, grammar! Its whole content's
one long string of accidents!

31
It's grammarians that the gods torment
and Homer's *fatal wrath*'s their instrument.

Monthly (if that!) the grudging nanny wraps
their measly pittance in papyrus scraps.
She nicks some, switches coins, and not content
holds out her grasping claws for 10 per cent,
then lays at teacher's feet a screw of stuff
like paper poppies on a cenotaph.

Just get one loving father to agree
to pay (in decent gold!) a *yearly* fee,
the eleventh month, just when it's almost due,
he'll hire a 'better teacher' and fire you.

Your food and lodging gone, he's got the gall
to crack after-dinner jokes about it all.

32
Nouns *and* poor grammarians decline.
I'm selling off these rotten books of mine,
my Pindar, my Callimachus, the lot.
I'm a bad 'case'. It's poverty I've got.
Dorotheus has given me the sack
and slanders me behind my back.

Help me, Theon, or all that'll stand
between poverty and me's an &

33

Poor little donkey! It's no joke
being a pedant's not a rich man's moke
preened in the palace of the alabarch.

Exist on all the *carets* that I mark
in pupils' proses, little donkey, stay
with me patiently until the day
I get my (patience's first morpheme) pay.

34

This is my mule, a poor long-suffering hack
   with iambic front legs and trochaic back.

Backwards or forwards, he'll take you home
   both ways together like a palindrome.

35

I need mulled wine. Mull? Mull?
O your etymology's a load of bull!

I don't care if it is the Hebrides,
all I need is more mulled vino, *please.*

Old Norse, Gaelic or Teutonic,
it's still a first-rate stomach tonic.

You fetch the lexicon. Mull! Schmull!
Stuff etymology, when my cup's full.

36

A grammarian's daughter had a man
then bore a child m. f. & n.

37

You brainless bastard! O you stupid runt!
Such showing off and you so ignorant!
When the talk's linguistics, you look bored;
your specialism's Plato. Bloody fraud!
Someone says 'Ah, Plato!' then you duck
behind some weighty new phonetics book.

Linguistics! Plato Studies! Dodge and switch,
you haven't a clue, though, which is which.

38

The ignorant man does well to shut his trap
and hide his opinions like a dose of clap.

39

Menander's right, and thought's most fertile soil
  's serendipity, not midnight oil.

40

A lifetime's teaching grammar come to this –
  returned as member for Necropolis!

41. *On Gessius*

I

Fate didn't hustle Gessius to his death.
He ran there well before it, out of breath.

II

A mortal's better off not deified
or arrogantly over-elevated.

Look at Gessius, always dissatisfied,
puffed up first, and then deflated.

III

Two crystal-gazers gazed and prophesied
a consulate for Gessius. There wasn't and he died.

Mankind, self-destructive, puffed up with vanities,
even Death itself can't put you wise.

IV

Neglect of *Nothing in excess*
landed Gessius in this pretty mess.
Erudite he may be but a loon
thinking he could reach the moon.
Bellerophon spurred his mount too far
to learn what heavenly bodies are;
he had youth and strength, and he was on
winged Pegasus, was Bellerophon.

Gessius has nothing. Poor Gessius, I fear
hasn't the energy for diarrhoea!

42. *Maurus*

The politician's elephantine conk's
amazing, amazing too the voice that honks
through blubber lips (1 lb. net each)
spouting his loud, ear-shattering speech.

43

Where's the public good in what you write,
raking it in from all that shameless shite,

hawking iambics like so much *Betterbrite*?

44

Better the hangman's noose than surgeon's knife.
The executioner takes life for life
in legalized hatred for those who kill –

the surgeon does you in and sends a bill!

45
There's that old saying: *Ex-domestics can't*
run houses of their own. My equivalent

's: *An advocate's no judge* though he's
as great a pleader as Isocrates.

Those who sell eloquence like common whores
'll foul pure Justice with their dirty paws.

46
𝔐𝔢𝔦𝔫 𝔅𝔯𝔢𝔞𝔰𝔱, 𝔪𝔢𝔦𝔫 ℭ𝔬𝔯𝔰𝔢𝔱 𝔲𝔫𝔡 𝔪𝔢𝔦𝔫 𝔏𝔢𝔤𝔰
𝔍𝔞 𝔡𝔢𝔡𝔦𝔠𝔞𝔱𝔢𝔰 𝔱𝔬 𝔍𝔲𝔦𝔠𝔢 𝔩𝔦𝔨𝔢 𝔞𝔩𝔩 𝔤𝔲𝔱 𝔊𝔯𝔦𝔢𝔤𝔰.

47
I was promised a horse but what I got instead
was a tail, with a horse hung from it almost dead.

48
Thanks for the haggis. Could you really spare
    such a huge bladder so full of air?

49
When you send out invitations, don't ask me.
It's rare fillets that I like not filigree.
A piece of pumpkin each! The table creaks
not with the weight of food but your antiques.

Save your *soirées* for connoisseurs who'll notch
their belts in tighter for a chance to watch
the long procession of your silverware,
for art's sake happy just to starve and stare,
and, for some fine piece to goggle at, forgo
all hope of eating, if the hallmarks show.

50

You invite me out, but if I can't attend
I've had the honour and I'm more your friend.

The heart's no gourmet, no it feels
honour stays hunger more than meals.

51
women all
cause rue

but can be nice
on   occasional

moments   two
to   be   precise

in   bed

& dead

52
Cuckolded husbands have no certain sign
that trusted wives are treacherous, *like mine.*
The ugly woman's not *de facto* pure,
nor every beauty fast. You're never sure.
The beddable girl, though every bidder woos
with cash and comfort's likely to refuse.
There's many a plain nympho who bestows
expensive gifts on all her gigolos.

The serious woman, seemingly man-shy
and never smiling, does that mean chastity?
Such gravity's worn only out of doors;
at home, in secret, they're all utter whores.

The chatty woman with a word for all
may well be chaste, though that's improbable.
Even old age gets goaded into lust;
senility's no guarantee. What can we trust?

I've got twelve gods to swear my honour by,
she, convenient Christianity!

53
The theft of fire. Man's worst bargain yet.
Zeus created Woman, He was that upset!

A woman desiccates a man with cares
and soon gives golden youth his first grey hairs.

But Zeus's married life in Heaven above
's no cloudy mattress of ambrosial love.

Zeus with Hera of the golden throne
longs to be divorced and on His own.

He often has to shove Her from the sky
to a dog-house cumulus to sulk and cry.

Homer knew this well and shows the two
squabbling on Olympus as mere mortals do.

Thus a woman nags and haggles though she lies
beside the Deity of Deities.

54
Man stole fire, and Zeus created flame
much fiercer still. Woman was its name.

Fire's soon put out, but women blaze
like volcanic conflagrations all our days.

55

The women all shout after me and mock:
Look in the mirror, you decrepit wreck!
But I'm too near the end to give a toss
for trivia like grey temples and hair-loss.

A nice, fresh deodorant, some aftershave
for banishing the bad smell of the grave,
a few bright flowers in my falling hair,
a good night's drinking, and I just don't care.

56

When he comes up to the bedroom
and switches on the light,
the poor man with the ugly wife
stares out into the night.

57

Zeus isn't such a raving Casanova
if he's seen this girl and passed her over.

No galloping bull or strong-winged giant swan
to get his hands on this proud courtesan,

who's Leda, Europa, Danaë all rolled
into one, worth ten showers of his gold.

Are courtesans too common to seduce
and only royal virgins fit for Zeus?

58

From Alexandria to Antioch.
From Syria to Italy: no luck!

Between the Tiber and the Nile
not one man to lead you up the aisle.

'Hope springs eternal . . .' though. Good luck, my dear,
husband-hunting through the Gazetteer.

59

With a son called Eros and a wife whose name
's Aphrodite, no wonder that you're lame!

60

Mere ants and gnats and trivia with stings
vent their aggression like all living things,
but you, you think that *I* ought to be meek,
lay myself open, 'turn the other cheek',
not even verbal comebacks, but stay dumb
and choking on my gag till Kingdom Come!

61

Boast you don't obey the wife, I'll say that's balls.
You're a man aren't you, and not a rock or log?
You suffer too. You know what bugs us all 's
being the husband and the underdog.

But say: *She doesn't slipper me or sleep around;
no turning a blind eye*, then, *if* that's true,
your bondage isn't bad, being only bound
to one who's chaste and not *too* hard on you.

62

A drink to drown my sorrows and restart
    the circulation to my frozen heart!

63. *On a Temple of Fortune turned into a tavern*

I

Agh, the world's gone all to fuck
when Luck herself's run out of luck!

Fortune, fortune maker/breaker,
human nature cocktail-shaker,

goddess once, and now a barmaid
's not too drastic change of trade!

You'll do nicely where you are
behind the counter of *The Fortune Bar*,

metamorphosed to 'mine host'
the character that suits you most.

III

Fortune, can you hear them making fun,
all the mortals, now you're one?

This time you've really gone too far
blotting out your own bright star.

Once queen of a temple, now you're old
you serve hot toddies to keep out the cold.

Well might you complain, now even you
suffer from yourself as mere men do.

64

The blacksmith's quite a logical man
to melt an Eros down and turn
the God of Love into a frying pan,
something that can also burn.

65
Knocked off his pedestal! THEY've
done *this* to Heracles?
Flabbergasted I began to rave
and went down on my knees:

Giant, whose birth took three whole days,
whose image stands at each crossroad,
you to whom the whole world prays,
our Champion, KOed?

That night he stood at my bed-end
and smiled and said: *I can't complain.*
The winds of change are blowing, friend,
your god's a weather-vane.

66. *Marina's House*
'Baptized' Olympians live here in peace,
spared Treasury furnace and coiner's mould,
the fires of revolution and small change.

67. *Hypatia*
Searching the zodiac, gazing on Virgo,
knowing your province is really the heavens,
finding your brilliance everywhere I look,
I render your homage, revered Hypatia,
teaching's bright star, unblemished, undimmed.

68. *On Monks*
Solitaries? I wonder whether
real solitaries live together?

Crowds of recluses? Pseuds,
pooling all their 'solitudes'.

69. *The Spartan Mother*

A Spartan lad fled from the war.
He didn't want no bullet.
He isn't home two ticks before
his mam's dagger's at his gullet.

She prods him with her stiletto blade
and pricks his yeller belly:
What, a son of mine afraid?
Yer spineless little jelly.

If you're allowed to stay alive,
you miserable little crumb,
think how your rotten coward's skive
brings shame on your old mum.

That's if you don't die. If you do
'A mum's a proper martyr'
's what they'll say, but (she ran him through)
no shame for me or Sparta.

70. *The Murderer & Sarapis*

A murderer spread his palliasse
beneath a rotten wall
and in his dream came Sarapis
and warned him it would fall:

Jump for your life, wretch, and be quick!
One more second and you're dead.
He jumped and tons of crumbling brick
came crashing on his bed.

The murderer gasped with relief,
he thanked the gods above.
It was his innocent belief
they'd saved him out of love.

But once again came Sarapis
in the middle of the night,
and once more uttered prophecies
that set the matter right:

Don't think the gods have let you go
and connive at homicide.
We've spared you that quick crushing, so
we can get you crucified.

US MARTIAL

1

Not Afro- not crewcut
& no way out new cut
but something betwixt and between.

Avoid looking too hippy
or boondocks Mississippi
& try if you can to keep clean.

Shave so close but no closer
no *eau-de-mimosa*,
be macho, not mucho, enough.

I'm a little bit wary
or hirsute and hairy
& your sort of chestrug's so rough –

EVERYWHERE'S
just a jungle of hairs
your legs, your back, your behind,

but one place nothing sprouts
as all growth's been plucked out 's,
Mr REDNECK, your mind!

2

What'mmmIdoin'? slurs Lyris, feigning shock.

I'll tell you what you're doing: YOU
are doing what you always do,
even when you're sober   SUCKING COCK!

3

The tart passed round for sweet's so hot
no one touches it. No one, but NOT
Sabidius whose greed burns more.
He blows on it 1-2-3-4.
It's cool. Still no one touches it –

Sabidius's breath turns all to shit.

4

Again, after free-loading
your doggy-bag's exploding
as if you'd got to feed the whole Bronx Zoo.

So next time I dine at *Sardi's*
send your St Bernard, he's
bringing home a bastard-bag for you!

5

Screw old women? Sure I do! But YOU
you're one step further on, more corpse, than crone
and necrophilia I'm not into!

Hecuba, Niobe, both of them I'd screw
till one became a bitch, the other stone.

6

You serve me plonk, and you drink *reservé.*

My taste-buds back away from mine's bouquet.

7. *Scentsong*

for Gellia

You swing past, a pong typhoon,
a *parfumerie* afflatus,
wafts over us and makes us swoon.
What brand do you use to bait us?

Dior? One of *Fabergé's?*
Frogshit (*Chanel* no.2)!
Maybe your shower or bidet's
been plumbed to pipe out *Patou.*

You don't need *Nina Ricci*
or *Givenchy* creations
I think your perfume's peachy
and just like my Dalmatian's.

8

You're fucking Aufidia, your ex
who's married to the guy who gave *you* grounds.
Adultery's the one way you get sex.
You only get a hard-on out of bounds.

9. *Twosum*

Add one and one together and make TWO:
that boy's sore ass + your cock killing you.

10

A slight cold or a touch of flu,
but when THE SPECIALIST and all his crew
of a 100 students once are through,
and every inch of me's been handled twice
by a hundred medics' hands as cold as ice
the pneumonia I didn't have I DO!

11

Musclion balances dumb-bells on his nose.
Ninus the muscleman can lift the weight
of 7 little boys, and sometimes 8,
but what Stella can bring off gets my *bravos*
(incredible the heights that she can reach!)
10 girls with 2 hands, 1 finger each!

12. *Paula*

She doesn't feel 3
parts in Comedy
quite do.

4's more & merrier!
She hopes the spear-carrier
comes on too!

13

Time makes enormous differences
between the past and present tenses,
the long way that I did is from I do.

I *love* Glycera, Lycoris. I love*d* you.

14

The 'miracle restorer' you employ
that puts the black gleam where your hair was thin
's from your trichologist, the shoeshine boy
and comes in dollops from his polish tin.

15. *To Bassara*

She likes the winter season
when there's lots of ice and snow
because it gives her reason
to hold a fashion show.

She loves the weather when it stinks
and no sooner does it freeze
than out come musquashes and minks
and chic *pendant* and *après-skis*.

I don't flaunt $$$ on my back
or keep a wardrobe like a zoo,
only one threadbare anorak
the winter blows right through,

so if you really want to be
more noticed in your clothes
and at the same time fair on me
please stay in when it snows,

but when I can sit out in my shorts
and sip a long iced drink,
then you dress up for winter sports
and run around in mink.

16. *The Joys of Separation*
She wants more and more and more new men in her.

He finally finishes *Anna Karenina*.

17. *Sandwich Bawd Swing Song*
Pa's sugar and oil shares run to eight zeros,
Deep South/mouth lady, very Southern Belle-y,
and all you seem to want's two well-hung heroes
for the sort of sandwich sold at no deli.

Texans unite! Quit lynching and start swinging!
By 'wanting a sandwich' I take it you mean
(this next line really should be Elvis singing)
yuh wantuh coupluh felluhs to be fucked between!

Wish you two blacks for your lickerish allsort.
I think you'll find, missy, these two'll do,
though not your antebellum beck-and-call sort,
they're well up to filling a *trou* or two.

Or renta-penta-studs (SSSR!)
reds *in* bed not under that last all night
pumping seed (wherever) like warm caviar,
Cossacks Casanova 'd dub Stakhanovite!

Black power, baby, or hammer & sickle?

Piebald's perfect! A one-of-each threesome!

one buttered Ruski, one pumpernickel.

Two provisos: 1. Leave off the pickle.

2. Tell the sons-a-bitches to leave me some!

I translated these poems of Marcus Valerius Martialis (AD *c.*40–
*c.*104) in the first few days of March 1981 and in my study in apt.
841 of the Hotel Ansonia on 73rd and Broadway, New York. From an
upper storey the stone head of a satyr looked in on my labours. His
stare and the eyes of his co-satyrs taking in the multifarious life of New
York City and missing nothing combined to season these versions.
                              (T.H., Hotel Ansonia, New York, March 1981)

References

This table gives references to the book and poem number of the
originals in the work of Marcus Valerius Martialis:

1	2.16	7	3.55	13	6.40
2	2.73	8	3.70	14	5.41
3	3.17	9	3.71	15	6.59
4	3.23	10	5.9	16	7.100
5	3.32	11	5.12	17	8.83
6	3.49	12	6.6		

Sentences

1. *Brazil*

Even the lone man
in his wattle lean-to,
the half-mad women
in their hive of leaves,
pitched at the roadside
by a low shared fire
so near the shoulder
that their tethered goat
crops only half-circles
of tough, scorched turf,
and occasional tremors
shake ash from the charcoal,
live for something more
than the manioc and curds
they're preparing,
barely attentive to speech
as they strain
through the oppressive midday drowse,
or, at night, through the noise
of the insects drilling into them
the lessons of loneliness
or failed pioneering
over miles of savannah,
for the punctual Bahia-Rio
coaches as they come
to the village of Milagres
they are outcasts from
for a quick *cafezinho*,
a quick piss,
edible necklaces
and caged red birds.

2. *Fonte Luminosa*

Walking on the Great North Road
with my back towards London
through showers of watery sleet,
my cracked rubber boot soles
croak like African bullfrogs
and the buses and lorries that swish
like a whiplash laid on and on
without intermission or backswing
send a spray splashing over
from squelching tyres skywards
STOP red, GO green, CAUTION
amber, and at the crossing
where you had your legs crushed
I remember the *fonte luminosa*,
Brasilia's musical geyser
spurting a polychrome plumage,
the fans of rich pashas,
a dancer's dyed ostriches,
making parked Chevrolets
glisten, people seem sweaty,
and when yellowing, loppy Terezinha,
the eldest, though your age,
of the children all huddled
under the fancy ramp entrance
of the National Theatre,
comes and scoops from the churned
illuminated waters a tinful
for drinking and cooking and goes
gingerly to ingenious roads
where cars need never once
stop at Belishas or crossings,
intersect, crash, or slow down,
the drops that she scatters

are not still orange or purple,
still greenish or gorgeous
in any way, or still gushing,
but slightly clouded like quartz,
and at once they're sucked back
into Brazil like a whelk
retracting, like the tear
that drains back into your eye
as once more you start coming through
the rainbowing spindrift and fountains
of your seventh anaesthesia.

3. *Isla de la Juventud*

The fireflies that women
once fattened on sugar
and wore in their hair
or under the see-through
parts of their blouses
in Cuba's *Oriente,*
here seem to carry
through the beam where they cluster
a brief phosphorescence
from each stiff corpse
on the battlefields that look
like the blown-up towel
of a careless barber,
its nap and its bloodflecks,
and if you were to follow,
at Santa Fe's open-air
cinema's Russian
version *War & Peace,*
the line of the dead
to the end, corpses,
cannons and fetlocks,
scuffing the red crust
with your snowboots,
or butt-end of your rifle,
you would enter an air
as warm as the blankets
just left by a lover,
yours, if you have one,
an air full of fireflies,
bright after-images,
and scuffed Krasnoe snow
like unmeltable stars.

4. *On the Spot*

for Miroslav Holub,
Havana, August 1969

Watching the Soviet subs surface
at the side of flagged battleships
between Havana harbour and the USA
I can't help thinking how the sword
has developed immensely,
how only nomads in deserts
still lop heads off with it,
while the pen is still only
a point, a free ink-flow
and the witness it has to keep bearing.

Miroslav, you must remember
there'd be no rumba now,
if the blacks who made Cuba
had not somehow evolved
either when shackled or pegged
or grouped for a whiplash harangue
or under the driver's bluebottle eye
following their own eyes flicking,
flies dying in jam-jars
jerking all over –

   Think
of those trapped pupils let loose,
the offal they'd flock to,
O have to, being so hungry,
History inescapable, high,
necessary, putrescent,
unburied, still not picked over,
only the balls of it gnawed at –

had not evolved as I said,
together, somehow, with slight spasms
of only the nipples or haunches,
a calf-muscle tugging the chain taut,
the art of dancing on the spot
without ever being seen to be moving,
not a foot or a hand out of place.

Voortrekker

A spoor from a kraal. Then grass
greens the turd of the carnivore
gone all gums. So the sick Boer
lays on with the whip less.

Panic in him and round him
like a wind-flapped tilt –
only the sable sons of Ham
cram Death's dark veld.

Coupled together in God's span,
outnumbered many times over,
ox, dog, Hottentot, Caffre,
and just one Christian man.

The Bonebard Ballads

1. *The Ballad of Babelabour*

'This Babylonian confusion of words results from their being the language of men who are going down.'

(Bertolt Brecht)

What ur-𝕾𝖕𝖗𝖆𝖈𝖍𝖊 did the labour speak?
ur ur ur to t'master's 𝕾𝖕𝖗𝖆𝖈𝖍𝖊
the hang-cur ur-grunt of the weak
the unrecorded urs of gobless workers

Their snaptins kept among their turds
they labour   eat and shit
with only grunts not proper words
raw material for t'poet

They're their own meat and their own dough
another block   another
a palace for the great Pharaoh
a prison for their brothers

Whatever name's carved on those stones
it's not the one who labours
an edifice of workers' bones
for one who wants no neighbours

Nimrod's nabobs like their bards
to laud the state's achievements
to eulogize his house of cards
and mourn the king's bereavements

The treasurer of 𝕾𝖕𝖗𝖆𝖈𝖍𝖊'𝖘 court
drops the bard his coppers
He knows that poets aren't his sort
but belong to the ur-crappers

Ur-crappers tongueless bardless nerks
your condition's shitty
no time for yer Collected Works
or modulated pity

but ur ur ur ur ur ur urs
sharpened into 𝕾𝖕𝖗𝖆𝖈𝖍𝖊
revurlooshunairy vurse
uprising nacker starkers

by the time the bards have urd
and urd and urd and 𝕾𝖕𝖗𝖆𝖈𝖍𝖊red
the world's all been turned into *merde*
& Nimrod's Noah'sarkered

sailing t'shit in t'ship they urd at
no labour can embark her
try and you'll get guard-dog grrred at
the shitship's one class: 𝕾𝖕𝖗𝖆𝖈𝖍𝖊

Bards & labour left for dead
the siltworld's *neue neue*
bard   the HMV doghead
in that *negra negra* Goya.

(See the picture 'A Dog Buried in the Sand' among the Black Paintings
of Goya in the Prado.)

2. *The Ballad of the Geldshark*

(from Aeschylus)

Geldshark Ares god of War
broker of men's bodies
usurer of living flesh
corpse-trafficker that god is –

give to War your men's fleshgold
and what are your returns?
kilos of cold clinker packed
in army-issue urns

wives   mothers   sisters each one scans
the dogtags on the amphorae
which grey ashes are my man's
they sift the jumbled names and cry:

My husband sacrificed his life
My brother battle-martyr
Aye   for someone else's wife
Helen   whore of Sparta

whisper   mutter   belly-aching
the people's beef and bile: *This war's*
been the clanchiefs' making
the ruling clanchiefs' so-called 'cause'.

Where's my father   husband   boy?
where do all our loved ones lie?

six feet under near the Troy
they died to occupy.

3. 'Flying down to Rio':

A Ballad of Beverly Hills

Big mouth of the horn of plenty
horny   horny Hollywood
Food   flesh   fashion *cognoscenti*
grudge the midge her mite of blood

Fat bugs fry and small gnats ping
against *Insectecutor* bars
so no slight unsightly sting
blemishes the flesh of stars

Don't adjust the skew-whiff Manet
you'll touch off the thief device
monitored each nook and cranny
of this closed-circuit paradise

but tonight she's feeling spooky
plucking plasmic plectra strike her
nervestrings like a bop bazouki
boogie-woogie balalaika

Divinely draped in Third World 'folk art'
(Locations where the labour's cheap!)
unaware she'll soon join Bogart
big C first and then big sleep

Brown tits ⅞ on show'll
scotch the lies they're not her own
Death's the only gigolo'll
rumble that they're silicone

Death   the riveting romancer
in sheerest X-ray underwear
nimble-footed fancy dancer
bonier than Fred Astaire

Girning atcha *gotcha gotcha*
(on his dance card once you're born)
cold carioca or chill cha-cha
charnelwise to Forest Lawn

Or choker sheikh whose robes hang loose
O worse than loss of honour fate!
His kisser sags from black burnous
your veils are blue barbiturate

Freeway skiddy with crashed star's gore
(fastlivingwecanshow'em!)
the jelling jugular 'll pour
at least a jereboam . . .

Places that you once changed planes at
or hardened second units shot
this afterlife eternal flat
horizonless back lot

places   faces from your worst dream
say   starvelings of Recife
who made your slimmer's body seem
embarrassingly beefy

On such locations old at twenty
boys grub green crabs from grey mud –
big mouth of the horn of plenty
horny   horny Hollywood.

Social Mobility

Ah, the proved advantages of scholarship!
Whereas his dad took cold tea for his snap,
he slaves at nuances, knows at just one sip
Château Lafite *from* Château Neuf du Pape.

THE SCHOOL OF ELOQUENCE

'In 1799 special legislation was introduced "utterly suppressing and prohibiting" by name the London Corresponding Society and the United Englishmen. Even the indefatigable conspirator, John Binns, felt that further national organization was hopeless ... When arrested he was found in possession of a ticket which was perhaps one of the last "covers" for the old LCS: *Admit for the Season to the School of Eloquence.*'

(E. P. Thompson, *The Making of the English Working Class*)

Nunc mea Pierios cupiam per pectora fontes
Irriguas torquere vias, totumque per ora
Volvere laxatum gemino de vertice rivum;
Ut, tenues oblita sonos, audacibus alis
Surgat in officium venerandi Musa parentis.
Hoc utcunque tibi gratum, pater optime, carmen
Exiguum meditatur opus, nec novimus ipsi
Aptius a nobis quae possint munera donis
Respondere tuis, quamvis nec maxima possint
Respondere tuis, nedum ut par gratia donis
Esse queat, vacuis quae redditur arida verbis . . .

Si modo perpetuos sperare audebitis annos,
Et domini superesse rogo, lucemque tueri,
Nec spisso rapient oblivia nigra sub Orco,
Forsitan has laudes, decantatumque parentis
Nomen, ad exemplum, servo servabitis aevo.

(John Milton, 1637)

Heredity

How you became a poet's a mystery!
Wherever did you get your talent from?
I say: I had two uncles, Joe and Harry –
one was a stammerer, the other dumb.

On Not Being Milton

for Sergio Vieira & Armando Guebuza (*Frelimo*)

Read and committed to the flames, I call
these sixteen lines that go back to my roots
my *Cahier d'un retour au pays natal*,
my growing black enough to fit my boots.

The stutter of the scold out of the branks
of condescension, class and counter-class
thickens with glottals to a lumpen mass
of Ludding morphemes closing up their ranks.
Each swung cast-iron Enoch of Leeds stress
clangs a forged music on the frames of Art,
the looms of owned language smashed apart!

Three cheers for mute ingloriousness!

Articulation is the tongue-tied's fighting.
In the silence round all poetry we quote
Tidd the Cato Street conspirator who wrote:

Sir, I Ham a very Bad Hand at Righting.

Note. An 'Enoch' is an iron sledge-hammer used by the Luddites to smash the frames which were also made by the same Enoch Taylor of Marsden. The cry was: 'Enoch made them, Enoch shall break them!'

The Rhubarbarians

Those glottals glugged like poured pop, each
rebarbative syllable, remembrancer, raise
'mob' *rhubarb-rhubarb* to a tribune's speech
crossing the crackle as the hayricks blaze.

The gaffers' blackleg Boswells at their side.
Horsfall of Ottiwells, if the bugger could,
'd've liked to (exact words recorded) *ride
up to my saddle-girths in Luddite blood.*

What t'mob said to the cannons on the mills,
shouted to soldier, scab and sentinel
's silence, parries and hush on whistling hills,
shadows in moonlight playing knurr and spell.

It wasn't poetry though. Nay, wiseowl Leeds
pro rege et lege schools, nobody needs
your drills and chanting to parrot right
the *tusky-tusky* of the pikes that night.

II

(On translating Smetana's *Prodaná Nevěsta* for the Metropolitan
Opera, New York.)

'One afternoon the Band Conductor up on his stand
Somehow lost his baton it flew out of his hand
So I jumped in his place and conducted the band
With mi little stick of Blackpool Rock!'
(George Formby)

Finale of Act II. Though I resist
blurring the clarity of *hanba* (shame)
not wanting the least nuance to be missed
syllables run to rhubarb just the same . . .

Sorry, dad, you won't get that quatrain
(I'd like to be the poet my father reads!)
It's all from you once saying on the train
how most of England's rhubarb came from Leeds.

Crotchets and quavers, rhubarb silhouettes,
dark-shy sea-horse heads through waves of dung!
Rhubarb arias, duets, quartets
soar to precision from our common tongue.

The uke in the attic manhole once was yours!

Watch me on the rostrum wave my arms –

mi little stick of Leeds grown *tusky* draws
galas of rhubarb from the Met-set palms.

Note. Tusky: the Leeds word for rhubarb.

Study

Best clock. Best carpet. Best three chairs.

For deaths, for Christmases, a houseless aunt,
for those too old or sick to manage stairs.

I try to whistle in it but I can't.

Uncle Joe came here to die. His gaping jaws
once plugged in to the power of his stammer
patterned the stuck plosive without pause
like a d-d-damascener's hammer.

Mi aunty's baby still. The dumbstruck mother.
The mirror, tortoise-shell-like celluloid
held to it, passed from one hand to another.
No babble, blubber, breath. The glass won't cloud.

The best clock's only wound for layings out
so the stillness isn't tapped at by its ticks.
The settee's shapeless underneath its shroud.

My mind moves upon silence and *Aeneid* VI.

Me Tarzan

Outside the whistled gang-call, *Twelfth Street Rag*,
then a Tarzan yodel for the kid who's bored,
whose hand's on his liana . . . no, back
to Labienus and his flaming sword.

Off laikin', then to t'fish 'oil all the boys,
off tartin', off to t'flicks but on, on, on,
the foldaway card table, the green baize,
De Bello Gallico and lexicon.

It's only his jaw muscles that he's tensed
into an enraged *shit* that he can't go;
down with polysyllables, he's against
all pale-face Caesars, *for* Geronimo.

He shoves the frosted attic skylight, shouts:

Ah bloody can't ah've gorra Latin prose.

His bodiless head that's poking out 's
like patriarchal Cissy-bleeding-ro's.

Wordlists

'There was only one more thing which had to be done, a last message to leave behind on the last day of all: and so he gathered up his strength in the midst of a long stretch of silence and framed his lips to say to me quite clearly the one word *Dictionary*.'

(*The Life of Joseph Wright*, 1858–1930)

I

Good parrots got good marks. I even got
a 100 in Divinity (posh schools' RI),
learned new long words and (wrongly stressed) *harlót*
I asked the meaning of so studiously.

I asked mi mam. She said she didn't know.
The Classics/RI master hummed and hawed.
(If only he'd've said it was a pro!)
New words: 'venery', 'VD' and 'bawd'!

Sometime ... er ... there's summat in that drawer ...

photograph foetuses, a pinman with no prick,
things I learned out laiking years before
they serialized 'Life' in the *Sunday Pic*.

Words and wordlessness. Between the two
the gauge went almost ga-ga. No RI,
no polysyllables could see me through,
come glossolalia, dulciloquy.

II

The *Funk & Wagnalls*? Does that still survive?
Uncle Harry most eloquent deaf-mute
jabbed at its lexis till it leaped to life
when there were Tory errors to confute.

A bible paper bomb that dictionary.
I learned to rifle through it at great speed.
He's dead. I've studied, got the *OED*
and other tongues I've slaved to speak or read:

L & S dead Latin, L & S dead Greek,
one the now dead lexicographer gave me,
Ivan Poldauf, his English-Czech *slovník*;
Harrap's French 2 vols, a Swahili,
Cabrera's Afro-Cuban *Anagó*,
Hausa, Yoruba, both R. C. Abraham's –

but not the tongue that once I used to know
but can't bone up on now, and that's mi mam's.

III

The treasure found here on this freezing shore,
with last-war tanktraps, and oil-clagged birds,
the morning shivery, the seawinds raw,
is the memory of a man collecting words.

Crushed scallops, washed up hard hats, shit, what fitter
thesaurus trove of trashes could he wish,
our lexicographer and *Doctor Litter-*
arum netting a fine but unexpected fish?

His heart beat faster when a living mouth
(the jotting said a 'fishwife's') used the old
and, for him forgotten in his flit down South,
border word *yagach* to describe the cold.

Though society 's not like the *OED*
and the future 's just as yagach as the day,
I celebrate beside the same bleak sea
James Murray, and a scholar's clarion call
that set those sharp speech combers on their way:

Fling our doors wide! all, all, not one, but all!

Classics Society

(Leeds Grammar School 1552–1952)

The grace of Tullies eloquence doth excell
any Englishmans tongue . . . my barbarous stile . . .

The tongue our leaders use to cast their spell
was once denounced as 'rude', 'gross', 'base' and 'vile'.

How fortunate we are who've come so far!

We boys can take old Hansards and translate
the British Empire into SPQR
but nothing demotic or too up-to-date,
and *not* the English that I speak at home,
not Hansard standards, and if Antoninus
spoke like delinquent Latin back in Rome
he'd probably get gamma double minus.

And so the lad who gets the alphas works
the hardest in his class at his translation
and finds good Ciceronian for Burke's:

a dreadful schism in the British nation.

National Trust

Bottomless pits. There's one in Castleton,
and stout upholders of our law and order
one day thought its depth worth wagering on
and borrowed a convict hush-hush from his warder
and winched him down; and back, flayed, grey, mad, dumb.

Not even a good flogging made him holler!

O gentlemen, a better way to plumb
the depths of Britain's dangling a scholar,
say, here at the booming shaft at Towanroath,
now National Trust, a place where they got tin,
those gentlemen who silenced the men's oath
and killed the language that they swore it in.

The dumb go down in history and disappear
and not one gentleman 's been brought to book:

Mes den hep tavas a-gollas y dyr

(Cornish) –
             'the tongueless man gets his land took.'

The Ode Not Taken

C. T. Thackrah (1799–1833)

Dissecting corpses with Keats at Guy's,
Leeds-born Thackrah shared the poet's TB.
Cadavers that made Keats poeticize
made Thackrah scorn the call of poetry.

Praising the Classics to the *Lit. & Phil.*,
versed in Greek and Latin, and Eng. Lit.,
he scribbled no sonnets on the scribbling mill
but penned descriptions of the scribblers' shit.
Could write hexameters by Virgil's rules,
and parrot Latin epics but he chose
flax-hecklers' fluxes with their 'gruelly' stools,
the shit of Yorkshire operatives, in prose.

But there are pentameters in Thackrah's tract,
the found iambics no prose can destroy,
which want to stop the heart with simple fact:

we do not find old men in this employ.

Them & [uz]

for Professors Richard Hoggart & Leon Cortez

I

αἰαῖ, ay, ay! . . . stutterer Demosthenes
gob full of pebbles outshouting seas –

4 words only of *mi 'art aches* and . . . 'Mine's broken,
you barbarian, T. W.!' *He* was nicely spoken.
'Can't have our glorious heritage done to death!'

I played the Drunken Porter in *Macbeth*.

'Poetry's the speech of kings. You're one of those
Shakespeare gives the comic bits to: prose!
All poetry (even Cockney Keats?) you see
's been dubbed by [Λs] into RP,
Received Pronunciation, please believe [Λs]
your speech is in the hands of the Receivers.'

'We say [Λs] not [ʊz], T. W.!' That shut my trap.
I doffed my flat a's (as in 'flat cap')
my mouth all stuffed with glottals, great
lumps to hawk up and spit out . . . *E-nun-ci-ate!*

So right, yer buggers, then! We'll occupy
your lousy leasehold Poetry.

I chewed up Littererchewer and spat the bones
into the lap of dozing Daniel Jones,
dropped the initials I'd been harried as
and used my *name* and own voice: [uz] [uz] [uz],
ended sentences with by, with, from,
and spoke the language that I spoke at home.
RIP RP, RIP T. W.
I'm *Tony* Harrison no longer you!

You can tell the Receivers where to go
(and not aspirate it) once you know
Wordsworth's *matter/water* are full rhymes,
[uz] can be loving as well as funny.

My first mention in the *Times*
automatically made Tony Anthony!

Working

Among stooped getters, grimy, knacker-bare,
head down thrusting a 3 cwt corf
turned your crown bald, your golden hair
chafed fluffy first and then scuffed off,
chick's back, then eggshell, that sunless white.
You strike sparks and plenty but can't see.
You've been underneath too long to stand the light.
You're lost in this sonnet for the bourgeoisie.

Patience Kershaw, bald hurryer, fourteen,
this wordshift and inwit's a load of crap
for dumping on a slagheap, I mean
th'art nobbut summat as wants raking up.

I stare into the fire. Your skinned skull shines.
I close my eyes. That makes a dark like mines.

Wherever hardship held its tongue the job
's breaking the silence of the worked-out-gob.

Note. 'Gob': an old Northern coal-mining word for the space left after
the coal has been extracted. Also, of course, the mouth, and speech.

Cremation

So when she hears him clearing his throat
every few seconds she's aware what he's raking
's death off his mind; the next attack. The threat
of his dying has her own hands shaking.

The mangle brought it on. Taking it to bits.
She didn't need it now he'd done with pits.

A grip from behind that seems to mean *don't go*
tightens through bicep till the fingers touch.
His, his dad's and *his* dad's lifetime down below
crammed into one huge nightshift, and too much.

He keeps back death the way he keeps back phlegm
in company, curled on his tongue. Once left alone
with the last coal fire in the smokeless zone,
he hawks his cold gobful at the brightest flame,
too practised, too contemptuous to miss.

Behind the door she hears the hot coals hiss.

TWO

Book Ends

I

Baked the day she suddenly dropped dead
we chew it slowly that last apple pie.

Shocked into sleeplessness you're scared of bed.
We never could talk much, and now don't try.

You're like book ends, the pair of you, she'd say,
Hog that grate, say nothing, sit, sleep, stare . . .

The 'scholar' me, you, worn out on poor pay,
only our silence made us seem a pair.

Not as good for staring in, blue gas,
too regular each bud, each yellow spike.

A night you need my company to pass
and she not here to tell us we're alike!

Your life's all shattered into smithereens.

Back in our silences and sullen looks,
for all the Scotch we drink, what's still between 's
not the thirty or so years, but books, books, books.

II

The stone's too full. The wording must be terse.
There's scarcely room to carve the FLORENCE on it –

Come on, it's not as if we're wanting verse.
It's not as if we're wanting a whole sonnet!

After tumblers of neat *Johnny Walker*
(I think that both of us we're on our third)
you said you'd always been a clumsy talker
and couldn't find another, shorter word
for 'beloved' or for 'wife' in the inscription,
but not too clumsy that you can't still cut:

You're supposed to be the bright boy at description
and you can't tell them what the fuck to put!

I've got to find the right words on my own.

I've got the envelope that he'd been scrawling,
mis-spelt, mawkish, stylistically appalling
but I can't squeeze more love into their stone.

Confessional Poetry

for Jeffrey Wainwright

When Milton *sees* his 'late espoused saint'
are we sure the ghost's wife 1 or 2?
Does knowing it's himself beneath the paint
make the Rembrandts truer or less true?

But your father was a simple working man,
they'll say, *and didn't speak in those full rhymes.*
His words when *they came would scarcely scan.*

Mi dad's did scan, like yours do, many times!

That quarrel then in Book Ends II *between*
one you still go on addressing as 'mi dad'
and you, your father comes across as mean
but weren't the taunts you flung back just as bad?

We *had* a bitter quarrel in our cups
and there *were* words between us, yes,
I'm guilty, and the way I make it up 's
in poetry, and that much I confess.

Next Door

I

Ethel Jowett died still hoping not to miss
next year's *Mikado* by the D'Oyly Carte.
For being her 'male escort' (9!) to this
she gave my library its auspicious start:

The Kipling Treasury. My name. The date:
Tony Harrison   1946
in dip-in-penmanship type copperplate
with proper emphasis on thins and thicks.

Mi mam was 'that surprised' how many came
to see the cortège off and doff their hats –
All the 'old lot' left gave her the same
bussing back from 'Homes' and Old Folk's Flats.

Since mi mam dropped dead mi dad's took fright.

His dicky ticker beats its quick retreat:

It won't be long before Ah'm t'only white!

Or t'Town Hall's thick red line sweeps through t'whole
    street.

II

Their front garden (8 × 5) was one of those
the lazier could write off as 'la-di-dah'.
Her brother pipesmoked greenfly off each rose
in summer linen coat and Panama.

Hard-faced traders tore her rooms apart.
Litter and lavender in ransacked drawers,
the yearly programmes for the D'Oyly Carte.
'Three Little Maids' she'd marked with '4 encores!'

Encore! No more. A distant relative
roared up on a loud bike and poked around.
Mi mam cried when he'd gone, and spat out: *Spiv!*

I got Tennyson and Milton leather-bound.

The Sharpes came next. He beat her, blacked her eye.
Through walls I heard each blow, each *Cunt! Cunt! Cunt!*

The Jowetts' dahlias were left to die.

Now mi dad's the only one keeps up his front.

Also the only one who shifts his snow
and him long past his three score years and ten.

You *try* to understand: *Their sort don't know.*
They're from the sun. But wait till they're old men.

But if some from out that 'old lot' still survive
and, shopping for essentials, shuffle past,
they'll know by your three clear flags that you're alive
and, though you'll never speak, they're not the last.

Outside your clearing your goloshes slip.
The danger starts the moment you're next door –
the fall, the dreaded 'dislocated hip',
the body's final freeze-up with no thaw.

If you weren't scared you'd never use the phone!

The winter's got all England in its vice.

All night I hear a spade that scrapes on stone
and see our street one skidding slide of ice.

IV

All turbans round here now, forget flat caps!

They've taken over everything bar t'CO-OP.
Pork's gone west, chitt'lins, trotters, dripping baps!
And booze an' all, if it's a Moslem owns t'new shop.

Ay, t'Off Licence, that's gone Paki in t'same way!
(You took your jug and bought your bitter draught)
Ah can't get over it, mi dad'll say,
smelling curry in a pop shop. Seems all daft.

Next door but one this side 's front room wi t'
Singers *hell for leather all day long 's*
some sort o' sweatshop bi the looks on it
running up them dresses . . . them . . . sarongs!

Last of the 'old lot' still left in your block.
Those times, they're gone. The 'old lot' can't come back.

Both doors I notice now you double lock –

he's already in your shoes, your next-door black.

Long Distance

I

Your bed's got two wrong sides. Your life's all grouse.
I let your phone-call take its dismal course:

Ah can't stand it no more, this empty house!

Carrots choke us wi'out your mam's white sauce!

Them sweets you brought me, you can have 'em back.
Ah'm diabetic now. Got all the facts.
(The diabetes comes hard on the track
of two coronaries and cataracts.)

Ah've allus liked things sweet! But now ah push
food down mi throat! Ah'd sooner do wi'out.
And t'only reason now for beer 's to flush
(so t'dietitian said) mi kidneys out.

When I come round, they'll be laid out, the sweets,
Lifesavers, my father's New World treats,
still in the big brown bag, and only bought
rushing through JFK as a last thought.

II

Though my mother was already two years dead
Dad kept her slippers warming by the gas,
put hot-water bottles her side of the bed
and still went to renew her transport pass.

You couldn't just drop in. You had to phone.
He'd put you off an hour to give him time
to clear away her things and look alone
as though his still raw love were such a crime.

He couldn't risk my blight of disbelief
though sure that very soon he'd hear her key
scrape in the rusted lock and end his grief.
He *knew* she'd just popped out to get the tea.

I believe life ends with death, and that is all.
You haven't both gone shopping; just the same,
in my new black leather phone book there's your name
and the disconnected number I still call.

Flood

His home address was inked inside his cap
and on every piece of paper that he carried
even across the church porch of the snap
that showed him with mi mam just minutes married.

But if ah'm found at 'ome (he meant found dead)
turn t'water off. Through his last years he nursed,
more than a fear of dying, a deep dread
of his last bath running over, or a burst.

Each night towards the end he'd pull the flush
then wash, then in pyjamas, rain or snow,
go outside, kneel down in the yard, and push
the stopcock as far off as it would go.

For though hoping that he'd drop off in his sleep
he was most afraid, I think, of not being 'found'
there in their house, his ark, on firm Leeds ground
but somewhere that kept moving, cold, dark, deep.

The Queen's English

Last meal together, Leeds, the Queen's Hotel,
that grandish pile of swank in City Square.
Too posh for me! he said (though he dressed well)
If you weren't wi' me now ah'd nivver dare!

I knew that he'd decided that he'd die
not by the way he lingered in the bar,
nor by that look he'd give with one good eye,
nor the firmer handshake and the gruff *ta-ra*,
but when we browsed the station bookstall sales
he picked up *Poems from the Yorkshire Dales* –

*'ere tek this un wi' yer to New York
to remind yer 'ow us gaffers used to talk.
It's up your street in't it? ah'll buy yer that!*

The broken lines go through me speeding South –

As t'Doctor stopped to oppen woodland yat . . .
and
     wi' skill they putten wuds reet i' his mouth.

Aqua Mortis

Death's elixirs have their own golden gleam.
I see you clearly: one good, failing eye's
on morning piss caught clumsily 'midstream'
it's your first task of the day to analyse.

Each day dawns closer to the last *eureka*,
the urine phial held up to clouding rays
meaning all solutions in life's beaker
precipitate one night from all our days.

Alchemists keep skulls, and you have one
that stretches your skin taut and moulds your face,
and instead of a star sphere for sense of space
there's the transatlantic number of your son,
a 14-digit spell propped by the phone
whose girdling's giddy speed knocks spots off Puck's
but can't re-eye dry sockets or flesh bone.

My study is your skull. *I'll burn my books.*

Grey Matter

The ogling bottle cork with tasselled fez
bowing and scraping, rolling goo-goo eyes is
gippo King Farouk, whose lewd leer says:

I've had the lot, my lad, all shapes and sizes!

One night we kept him prancing and he poured,
filtered through his brains, his bulk of booze.
The whisky pantaloons sans sash or cord
swashed dad to the brink of twin taboos.
As King Farouk's eyes rolled, dad rolled his own:
That King Farouk! he said, and almost came
(though in the end it proved too near the bone)
to mentioning both sex and death by name.

I wake dad with what's left. King Leer's stare
stuck, though I shake him, and his fixed Sphinx smile
take in the ultimate a man can bear
and that dry Nothingness beyond the Nile.

An Old Score

Capless, conscious of the cold patch on my head
where my father's genes have made me almost bald
I walk along the street where he dropped dead,
my hair cut his length now, although I'm called
poet, in my passport.

                  When it touched my ears
he dubbed me *Paganinny* and it hurt.
I did then, and do now, choke back my tears –

Wi' 'air like that you ought to wear a skirt!

If I'd got a violin for every day
he'd said *weer's thi fiddle?* at my flowing hair
I'd have a whole string orchestra to play
romantic background as once more I'm there
where we went for my forced fortnightly clip
now under new, less shearing, ownership,
and in the end it's that that makes me cry –

JOE'S SALOON's become KURL UP & DYE!

Still

Tugging my forelock fathoming Xenophon
grimed Greek exams with grease and lost me marks,
so I whisper when the barber asks *Owt on?*
No, thank you! YES! Dad's voice behind me barks.

They made me wear dad's hair-oil to look 'smart'.
A parting scored the grease like some slash scar.
Such aspirations hair might have for ART
were lopped, and licked by dollops from his jar.

And if the page I'm writing on has smears
they're not the sort to lose me marks for mess
being self-examination's grudging tears
soaked into the blotter, Nothingness,
on seeing the first still I'd ever seen
of Rudolph Valentino, father, O
now, *now* I know why you used *Brilliantine*
to slick back your black hair so long ago.

A Good Read

That summer it was Ibsen, Marx and Gide.

I got one of his you-stuck-up bugger looks:

ah sometimes think you read too many books.
ah nivver 'ad much time for a good read.

Good read! I bet! Your programme at United!
The labels on your whisky or your beer!
You'd never get unbearably excited
poring over Kafka or King Lear.
The only score you'd bother with 's your darts,
or fucking football . . .

                              (All this in my mind.)

I've come round to your position on 'the Arts'
but put it down in poems, that's the bind.

These poems about you, dad, should make good reads
for the bus you took from Beeston into town
for people with no time like you in Leeds –

once I'm writing I can't put you down!

Isolation

I cried once as a boy when I'd to leave her
at Christmas in the fourth year of the War,
taken to Killingbeck with scarlet fever,
but don't cry now, although I see once more
from the window of the York–Leeds diesel back
for her funeral, my place of quarantine,

and don't, though I notice by the same railtrack
hawthorns laden with red berries as they'd been
when we'd seen them the day that we returned
from the hospital on this same train together
and she taught me a country saying that she'd learned
as a child: *Berries bode bad winter weather!*

and don't, though the fresh grave's flecked with sleet,
and dad, with every fire back home switched on, 's frozen,
       and don't,
            until I hear him bleat
round the ransacked house for his long johns.

Continuous

James Cagney was the one up both our streets.
His was the only art we ever shared.
A gangster film and choc ice were the treats
that showed about as much love as he dared.

He'd be my own age now in '49!
The hand that glinted with the ring he wore,
his father's, tipped the cold bar into mine
just as the organist dropped through the floor.

He's on the platform lowered out of sight
to organ music, this time on looped tape,
into a furnace with a blinding light
where only his father's ring will keep its shape.

I wear it now to Cagneys on my own
and sense my father's hands cupped round my treat –

they feel as though they've been chilled to the bone
from holding my ice cream all through *White Heat*.

Clearing

The ambulance, the hearse, the auctioneers
clear all the life of that loved house away.
The hard-earned treasures of some 50 years
sized up as junk, and shifted in a day.

A stammerer died here and I believe
this front room with such ghosts taught me my trade.
Now strangers chip the paintwork as they heave
the spotless piano that was never played.
The fingerprints they leave mam won't wipe clean
nor politely ask them first to wipe their boots,
nor coax her trampled soil patch back to green
after they've trodden down the pale spring shoots.

I'd hope my mother's spirit wouldn't chase
her scattered household, even if it could.
How could she bear it when she saw no face
stare back at her from that long polished wood?

II

The landlord's glad to sell. The neighbourhood,
he fears, being mostly black, 's now on the skids.
The gate my father made from bread-tray wood
groans at the high jinks of Jamaican kids.

Bless this house's new black owners, and don't curse
that reggae booms through rooms where you made hush
for me to study in (though I wrote verse!)
and wouldn't let my sister use the flush!

The hearse called at the front, the formal side.
Strangers used it, doctors, and the post.
It had a show of flowers till you died.
You'll have to use the front if you're a ghost,
though it's as flat and bare as the back yard,
a beaten hard square patch of sour soil.

Hush!
                Haunt me, and not the house!
                                        I've got to lard
my ghosts' loud bootsoles with fresh midnight oil.

Illuminations

I

The two machines on Blackpool's Central Pier,
The Long Drop and *The Haunted House* gave me
my thrills the holiday that post-war year
but my father watched me spend impatiently:

Another tanner's worth, but then no more!

But I sneaked back the moment that you napped.
50 weeks of ovens, and 6 years of war
made you want sleep and ozone, and you snapped:

Bugger the machines! Breathe God's fresh air!

I sulked all week, and wouldn't hold your hand.
I'd never heard you mention God, or swear,
and it took me until now to understand.

I see now all the piled old pence turned green,
enough to hang the murderer all year
and stare at millions of ghosts in the machine –

The penny dropped in time! Wish you were here!

II

We built and bombed Boche stalags on the sands,
or hunted for beached starfish on the rocks
and some days ended up all holding hands
gripping the pier machine that gave you shocks.
The current would connect. We'd feel the buzz
ravel our loosening ties to one tense grip,
the family circle, one continuous US!
That was the first year on my scholarship
and I'd be the one who'd make that circuit short.
I lectured them on neutrons and Ohm's Law
and other half-baked Physics I'd been taught.
I'm sure my father felt I was a bore!

Two dead, but current still flows through us three
though the circle takes for ever to complete –
eternity, annihilation, me,
that small bright charge of life where they both meet.

III

The family didn't always feel together.
Those silent teas with all of us apart
when no one spoke except about the weather
and not about his football or my art.

And in those silences the grating sound
of father's celery, the clock's loud tick,
the mine subsidence from deep underground,
mi mam's loose bottom teeth's relentless click.

And when, I'm told, St James's came to fetch her,
My teeth! were the final words my mother said.
Being without them, even on a stretcher,
was more undignified than being dead.

Ay! I might have said, *and put her in her box*
dressed in that long gown she bought to wear,
not to be outclassed by those posh frocks,
at her son's next New York première!

The Beast with Two Backs

Their sulks and marital misunderstanding
were often healed by hot lumbago balm.
I'd see one or the other cross the landing
to wash the pungent fire off a palm.
What may have kept them coupled through such days
was thinking that the worst of being alone 's
(though you can gratify yourself in other ways)
you can't rub your own back with *Dr Sloane's*.
In the rheumatic North in icy weather
dapper Dr Sloane with waxed mustachios
could keep my parents silently together
touching the parts they'd sooner not expose.

I hear you leave, the gate creak on the hinges
I've meant all year to oil. And now you've gone
and I've got the winter's first rheumatic twinges
and the tube of colourless gel – who'll rub it on?

Grog

Barring my begetting their flu grog-making
was one act that I'd say they'd truly share.
Worth being fluey for, like now, with body aching
that grog it took both parents to prepare.
Neither too much of the one nor of the other:
whisky enough to make a kid's tongue tingle,
honey not too cloying, father, mother,
concoct a brew where both their loves could mingle.
The whisky was Dad's solemn stewardship.
She added honey, cloves and lemon. Steam
perfumed with cinnamon rose as they'd sip
from the spoon they'd stir together with, a team.

My thermos flask of grog 's one way I try,
flu-racked and forsaken, to forget,
when waking drenched and half-delirious, why
the shape beside me 's mine roughed out in sweat.

Turns

I thought it made me look more 'working class'
(as if a bit of chequered cloth could bridge that gap!)
I did a turn in it before the glass.
My mother said: *It suits you, your dad's cap.*
(She preferred me to wear suits and part my hair:
You're every bit as good as that lot are!)

All the pension queue came out to stare.
Dad was sprawled beside the postbox (still VR),
his cap turned inside up beside his head,
smudged H A H in purple Indian ink
and Brylcreem slicks displayed so folk might think
he wanted charity for dropping dead.

He never begged. For nowt! Death's reticence
crowns his life's, and *me*, I'm opening my trap
to busk the class that broke him for the pence
that splash like brackish tears into our cap.

Punchline

No! Revolution never crossed your mind!
For the kids who never made it through the schools
the Northern working class escaped the grind
as boxers or comedians, or won the pools.

Not lucky, no physique, too shy to joke,
you scraped together almost 3 weeks' pay
to buy a cast-off uke that left you broke.
You mastered only two chords, G and A!

That's why when I've heard George Formby that I've wept.
I'd always wondered what that thing was for,
I now know was a plectrum, that you'd kept,
but kept hidden, in your secret condom drawer.

The day of your cremation which I missed
I saw an old man strum a uke he'll never play,
cap spattered with tossed dimes. I made a fist
round my small change, your son, and looked away.

Currants

An Eccles cake's my *petite madeleine*!

On Sundays dad stoked up for next week's bake
and once took me along to be 'wi' t'men'.

One Eccles needs the currants you could take
in a hand imagined cupped round a girl's breast.
Between barrels of dried fruit and tubs of lard
I hunched and watched, and thought of girls undressed
and wondered what it meant when cocks got hard.
As my daydream dropped her silky underclothes,
from behind I smelt my father next to me.

Sweat dropped into the currants from his nose:

Go on! 'ave an 'andful. It's all free.

Not this barrel though. Your sweat's gone into it.
I'll go and get my handful from another.

I saw him poise above the currants and then spit:

Next Sunday you can stay 'ome wi' yer mother!

II

At dawn I hear him hawk up phlegm and cough
before me or my mother are awake.
He pokes the grate, makes tea, and then he's off
to stoke the ovens for my Eccles cake.

I smell my father, wallowing in bed,
dripping salt no one will taste into his dough,
and clouds of currants spiral in my head
and like drowsy autumn insects come and go
darkening the lightening skylight and the walls.

My veins grow out of me like tough old vines
and grapes, each bunch the weight of a man's balls
picked by toiling Greeks and Levantines,
are laid out somewhere open air and warm
where there might be also women, sun, blue sky

overcast as blackened currants swarm
into my father's hard 'flies' cemetery'.

Note. An Eccles cake was called a 'flies' cemetery' by children.

Breaking the Chain

The mams pig-sick of oilstains in the wash
wished for their sons a better glass of gear,
'wear their own clothes into work' but not go posh,
go up a rung or two but settle near.

This meant the drawing office to the dads,
same place of work, but not blue-collar, white.
A box like a medal case went round the lads
as, one by one, their mams pushed them as 'bright'.

My dad bought it, from the last dad who still owed
the dad before, for a whole week's wage and drink.
I was brought down out of bed to have bestowed
the polished box wrapped in the *Sporting Pink*.

Looking at it now still breaks my heart!
The gap his gift acknowledged then 's as wide as
eternity, but I still can't bear to part
with these never passed on, never used, dividers.

Changing at York

A directory that runs from B to V,
the Yellow Pages' entries for HOTELS
and TAXIS torn out, the smell of dossers' pee,
saliva in the mouthpiece, whisky smells –
I remember, now I have to phone,
squashing a *Daily Mail* half full of chips,
to tell the son I left at home alone
my train's delayed, and get cut off by the pips,
how, phoning his mother, late, a little pissed,
changing at York, from some place where I'd read,
I used 2p to lie about the train I'd missed
and ten more to talk my way to some girl's bed
and, in this same kiosk with the stale, sour breath
of queuing callers, drunk, cajoling, lying,
consoling his grampa for his granny's death,
how I heard him, for the first time ever, crying.

Marked with D.

When the chilled dough of his flesh went in an oven
not unlike those he'd fuelled all his life,
I thought of his cataracts ablaze with Heaven
and radiant with the sight of his dead wife,
light streaming from his mouth to shape her name,
'not Florence and not Flo but always Florrie'.
I thought how his cold tongue burst into flame
but only literally, which makes me sorry,
sorry for his sake there's no Heaven to reach.
I get it all from Earth my daily bread
but he hungered for release from mortal speech
that kept him down, the tongue that weighed like lead.

The baker's man that no one will see rise
and England made to feel like some dull oaf
is smoke, enough to sting one person's eyes
and ash (not unlike flour) for one small loaf.

The Icing Hand

That they lasted only till the next high tide
bothered me, not him whose labour was to make
sugar lattices demolished when the bride,
with help from her groom's hot hand, first cut the cake.

His icing hand, gritty with sandgrains, guides
my pen when I try shaping memories of him
and his eyes scan with mine those rising tides
neither father nor his son could hope to swim.

His eyes stayed dry while I, the kid, would weep
to watch the castle that had taken us all day
to build and deck decay, one wave-surge sweep
our winkle-stuccoed edifice away.

Remembrance like iced cake crumbs in the throat,
remembrance like windblown Blackpool brine
overfills the poem's shallow moat
and first, ebbing, salts, then, flowing, floods this line.

Deep and Crisp and Even

Till they wore out I'd even wear Dad's whites
to look the part and make puff pastry in.
I take a whisky on these wintry nights
like he did 'for mi 'eart', and *Warfarin*.

I step most in my Dad's shoes, though, when I bake
but unlike him can't stand the kitchen's heat,
It's just stopped snowing and I need a break,
a breath of cold air in the whitened street.

Someone's already been and left a track
of patterns stamped in snow from welly soles
so makes my trudging easier there and back
planting my own steps in the printed holes.

The baker's son's puff pastry, cake or scone
won't match his Dad's however hard he tries.

Each scrunched criss-cross sole-print leaves my own
like the dusted lattice crusts on our fruit pies.

A Piece of Cake

This New York baker's bread 's described as 'Swiss'
though it's said there's something Nazi in their past.
But the cheesecake that they make 's the best there is.
It's made fresh every day and sells out fast.

My kids are coming so I buy one too,
and ask for a WELCOME frosted on the top.
I watch the tube squeeze out the script in blue.
It has my father's smell, this German's shop,
as he concentrates on his ice craftsmanship
that cost him weeks of evenings to complete,
a cake with V signs, Spitfires, landing strip,
that took too many pains to cut and eat
to welcome home a niece back from the WAAFs.

Already I feel the cake stick in my throat!

The icing tube flows freely and then coughs.

The frosting comes out Gothic and reads: ꜩꝏꜩ!

A Close One

Hawsers. Dirigibles. Searchlight. *Messerschmitts.*
Half let go. Half rake dark nowt to find . . .

Day-old bereavement debris of a blitz
there's been no shelter from, no *all clear* whined.

Our cellar 'refuge room' made anti-gas.
Damp sand that smelled of graves not Morecambe Bay.
Air Raid Precautions out of *Kensitas.*
A Victory jig-saw on Fry's Cocoa tray.
Sandwiches. Snakes & Ladders. Thermos flask.

Sirens, then silences, then bombers' drone.
Long whistles. Windows gone. Each time I'd ask
which one was the Jerry, which our own.

How close we were with death's wings overhead!

How close we were not several hours ago.

These lines to hold the still too living dead –

my Redhill container, my long-handled hoe.

'Testing the Reality'

I could count to a ragged 20 but no higher.
The flocking birds she taught me numbers by
so crammed church roof and belfry, cross and spire
their final taking off blacked Beeston's sky.

There must have been 10,000 there or more.
They picketed piercingly the passing of each day
and shrilly hailed the first new light they saw
and hour after hour their numbers grew
till, on a Sunday morning, they all flew away
as suddenly as her 70 years would do.

The day that fledged her with the wings of night
made all her days flock to it, and as one
beyond all sight, all hearing, taste, smell, touch,
they soared away and, soaring, blocked the light
of what they steered their course by from her son,
the last soul still unhatched left in the clutch.

The Effort

'The atom bomb was in manufacture before the first automatic washing machine.'

(Tillie Olsen, *Silences*)

They took our iron railings down to dump
on Dresden as one more British bomb,
but mam cajoled the men to leave a stump
to hitch the line she hung the washing from.
So three inches didn't end in German flesh.
It was the furthest from surrender when she flew
a rope full of white Y-fronts, dazzling, fresh
from being stewed all day with dolly blue
in the cellar set-pot. Her ferocious pride
would only let quite spotless clothes outside.

Washes that made her tender hands red raw
we do nowadays in no time by machine.
No one works so hard to keep things clean
so it's maybe just as well she'd got to die
before the latest in bombardments and before
our world of minimum iron and spin dry.

Bye-Byes

The judder of energy when I jump
I laugh to see immediately pass
into the titmouse wired to a mossy stump
who taps his blunt beak on the dusty glass.

She wants me to leave 'this minute' but I won't
drawn to the faded feathers in glass cases
where grown-ups see what toddlers like me don't,
imposed on stuffed creation, their own faces.

Say bye-bye, our Tony, that's enough!
We've got to buy some liver for dad's tea,
Say bye-bye . . . sanderling, bye-bye . . . ruff!
I won't say anything, and wriggle free.

Sensing her four-year-old's about to cry
she buys me a postcard with the dodo on it.
43 years on this filial sonnet
lets the tears she staunched then out: Bye-bye!

Blocks

A droning vicar bores the congregation
and misquotes *Ecclesiastes* Chapter 3.
If anyone should deliver an oration
it should be me, her son, in poetry.

All the family round me start to sob.
For all my years of Latin and of Greek
they'd never seen the point of 'for a job',
I'm not prepared to stand up now and speak.

A time to . . . plough back into the soil
the simple rhymes that started at her knee,
the poetry, that 'sedentary toil'
that began, when her lap was warm, with ABC.

Blocks with letters. Lettered block of stone.
I have to move the blocks to say farewell.

I hear the family cry, the vicar drone
and VALE, MATER 's all that I can spell.

Jumper

When I want some sort of human metronome
to beat calm celebration out of fear
like that when German bombs fell round our home
it's my mother's needles, knitting, that I hear,
the click of needles steady though walls shake.
The stitches, plain or purl, were never dropped.
Bombs fell all that night until daybreak
but, not for a moment, did the knitting stop.
Though we shivered in the cellar-shelter's cold
and the whistling bombs sent shivers through the walls
I know now why she made her scared child hold
the skeins she wound so calmly into balls.

We open presents wrapped before she died.
With that same composure shown in that attack
she'd known the time to lay her wools aside –

the jumper I open 's shop-bought, and is black!

Bringing Up

It was a library copy otherwise
you'd've flung it in the fire in disgust.
Even cremation can't have dried the eyes
that wept for weeks about my 'sordid lust'.

The undertaker would have thought me odd
or I'd've put my book in your stiff hand.
You'd've been embarrassed though to meet your God
clutching those poems of mine that you'd like banned.

I thought you could hold my *Loiners*, and both burn!

And there together in the well wrought urn,
what's left of you, the poems of your child,
devoured by one flame, unreconciled,
like soots on washing, black on bone-ash white.

Maybe you see them in a better light!

But I still see you weeping, your hurt looks:

You weren't brought up to write such mucky books!

Timer

Gold survives the fire that's hot enough
to make you ashes in a standard urn.
An envelope of coarse official buff
contains your wedding ring which wouldn't burn.

Dad told me I'd to tell them at St James's
that the ring should go in the incinerator.
That 'eternity' inscribed with both their names is
his surety that they'd be together, 'later'.

I signed for the parcelled clothing as the son,
the cardy, apron, pants, bra, dress –

the clerk phoned down: *6-8-8-3-1?*
Has she still her ring on? (Slight pause) *Yes!*

It's on my warm palm now, your burnished ring!

I feel your ashes, head, arms, breasts, womb, legs,
sift through its circle slowly, like that thing
you used to let me watch to time the eggs.

Under the Clock

Under Dyson's clock in Lower Briggate
was where my courting parents used to meet.
It had a Father Time and *Tempus Fugit*
sticking out sideways into the street
above barred windows full of wedding bands,
'eternities' to be inscribed with names,
like that I felt on dad's when we held hands,
or on mam's crumbling finger in cremation's flames.

Today back on Briggate I stopped and saw
the red hands on the Roman XII and V
those lovers won't meet under any more,
glad stooping Father Time and I survive.
I see the scythe, the hourglass, the wings,
the Latin you'd proudly ask me to construe
and think of the padded boxes with your rings,
under the clock to keep our rendezvous.

Fireguard

The best wood to make chips with for our fire
was from bakehouse boxes Dad brought smeared with lard.
It had a whiplash crack. Its sparks leaped higher.
You had to look sharpish with the fireguard.

Primed with *Posts* Mam plaited the greased chips
lit with a purple sputter and deep hiss.
More than childhood's pier-machines or sherbet dips
this fire I learned to lay 's what I most miss,
though my hands got clarted with thick lard and slack
and newsprint from the crumpled *Yorkshire Post*,
and made the white bread finger-marked and black
when I used the fire I'd lit to make us toast.

Why can't my memory home in on just that?
Through the griefguard round the glow we all sat near
burst sputterings of polished pine and fat,
then smoke I crane my neck at to watch clear.

Fire-Eater

My father speaking was like conjurors I'd seen
pulling bright silk hankies, scarves, a flag
up out of their innards, red, blue, green,
so many colours it would make me gag.

Dad's eldest brother had a shocking stammer.
Dad punctuated sentence ends with but . . .
Coarser stuff than silk they hauled up grammar
knotted together deep down in their gut.

Theirs are the acts I nerve myself to follow.
I'm the clown sent in to clear the ring.
Theirs are the tongues of fire I'm forced to swallow
then bring back knotted, one continuous string
igniting long-pent silences, and going back
to Adam fumbling with Creation's names,
and though my vocal chords get scorched and black
there'll be a constant singing from the flames.

Pain-Killers

I

My father haunts me in the old men that I find
holding the shop-queues up by being slow.
It's always a man like him that I'm behind
just when I thought the pain of him would go
reminding me perhaps it never goes,
with his pension book kept utterly pristine
in a plastic wrapper labelled *Pantihose*
as if they wouldn't pay if it weren't clean,

or learning to shop so late in his old age
and counting his money slowly from a purse
I'd say from its ornate clasp and shade of beige
was his dead wife's glasses' case. I curse,
but silently, secreting pain, at this delay,
the acid in my gut caused by dad's ghost –
I've got aerogrammes to buy. My love's away!
And the proofs of *Pain-Killers* to post!

II

Going for pills to ease the pain I get
from the Post Office on Thursdays, Pension Day,
the chemist's also gives me cause to fret
at more of my dad's ghosts, and more delay
as they queue for their prescriptions without hopes
and go looking for the old cures on the shelves,
stumbling into pyramids of scented soaps
they once called cissy when they felt 'themselves'.

There are more than in the Post Office in BOOTS
and I try to pass the time behind such men
by working out the Latin and Greek roots
of cures, the *san-* that's in *Sanatogen*,
compounds derived from *derm-* for teenage spots,
suntan creams and lotions prefixed *sol-*
while a double of my dad takes three wild shots
at pronouncing PARACETAMOL.

Background Material

My writing desk. Two photos, mam and dad.
A birthday, him. Their ruby wedding, her.
Neither one a couple and both bad.
I make out what's behind them from the blur.

Dad's in our favourite pub, now gone for good.
My father and his background are both gone,
but hers has my Welsh cottage and a wood
that still shows these same greens eight summers on,
though only the greenness of it 's stayed the same.

Though one of them 's in colour and one 's not,
the two are joined, apart from their shared frame,
by what, for photographers, would mar each shot:

in his, if you look close, the gleam, the light,
me in his blind right eye, but minute size –

in hers, as though just cast from where I write,
a shadow holding something to its eyes.

THREE

Self Justification

Me a poet! My daughter with maimed limb
became a more than tolerable sprinter.
And Uncle Joe. Impediment spurred him,
the worst stammerer I've known, to be a printer.

He handset type much faster than he spoke.
Those cruel consonants, *m*s, *p*s, and *b*s
on which his jaws and spirit almost broke
flicked into order with sadistic ease.

It seems right that Uncle Joe, 'b-buckshee
from the works', supplied those scribble pads
on which I stammered my first poetry
that made me seem a cissy to the lads.

Their aggro towards me, my need of them 's
what keeps my would-be mobile tongue still tied –

aggression, struggle, loss, blank printer's ems
by which all   eloquence   gets justified.

Divisions

All aggro in tight clothes and skinhead crops
they think that like themselves I'm on the dole.
Once in the baths that mask of 'manhood' drops.
Their decorated skins lay bare a soul.

Teenage dole-wallah piss-up, then tattoos.
Brown Ale and boys' bravado numbs their fright –
MOTHER in ivy, blood reds and true blues
against that North East skin so sunless white.

When next he sees United lose a match,
his bovvers on, his scarf tied round his wrist,
his rash NEWCASTLE RULES will start to scratch,
he'll aerosol the walls, then go get pissed . . .

So I hope the TRUE LOVE on your arm stays true,
the MOTHER on your chest stays loved, not hated.

But most I hope for jobs for all of you –

next year your tattooed team gets relegated!

II

Wartime bunkers, runways overgrown,
streets named for the town's two England caps;
cricket played with shovelblade and stone,
the daylight's rotten props near to collapse.

HEALTH (H changed to W) FOR ALL
with its *Never Have Another Haemorrhoid*
is all that decorates the tap-room wall
of this pub for pensioners and unemployed.

The Brewery that owns this place supports
only the unambiguously 'male'
Northern working-class spectator sports
that suit the image of its butch *Brown Ale*,
that puts hair on your chest, and makes you fight,
and when you're legless makes a man of you!

The *Brown Ale* drinkers watch me as I write:

one front door orange in a row all blue!

History Classes

Past scenic laybys and stag warning signs
the British borderlands roll into view.

They read: *Beware of Unexploded Mines!*
I tell my children that was World War II.

They want to walk or swim. We pick up speed.
My children boo the flash of each NO ENTRY:

High seas, and shooting, uniform or tweed,
Ministry of Defence, or landed gentry.

Danger flags from valley mills that throve,
after a fashion, on the Empire's needs.

Their own clothes spun in India they wove
the Colonel's khaki and the blue blood's tweeds.

Mill angelus, and church tower twice as high.
One foundry cast the work- and rest-day bells –

the same red cotton 's in the flags that fly
for ranges, revolutions, and rough swells.

Stately Home

'Behold Land-Interest's compound Man & Horse.'
(Ebenezer Elliott)

Those bad old days of 'rapine and of reif!'
Northumberland's peles still seeping with old wars –
this year's lawful lord and last year's thief,
those warring centaurs, scratch their unscabbed sores.

But here, horned koodoo and okapi skulls,
the family's assegais, a Masai shield,
the head of one of Chillingham's white bulls,
this month's *Tatler, Horse & Hound, The Field.*

Churned earth translucent Meissen, dusted Spode
displayed on Sundays for the pence it makes,
paintings of beasts they'd shot at or they'd rode,
cantered grabbed acres on, won local stakes,
once all one man's debatable demesne,
a day's hard ride from Cheviot to sea –

His scion, stretching back to Charlemagne,
stiff-backed, lets us put down 40p.

Lines to My Grandfathers

I

Ploughed parallel as print the stony earth.
The straight stone walls defy the steep grey slopes.
The place's rightness for my mother's birth
exceeds the pilgrim grandson's wildest hopes –

Wilkinson farmed Thrang Crag, Martindale.

Horner was the Haworth signalman.

Harrison kept a pub with home-brewed ale:

fell farmer, railwayman, and *publican*,

and he, while granma slaved to tend the vat
graced the rival bars 'to make comparisons',
Queen's Arms, the Duke of this, the Duke of that,
while his was known as just 'The Harrisons''.

He carried cane and *guineas*, no coin baser!
He dressed the gentleman beyond his place
and paid in gold for beer and whisky chaser
but took his knuckleduster, 'just in case'.

The one who lived with us was grampa Horner
who, I remember, when a sewer rat
got driven into our dark cellar corner
booted it to pulp and squashed it flat.

He cobbled all our boots. I've got his last.
We use it as a doorstep on warm days.
My present is propped open by their past
and looks out over straight and narrow ways:

the way one ploughed his land, one squashed a rat,
kept railtracks clear, or, dressed up to the nines,
with waxed moustache, gold chain, his cane, his hat,
drunk as a lord could foot it on straight lines.

Fell farmer, railwayman and publican,
I strive to keep my lines direct and straight,
and try to make connections where I can –

the knuckleduster's now my paperweight!

The Earthen Lot

for Alistair Elliot

'From Ispahan to Northumberland, there is no building that does not show the influence of that oppressed and neglected herd of men.'

(William Morris, *The Art of the People*)

Sand, caravans, and teetering sea-edge graves.

The seaward side's for those of lowly status.
Not only gales gnaw at their names, the waves
jostle the skulls and bones from their quietus.

The Church is a solid bulwark for their betters
against the scouring sea-salt that erodes
these chiselled sandstone formal Roman letters
to flowing calligraphic Persian odes,
singing of sherbet, sex in Samarkand,
with Hafiz at the hammams and harems,
O anywhere but bleak Northumberland
with responsibilities for others' dreams!

Not for the Northern bard the tamarinds
where wine is always cool, and *kusi* hot –

his line from Omar scrivened by this wind 's:

Some could articulate, while others not.

(Newbiggin-by-the-Sea, 1977)

Remains

for Robert Woof and Fleur Adcock

Though thousands traipse round Wordsworth's Lakeland shrine
imbibing bardic background, they don't see
nailed behind a shutter one lost line
with intimations of mortality
and immortality, but so discrete
it's never trespassed on 'the poet's' aura,
nor been scanned, as it is, five strong verse feet.

W. Martin's work needs its restorer,
and so from 1891 I use
the paperhanger's one known extant line
as the culture that I need to start off mine
and honour his one visit by the Muse,
then hide our combined labours underground
so once again it might be truly said
in words from Grasmere written by the dead:

our heads will be happen cold when this is found.

W. Martin
paperhanger
4 July 1891

Dichtung und Wahrheit

for Marcelino Dos Santos (*Frelimo*)
Dar-es-Salaam, 1971

Frelimo's fluent propagandist speaks
the cloven tongues of four colonial powers:
French and Spanish, Portuguese and ours,
plus Makonde *one* of Mozambique's,
and swears in each the war will soon be won.
He speaks of 'pen & sword', quotes Mao's phrase
about 'all power' the moment his guests gaze
on the 14–18 bronze with Maxim gun.

Dulciloquist Dos Santos, swear to them
whose languages you'll never learn to speak
that tongues of fire at a 1000 rpm
is not the final eloquence you seek.

Spondaic or dactylic those machines
and their dry scansions mean that truths get lost,

and a *pravda* empty as its magazines
is Kalashnikov PK 's flash Pentecost.

Sonnets for August 1945

1. The Morning After

I

The fire left to itself might smoulder weeks.
Phone cables melt. Paint peels from off back gates.
Kitchen windows crack; the whole street reeks
of horsehair blazing. Still it celebrates.

Though people weep, their tears dry from the heat.
Faces flush with flame, beer, sheer relief
and such a sense of celebration in our street
for me it still means joy though banked with grief.

And that, now clouded, sense of public joy
with war-worn adults wild in their loud fling
has never come again since as a boy
I saw Leeds people dance and heard them sing.

There's still that dark, scorched circle on the road.
The morning after kids like me helped spray
hissing upholstery spring wire that still glowed
and cobbles boiling with black gas tar for VJ.

II

The Rising Sun was blackened on those flames.
The jabbering tongues of fire consumed its rays.
Hiroshima, Nagasaki were mere names
for us small boys who gloried in our blaze.

The blood-red ball, first burnt to blackout shreds,
took hovering batwing on the bonfire's heat
above the *Rule Britannias* and the bobbing heads
of the VJ hokey-cokey in our street.

The kitchen blackout cloth became a cloak
for me to play at fiend Count Dracula in.
I swirled it near the fire. It filled with smoke.
Heinz ketchup dribbled down my vampire's chin.

That circle of scorched cobbles scarred with tar 's
a night-sky globe nerve-rackingly all black,
both hemispheres entire but with no stars,
an Archerless zilch, a Scaleless zodiac.

2. *Old Soldiers*

Last years of Empire and the fifth of War
and CAMP coffee extract on the kitchen table.
The Sikh that served the officer I saw
on the label in the label in the label
continuously cloned beyond my eyes,
beyond the range of any human staring,
down to amoeba, atom, neutron size
but the turbaned bearer never lost his bearing
and nothing shook the bottle off his tray.
Through all infinity and down to almost zero
he holds out and can't die or fade away
loyal to the breakfasting Scots hero.

But since those two high summer days
the US dropped the World's first A-bombs on,
from that child's forever what returns my gaze
is a last chuprassy with all essence gone.

3. *The Figure*

In each of our Blackpool photos from those years
and, I'll bet, in every family's South Pier snap,
behind the couples with their children on the pier, 's
the same figure standing in frayed suit and cap.

We'd come to plunge regardless in the sea,
ball-shrivellingly chill, but subs all gone,
gorge Mrs Moore's Full Board, now ration-free,
glad when *I-Speak-Your-Weight* showed pounds put on.

The first snap that I have 's from '45.
I've never seen a family group so glad
of its brief freedom, so glad to be alive,
no camera would have caught them looking sad.

He's there, in the same frayed suit, in '51,
that figure in each photo at the back
who sent us all sauntering towards the sun
and the tripod, and the biped draped in black.

4. *Black & White*

If we had the cameras then we've got today
since Oblivion, always deep, grew even deeper
the moment of the flash that made VJ
and the boom made almost pro ones so much cheaper,
I'd have snaps of me happy and pre-teen
in pale, affordable Fuji for the part
of innocence that never could have been
born just in time to see the World War start.

The ugly ducklings changed to sitting ducks!

Now everything gets clicked at the loud clock
the shots and shutters sound like 's Captain Hook's
ticking implacably inside the croc.

If he wants his shadow back the Peter Pan
who cowers since Hiroshima in us all
will have to keep returning to Japan
till the blast-cast shape walks with him off the wall.

5. *Snap*

Uncle Wilf in khaki but decapitated,
and he'd survived the jungle and the Japs,
so his grin 's gone when we all celebrated
Hirohito's empire in collapse.

My shorter father 's all in and looks glad
and full of euphoria he'd never found
before, or since, and I'm with the grocer's lad
two fingers turned the positive way round!

Innocence, that fraying Kirby wire
that briefly held the whole weight of the nation
over the common element of fire
that bonded the A-bomb blast to celebration,
our VJ bonfire to Jehovahspeak,
the hotline Jesus got instructions from,
and, at Pentecost, Apostles their technique
of saying in every language: *Ban the Bomb!*

6. First Aid in English

First Aid in English, my first grammar book
with a cross on the light blue cover of dark blue
drilled into a [?] of parrots that one rook
became a congregation when it's two.

We chanted gaggle, bevy, coven, herd
between the Nazi and the Japanese defeat.
Did even the dodo couple have its word
that became, in the last one's lifetime, obsolete?

Collective nouns but mostly bird or beast.
Ghetto and gulag weren't quite current then.
The fauna of our infancies decreased
as new nouns grew collectivizing men.

Cats in their clowder, lions in their pride,
but there's no aid in English, first or last,
for a [Fill in the Blank] of genocide
or more than one [Please Tick] atomic blast.

7. The Birds of Japan

Campi Phlegraei, Lake Nyos of Wum,
their sulphur could asphyxiate whole flocks
but combustibility had not yet come
to the femto-seconds of the *Fiat Nox*:
men made magma, flesh made fumaroles,
first mottled by the flash to brief mofettes
and Hiroshima's fast pressurizing souls
hissed through the fissures in mephitic jets.

Did the birds burst into song as they ignited
above billowing waves of cloud up in the sky,
hosannahs too short-lived to have alighted
on a Bomb-Age Bashō, or a Hokusai?

Apostles of that pinioned Pentecaust
of chirrupings cremated on the wing
will have to talk their ghosts down, or we're lost.
Until we know what they sang, who can sing?

Art & Extinction

'When I hear of the destruction of a species I feel as if all the works
of some great writer had perished.'

(Theodore Roosevelt, 1899)

1. The Birds of America

(i) *John James Audubon (1785–1851)*
The struggle to preserve once spoken words
from already too well-stuffed taxonomies
is a bit like Audubon's when painting birds,
whose method an admirer said was this:
Kill 'em, wire 'em, paint 'em, kill a fresh 'un!

The plumage even of the brightest faded.
The artist had to shoot in quick succession
till all the feathers were correctly shaded.

Birds don't pose for pictures when alive!
Audubon's idea of restraint,
doing the Pelican, was 25
dead specimens a day for *one* in paint.

By using them do we save words or not?

As much as Audubon's art could save a,
say, godwit, or a grackle, which he shot
and then saw 'multiplied by Havell's graver'.

(ii) *Weeki Wachee*

Duds doomed to join the dodo: the dugong,
talonless eagles, croc, gimp manatee,
here, courtesy Creation's generous strong,
the losers of thinned jungle and slicked sea.

Many's the proud chieftain used to strut
round shady clearings of dark festooned teak
with twenty cockatoo tails on his nut,
macaw plumes à la mode, rainforest chic.

Such gladrag gaudies safe in quarantine
and spared at least their former jungle fate
of being blowpiped for vain primitives to preen
now race a tightrope on one roller skate.

A tanned sophomore, these ghettoed birds' Svengali,
shows glad teeth, evolved for smiling, as macaws
perform their deft Darwinian finale
by hoisting the Stars and Stripes for our applause.

(iii) *Standards*

in hopeful anticipation of the bicentenary of the national emblem
of the United States of America, *Haliaaetus Falco Leucocephalus*,
1782–1982

'The bald eagle is likewise a large, strong, and very active bird, but
an execrable tyrant: he supports his assumed dignity and grandeur
by rapine and violence, extorting unreasonable tribute and subsidy
from the feathered nations.'

(William Bartram, *Travels*, 1791)

'Our standard with the eagle stands for us.
It waves in the breeze in almost every clime.'

(The flag, not *Falco Leucocephalus*
poised in its dying on the brink of time!)

Rejecting Franklin's turkey for a bird that *flies*
Congress chose the soaring eagle, called,
for its conspicuous white head, 'the bald'.

Now the turkey's thriving and the eagle dies!

When the last stinks in its eyrie, or falls slow,
when the very last bald eagle goes the way
of all the unique fauna, it won't know
the Earth it plummets to 's the USA.

But will still wing over nations as the ghost
on money, and the mountainous US Post.

much as sunlight shining through the British pound
showed PEACE with her laurels, white on a green ground.

2. *Loving Memory*

for Teresa Stratas

The fosses where Caractacus fought Rome
blend with grey bracken and become a blur
above the Swedish Nightingale's last home.

Somehow my need for you makes me seek her.

The Malverns darken as the dusk soaks in.
The rowan berries' dark red glaze grows dull.
The harvest moon's scraped silver and bruised tin
is only one night off from being full.

Death keeps all hours, but graveyards close at nights.
I hurry past the Malvern Hospital
where a nurse goes round small wards and puts on lights
and someone there's last night begins to fall.

'The oldest rocks this earth can boast', these hills,
packed with extinction, make me burn for you.

I ask two women leaving with dead daffodils:
Where's Jenny Lind's grave, please? They both say: *Who?*

3. *Looking Up*

for Philip, Terry, and Will Sharpe and the bicentenary of the birth
of Peter Mark Roget (1779–1869)

All day till it grows dark I sit and stare
over Herefordshire hills and into Wales.
Reflections of red coals thrown on the air
blossom to brightness as the daylight fails.

An uncharred cherry flaunts a May of flames.
Like chaffinches and robins tongues of fire
flit with the burden of Creation's names
but find no new apostle to inspire.

Bar a farmhouse TV aerial or two,
the odd red bus, the red Post Office van,
this must have been exactly Roget's view,
good Dr Roget, the *Thesaurus* man.

Roget died here, but 90 when he died
of natural causes, twice as old as me.

Of his six synonyms for suicide
I set myself alight with safe suttee.

4. Killing Time

Among death-protected creatures in a case,
'The Earth's Endangered Species' on display
at a jam-packed terminal at JFK,
killing time again, I see my face
with Hawksbill Turtle, scrimshawed spermwhale bone,
the Margay of the family *Felidae*,
that, being threatened, cost the earth to buy.

And now with scientists about to clone
the long-haired mammoth back from Soviet frost,
my reflection's on the species the World's lost,
or will be losing in a little while,
which, as they near extinction, grow in worth,
the leopard, here a bag and matching purse,
the dancing shoes that were Nile crocodile,

the last *Felis Pardalis* left on Earth,

the poet preserved beneath deep permaverse.

5. Dark Times

That the *Peppered Moth* was white and now is dark 's
a lesson in survival for Mankind.

Around the time Charles Darwin had declined
the dedication of *Das Kapital* by Marx
its predators could spot it on the soot,
but Industrial Revolution and Evolution taught
the moth to black its wings and not get caught
where all of Nature perished, or all but.

When lichens lighten some old smoke-grimed trees
and such as Yorkshire's millstacks now don't burn
and fish nose waters stagnant centuries,
can *Biston Carbonaria* relearn,

if Man's awakened consciousness succeeds
in turning all these tides of blackness back
and diminishing the need for looking black,

to flutter white again above new Leeds?

6. t'Ark

Silence and poetry have their own reserves.
The numbered creatures flourish less and less.
A language near extinction best preserves
the deepest grammar of our nothingness.

Not only dodo, oryx and great auk
waddled on their tod to t'monster ark,
but 'leg', 'night', 'origin' in crushed people's talk,
tongues of fire last witnessed mouthing: *dark!*

Now when the future couldn't be much darker,
there being fewer epithets for sun,
and Cornish and the Togoland *Restsprache*
name both the animals and hunter's gun,
celebrate before things go too far
Papua's last reported manucode,
the pygmy hippo of the Côte d'Ivoire,
and Upper Guinea's oviparous toad –

(or mourn in Latin their imminent death,
then translate these poems into *cynghanedd*.)

7. *The Poetry Lesson*

Its proboscis probes the basking monster's eye.
The *Flambeau*, whose ambrosia's salt dew
and nectars sucked from caymans' *lacrimae*,
survives on saurian secretions in Peru.

The blue fritillary of north Brazil
I saw uncurl the watchspring of its tongue
and, by syphoning or licking, have its fill
of goodnesses discarded in man's dung.
The question mark (complete with added dot)
crapped on the pavement in full public view
by cane-hooch-smashed emaciate was steaming hot
but ambrosia not shit to browsing Blue.

Both lessons in survival for fine words
to look for fodder where they've not yet looked –
be lepidoptera that browse on turds
or delicately drain the monster's duct.

8. *Dendrocopos Minor*

in memoriam Jocelyn Herbert, 1917–2003

I see in the lengthening *Endangered List*
the *po'ouli* of Hawaii's down to two.
Extinction's heartless fundamentalist,
who'll snuff loved local flora first snuffed you.

Abundant bluebells, doomed to disappear
with newly announced endangered British birds,
bloomed in cobalt clouds and filled the dell,
cerulean rapids walked on by two deer.
The day you died you stood there lost for words
till the two deer bolted off and broke the spell.

Drinking *retsina* there on your last day
toasting those bluebells we'd just seen we heard
then saw the woodpecker these figures say
is 'Britain's most rapidly declining bird'.

You, *Dendrocopos minor*, both burn bright,
its red head in your heart that final night.

On the Metre

I'm always quoting *le coeur bat l'iambe* –
Jean-Louis Barrault on the metre of Racine.
Blood recorded on an echocardiogram
in synch with karaoke squid shapes on the screen,
I hear now with a woman in white coat.
Though not iambic, more fluttery trochee,
the odd dochmaic, anapaest, I note
the verse in my pounding heart at least 's not free.

The beat 's in a blood wash, the sound 's more
a factory filled most hours but now forlorn
where a nightshift cleaner swabs a vast tiled floor
shoes 'll clatter on and echo come the dawn,
someone weary and worksick but in a hurry
with measured swishes from his sodden mop.

She switches off that sound like sloshing slurry
and I hear the tide of almost Alexandrines stop.

Gaps

Sitting in the ferry's stern, my son, my dad,
with a gap where I'd been till I took these snaps.
Both wear fur hats I'd brought from Leningrad
in Cold War days before the Wall's collapse.

Dad's, though his mates mocked, got lots of wear.
On his Leeds United terrace his bald head
was kept snug by Siberian brown bear.
My daughter 's got his hat, but Dad 's long dead.

My son's was made of rabbit and he gnawed
the fur off it in clumps when we saw *Jaws*.
He didn't need it in the locked hot ward,
his visions frightening as the First Gulf War's.

This snap 's a snatched but happy family scene,
bright New York winter sun between two showers
shining on both of them, and in between
the World Trade Center's unbombarded towers.

Listening to Sirens

Was it the air-raids that I once lived through
listening to sirens, then the bombers' drone
that makes the spring night charter to Corfu
wake me at 2, alarmed, alert, alone?
I watch its red light join the clustered stars
in the one bright clearing in the overcast
then plummet to become a braking car's
cornering deserted side-streets far too fast.

My lilac purples as the headlamps pass
and waft it in, that same lilac smell
that once was used to sweeten mustard gas
and induce men to inhale the fumes of hell.
A thin man from that War who lived round here
used to go berserk on nights like these,
cower, scream, and crap his pants with fear
whenever he scented lilac on the breeze.

Senses that have been blighted in this way
or dulled by dark winter long for the warm South,
some place we hollow out for holiday,
and nothing spoils the white wine in the mouth.
I drag my senses back into the dark
and think of those pale Geordies on their flight.
I'd still be oblivious when they disembark
dazzled by the blue and the bright light.

Facing North

'The North begins inside.'
        (Louis MacNeice)

God knows why of all rooms I'd to choose
the dark one facing North for me to write,
liking as I do air, light and views,
though there's air in the North wind that rocks the light
I have to keep on, all year round, all day;
nor why, despite a climate I profess to hate,
and years spent overseas, I stay,
and, when I start to pack, procrastinate.

The North wind's part of it and when it blows
my shutters rattle and the front door slams
like memory shutting out half what it knows.
Here I poured huge passion into aerogrammes,
the lightest paper loaded with new hope
and made the old pain seem, on looking back,
seen through the wrong end of the telescope
making it so small I soon lost track.

The window's open to the winter's chill,
to air, to breezes and strong gusts that blow
my paper lantern nothing will keep still
and let me make things happen in its O.
When the circle, where my hand moves over white
with red and green advances on black ink,
first swung like this it gave me such a fright
I felt I was on a ship about to sink.

Now years of struggle make me concentrate
when it throws up images of planets hurled,
still glowing, off their courses, and a state
where there's no gravity to hold the world.

I have to hold on when I think such things
and weather out these feelings so that when
the wind drops and the light no longer swings
I can focus on an Earth that still has men,

in this flooded orchestra where elbow grease,
deep thought, long practice and much sweat
gave me some inkling of an inner peace
I'd never found with women till I met
the one I wrote all those air letters for
and she's the one I'm needing as I see
the North wind once more strip my sycamore
and whip the last leaves off my elder tree.

Now when the wind flays my wild garden of its green
and blows, whistling through the flues, its old reminder
of the two cold poles all places are between,
though where she lives the climate's a lot kinder,
and starts the lightbulb swinging to and fro,
and keeps it swinging, switched off, back and forth,
I feel the writing room I'm leaving grow
dark, and then darker with the whole view North.

A Kumquat for John Keats

Today I found the right fruit for my prime,
not orange, not tangelo, and not lime,
nor moon-like globes of grapefruit that now hang
outside our bedroom, nor tart lemon's tang
(though last year full of bile and self-defeat
I wanted to believe no life was sweet)
nor the tangible sunshine of the tangerine,
and no incongruous citrus ever seen
at greengrocers' in Newcastle or Leeds
mis-spelt by the spuds and mud-caked swedes,
a fruit an older poet might substitute
for the grape John Keats thought fit to be Joy's fruit,
when, two years before he died, he tried to write
how Melancholy dwelled inside Delight,
and if he'd known the citrus that I mean
that's not orange, lemon, lime or tangerine,
I'm pretty sure that Keats, though he had heard
'of candied apple, quince and plum and gourd'
instead of 'grape against the palate fine'
would have, if he'd known it, plumped for mine,
this Eastern citrus scarcely cherry size
he'd bite just once and then apostrophize
and pen one stanza how the fruit had all
the qualities of fruit before the Fall,
but in the next few lines be forced to write
how Eve's apple tasted at the second bite,
and if John Keats had only lived to be,
because of extra years, in need like me,
at 42 he'd help me celebrate
that Micanopy kumquat that I ate
whole, straight off the tree, sweet pulp and sour skin –
or was it sweet outside, and sour within?
For however many kumquats that I eat
I'm not sure if it's flesh or rind that's sweet,

and being a man of doubt at life's mid-way
I'd offer Keats some kumquats and I'd say:
You'll find that one part's sweet and one part's tart:
say where the sweetness or the sourness start.
I find I can't, as if one couldn't say
exactly where the night became the day,
which makes for me the kumquat taken whole
best fruit, and metaphor, to fit the soul
of one in Florida at 42 with Keats
crunching kumquats, thinking, as he eats
the flesh, the juice, the pith, the pips, the peel,
that this is how a full life ought to feel,
its perishable relish prick the tongue,
when the man who savours life 's no longer young,
the fruits that were his futures far behind.
Then it's the kumquat fruit expresses best
how days have darkness round them like a rind,
life has a skin of death that keeps its zest.

History, a life, the heart, the brain
flow to the taste buds and flow back again.
That decade or more past Keats's span
makes me an older not a wiser man,
who knows that it's too late for dying young,
but since youth leaves some sweetnesses unsung,
he's granted days and kumquats to express
Man's Being ripened by his Nothingness.
And it isn't just the gap of sixteen years,
a bigger crop of terrors, hopes and fears,
but a century of history on this earth
between John Keats's death and my own birth –
years like an open crater, gory, grim,
with bloody bubbles leering at the rim;
a thing no bigger than an urn explodes
and ravishes all silence, and all odes,

Flora asphyxiated by foul air
unknown to either Keats or Lemprière,
dehydrated Naiads, Dryad amputees
dragging themselves through slagscapes with no trees,
a shirt of Nessus fire that gnaws and eats
children half the age of dying Keats . . .

Now were you twenty-five or -six years old
when that fevered brow at last grew cold?
I've got no books to hand to check the dates.
My grudging but glad spirit celebrates
that all I've got to hand are kumquats, John,
the fruit I'd love to have your verdict on,
but dead men don't eat kumquats, or drink wine,
they shiver in the arms of Proserpine,
not warm in bed beside their Fanny Brawne,
nor watch her pick ripe grapefruit in the dawn
as I did, waking, when I saw her twist,
with one deft movement of a sunburnt wrist,
the moon, that feebly lit our last night's walk
past alligator swampland, off its stalk.
I thought of moon-juice juleps when I saw,
as if I'd never seen the moon before,
the planet glow among the fruit, and its pale light
make each citrus on the tree its satellite.

Each evening when I reach to draw the blind
stars seem the light zest squeezed through night's black rind;
the night's peeled fruit the sun, juiced of its rays,
first stains, then streaks, then floods the world with days,
days, when the very sunlight made me weep,
days, spent like the nights in deep, drugged sleep,
days in Newcastle by my daughter's bed,
wondering if she, or I, weren't better dead,
days in Leeds, grey days, my first dark suit,
my mother's wreaths stacked next to Christmas fruit,
and days, like this in Micanopy. Days!

As strong sun burns away the dawn's grey haze
I pick a kumquat and the branches spray
cold dew in my face to start the day.
The dawn's molasses make the citrus gleam
still in the orchards of the groves of dream.
The limes, like Galway after weeks of rain,
glow with a greenness that is close to pain,
the dew-cooled surfaces of fruit that spent
all last night flaming in the firmament.
The new day dawns. O days! My spirit greets
the kumquat with the spirit of John Keats.
O kumquat, comfort for not dying young,
both sweet and bitter, bless the poet's tongue!
I burst the whole fruit chilled by morning dew
against my palate. Fine, for 42!

I search for buzzards as the air grows clear
and see them ride fresh thermals overhead.
Their bleak cries were the first sound I could hear
when I stepped at the start of sunrise out of doors,
and a noise like last night's bedsprings on our bed
from Mr Fowler sharpening farmers' saws.

Florida Frost

Cancer carried off his cherished wife
as Florida floundered in a freak harsh freeze
and let the Fahrenheit out of his life
never to gain back its lost degrees.
He still can't quite believe she's wholly lost.
He no more thought he'd see his dear one go
than that he'd see in Florida a frost
with that sudden drop last year to 12 below.

Grapefruit froze then splurted slush.
Unripe oranges were cold and hard.
Tears were shed for many a blighted bush
in every northern Florida backyard.
Pipless tangelos with loose zipper skins
flashed frozen segments with a sound like farts.
Burst pith with ice spikes like a hexer's pins
hammered in to atrophy those parts.

Literally glacé, ice-candied rind
rims the ruined kumquats with a shine,
moonshafts from shadows, they're the kind
served by Pluto to sad Proserpine.
Stacks of citrus branches burned all night
and glowed through the window of his sharpening shed
onto rows of glittering teeth that soon would bite
into more local orchards that were dead.

A man brought in his grandad's old two-hander –
felling an orchard was a chore to share,
a source of grief to grower goose and gander
so he asks his wife to go Dutch on despair.
Her grip on the other handle steels his nerves.
She hears, as the kumquat crown bows to the blade,
the boiling pock-pock of a life's preserves
then collapsing pantry shelves of marmalade.

He gets a different memory from the saw,
and feels the rhythms they once used in love,
though the bedsprings aren't so squeaky any more,
in the old two-hander that they pull and shove.
Gratified greed gives saws their grin.
Whether a moist juice dribbles down its jaw
or just a few dry crumbs stick to its chin,
any wood seems toothsome to a saw.

The moist eyes move from new cut stump to stump
of trees that never failed them, and just last year
fruited when she found her frightening lump
and the whole house reeked with jamming and joint fear.
Now he sharpens saws with relish for them both,
bitter that the bright oncologist maligned
their glorious groves by calling cancer 'growth'
and all day the whetted teeth have whined and dined.

Never had saws more venom in their bite.
Never did fruit trees struggle less to fall.
Why shouldn't Florida feel freezing blight
walk in from the groves and touch them all?
One Sunday his sense of loss sent him berserk –
another turkeyless repast to face alone.
He took the mower out and made short work
of everything his wife had ever grown.

Earth dragged down his darling and his dear
and considered it just recompense to toss
hydrangeas his direction once a year.
All Busch Gardens weren't worth such a loss.
What happened to vast acres north and west
of central Florida attacked his wife;
the icy Celsius gnawed at her breast
and robbed the Citrus State of half its life.

Skywriting

for David Hockney

The Californians read the sky aloud.
The Pasadena HAPPY turns to cloud!

My desk top's like a Californian pool.
Practice mirrors from the ballet school,
meditation group, karate class
dodge or lay doggo in my desk-top glass,
but the opposite gymnasia both let through
enough clear sky to flood the desk with blue
which, like purposeful deletions, smoketrails cross.

Such smoketrails would have been of sphagnum moss
if these aeroplanes were floats displayed
at Pasadena's New Year Rose Parade,
and in the air, plus HAPPY, there'd appear
as HAPPY starts dissolving, the NEW YEAR.
The seven puffs of white that made the Y
are disconnected cottonballs and sky.

As many floats as minutes are in hours
and nothing's used to make them but fresh flowers,
raw cotton (wool not being flora) sheep
go bleating round a hyacinth Bo-Peep.
A woodwardia howdah delicately sways
with jonquil rajahs turbaned with bouquets,
the Cross in crocus and in baby's breath
but no carnation Christ clamped to his death,
no battered nailheads of black onion seeds,
no spearthrust of poinsettia that bleeds.
A larkspur 'Swoonatra' in lunaria marquee
croons blue dendrobiums as do-re-mi,
a eucalyptus Calliope plays
furze and broom ta-ra-ra boom-de-ays.

Next day in Pasadena the parade
succumbs to seconds and to Centigrade.
Mange-stricken mane and stripes moult in the heat,
the tiger's marigolds, the lion's wheat.
Poinsettia and poppy start to wilt
and deMcPhersonize the floral kilt.
Stoned teenagers in New Year t-shirts steal
the gladioli from the glockenspiel.
What struts in a sticky palm an hour or so 's
no longer the snake's pupil but a rose.

Real gardens make imaginary toads
as purple biro marks make funeral odes,
roses one huge daffodil, the clover moons,
and ferns make bars with cedar bark spitoons.
Life made out of minutes rings as true
as floragraphs of Cherokee and Sioux,
and like igloos quilted out of eglantine
1980's made from '79!

The new depth of my desk top's like a pit's!

The first stars spike its black with silver spritz.
The twilight shandygaff's a little swish
of seltzer in a lake of liquorice.
Under plexiglass the crushed polestar
's a boot-buffed Coke top stuck in Broadway tar.
Half conquered, half unconquerable space
in total darkness now reflects my face.
The space where Apollo slid into Soyuz
cries out for some strong, some tireless muse.
Like Arabella spider, I too try,
trailing these blown lines across the sky,
the creator with small letter c,
to learn to spin new webs in zero G.

And these figures lowered through my eyes
out of and into ever darkening skies,
they're not the engrossed classes opposite
floating in free fall above my pit,
feeling each other's faces like the blind,
or trying to rein still a racing mind,
nor those who've spent the new decade's first weeks
mastering self-help anti-rape techniques –
Mummers from Allendale, that's who they are!
Glum guisers with halved hogsheads of lit tar,
in costumes culled from soccer and crusade
cast crackling casks to start the new decade.
The firebarrels make a New Year blaze
that sparks a chain of beacons that are days.
The tossed in barrels send a noisy hiss
up from the surface of my desk's abyss.
It's up to someone else, not me to write
HAPPY in this smoke across the night.

Exeunt the other mummers. 'In comes I'
sounding with short plumb my blackened sky,
blackface Narcissus whose spirit has to pass
over the desk with dark depths in its glass.

In the glass desk now no lightening spark
pricks through the shiny carbon of its dark.
Night caulked over the light's last penpoint chink.
The tarred creator stares at seas of ink,
and at the solstice of his silence cries aloud:

The Pasadena HAPPY turns to cloud!

And goes on repeating and repeating the same cry
until the seas of ink have all run dry.

The Call of Nature

Taos, New Mexico, 1980

for the 50th anniversary of the death of D. H. Lawrence (1885–1930)

Juniper, aspen, blue spruce, just thawing snow
on the Sangre de Cristo mountains of New Mexico.

The trick's to get that splendid view with all
those open spaces, without the hot-dog stall,
and those who shoot their photos as they pass
might well end up with billboards saying GAS!

The pueblo people live without TV
but will let you snap their houses, for a fee.
Their men get work as extras and are bussed
to ancestral battlefields to bite the dust.
And bussed, but to snap adobes, rubber necks
get excursion visits to 'the priest of sex'.
They stay put in the bus. They smell the pine
not spritzed from aerosols but genuine,
dense in the thin air of that altitude.
They've heard about his work, and that it's rude.
Back on the valley freeway at the first motel
they forget both noble Navajo and D.H.L.
Their call of nature ends through separate doors
branded in ranch pokerwork: BRAVES! SQUAWS!

Giving Thanks

Late last night on 77th I waited
to watch the Macy mammoths get inflated
and listen to the blear-eyed children cheer
as Kermit's leg or Snoopy's limp left ear
came out of their collapse, as gas was blown
through each sagged limb, now magically regrown.

Each mammoth stirs beneath its weighted net
straining for the sky it can't have yet,
impatient to be loosed out of the dark
over the browning trees of Central Park.

From yesterday I still can feel you blow
your love all through me like some helium
that restores my true proportions, head to toe,
and lifts my body skywards. When I come
I'm out of the sandbagged nets and soar away
into release and *my* Thanksgiving Day.

(Thanksgiving Day, 22 November 1979)

The Red Lights of Plenty

for the centenary of the death of Karl Marx, died London,
14 March 1883

'. . . et asperi
Martis sanguineas quae cohibet manus,
quae dat belligeris foedera gentibus
et cornu retinet devite copiam.'
(Seneca, *Medea* 62–5)

Though ageing and abused still half benign
this petrified PLENTY spilling from her horn
the Old World's edibles, the redskins' corn,
next to the Law Court's Fallout Shelter sign
the blacks and oranges of Hallowe'en.
All that motherly bounty turned to stone!
She chokes back tears of dribbling gasoline
for the future fates of countries like my own.

I stroll round Washington. November strews
red welcomes on the pavements from the trees
on Constitution and Independence Avenues
as if the least pedestrians were VIPs
or returning warlords lured inside to hack,
their lifeblood gushing out this hue of Fall
bulldozed by Buick and by Cadillac
to side drains too choked up to take it all.

Through two museums, *Science* and *Indian Arts*
something from deep below the car-choked street,
like thousands of Poe's buried tell-tale hearts
pounds with a bass and undissembled beat.
With NASA decals, necklaces by Navajo,
Japanese in groups come out to stare
at the demolition that they'd felt below
their feet, choking this chill Sunday air.

The American Wrecking Co.'s
repeatedly rammed iron wrecking ball
swinging in arcs of rhythmic tos and fros
against a scarcely-50-year-old, well-built wall
cracks cement from criss-cross steel supports,
and, floor by floor, once guaranteed to last
till time needs more museums, Justice Courts,
and enterprises space, collapses to the past.

A red light flashes many times a minute
on the Population Clock here in DC
to show the billions the World has in it
including those police, that black youth, me,
and, three years ago today, reached 4.5!
Each line of verse how many people born?
How many of these children will survive
crushed through the narrow end of PLENTY's horn?

And one red light for punished and for pitied
the FBI displays next to the time
flashes on whenever there's committed
somewhere in the States a serious crime,
as I imagine that it flashed on when the youth
I see handcuffed and then screeched away
to monuments of Justice, Order, Truth,
committed his, but what it was I couldn't say.

An All Souls' pumpkin rots on someone's porch.
It could be PLENTY's head, about to die,
her cornucopia a guttering torch
still hot enough to scorch the whole Earth dry.
This pumpkin lantern's gouged eyes glued
against some unbelievably bright glare
can't see, as I do, that young black pursued
then caught, the red lights hacking darkening air.

Leaves, some like menses, some volcanic hues,
whirl on successive wafts of hot CO
as Constitution and Independence Avenues
boom to the ball and chain's destructive blow
and, against Virginia, on Capital and Law
each sunset-reddened window one degree
of vast thermometers that, floor by floor,
chart our fever up to World War Three.

In a poem this long how many new souls born?
How many pendulum swings of wreckers' ball
that throbs beneath the White House on whose lawn
a giant vacuum's Hoovering the Fall?

The Heartless Art

in memoriam S. T., died 4 April 1985

Death is in your house, but I'm out here
sackclothing kumquats against the forecast freeze,
filling the hole you took two days to clear
of briars, beercans, and bleached, barkless trees,
with hackberry leaves, pine needles, stuff like that.
Next spring, when you're no longer here
we'll have the land grassed over and quite flat.

When the Southern sun starts setting it sets fast.
I've time to tip one more load if I run.
Because I know this light could be your last
I drain the day of every drop of sun.
The barrow wheel spins round with a clock's tick.
I hear, three fields away, a hunter's gun,
you, in the silence after, being sick.

I watched you, very weak, negotiate
the childproof pill jar, panting to draw breath,
and when you managed it you poured your hate
more on the poured-out contents than on death,
and, like Baptists uttering Beelzebub
syllable by syllable, spat *Meth-
a-done*, and there's also the poetic rub!

I've often heard my fellow poets (or those
who write in metres something like my own
with rhyme and rhythm, not in chopped-up prose
and brood on man's mortality) bemoan
the insufficiency of rhymes for death –
hence my syllabifying *Methadone*
instead of just saying that you fought for breath.

Maybe the main but not the only cause;
a piece of engineering I'll explain.
Each syllable *was* followed by a pause
for breathlessness, and scorn of drugs for pain.
Another reason, though, was to delay
the use of one more rhyme stored in my brain
that, alas, I'll have a use for any day.

I'd stored away this rhyme when we first met.
Knowing you crawled on hands and knees to prime
our water pump, I'll expiate one debt
by finally revealing that stored rhyme
that has the same relentlessness as death
and comes to every one of us in time
and comes to you this April full moon, SETH!

In return for all those oily working parts
you took the time and trouble to explain,
the pump that coughs, the saw that never starts,
I'll show you to distract you from the pain
you feel, except when napping, all the time
because you won't take drugs that dull the brain,
a bit about my metre, line and rhyme.

In Arthur Symons' *St Teresa* Nazaréth
is stressed on the last against its spoken flow
to engineer the contrast Jesus/Death.
Do I endorse that contrast? I don't, no!
To have a life on Earth and then want Heaven
seems like that all-night bar sign down below
that says that *Happy Hour*'s from 4 to 7.

Package lounges are like ambulances:
the Bourbon-bibber stares at us and glowers
at what he thinks are pained or pitying glances.
We don't see his face but he sees ours.

The non-dying don't see you but you see them
passing by to other rooms with flowers
as you fill the shining kidney with red phlegm.

I've left some spaces (   )¹
benumbed by morphia and *Methadone*
until the (   )² of April, (   )³
When I began these lines could I have known
that the nurse's registration of the time
you let your spirit go with one last groan
would help complete the first and third line rhyme?

Those bits I added later. Them apart
I wrote this *in memoriam* for Seth,
meant to show him something of my art,
almost a whole week before his death.
The last thing the dying want to read,
I thought, 's a poem, and didn't show it,
and you, not dying yet, why should you need
to know the final failure of the poet?

1. how you stayed alive
2. 4th
3. 10.05

The Fire-Gap

A Poem with Two Tails

The fire-patrol plane's tail-fins flash.
I see it suddenly swoop low,
or maybe it's scouting out the hash
some 'crackers' round here grow.
There's nothing on our land to hide,
no marijuana here,
I think the patrol's quite satisfied
the fire-gap's bulldozed clear.
I'm not concerned what's in the air
but what's beneath my feet.
This fire-gap I walk on 's where
the snake and I will meet.
Where we live is much the same
as other land in the US,
half kept cultivated, tame,
and half left wilderness,
and living on this fire-gap
between wilderness and tilled
is the snake my neighbours want to trap;
they want 'the motherfucker' killed.
One man I know round here who's mean
would blast the hole with dynamite
or flood the lair with gasoline
and maybe set the woods alight.
Against all truculent advice
I've let the rattler stay,
and go each day with my flask of ice
to my writing shed this way.
I think the land's quite big enough
to contain both him and me
as long as the odd, discarded slough
is all of the snake I see.

But I'm aware that one day on this track
there'll be, when I'm least alert,
all six feet of diamondback
poised to do me mortal hurt,
or I might find its shrugged-off shed –
'clothes on the beach', 'gone missing',
and just when I supposed him dead
he's right behind me, hissing.
Although I know I risk my neck
each time I pass I stare
into the gopher hole to check
for signs the rattler's there.
I see the gopher's pile of dirt
with like rope-marks dragged through
and I'm at once on the alert
for the killer of the two.
Is it perverse of me to start
each morning as I pass the hole
with a sudden pounding of my heart,
my fear out of control,
my Adam's apple in a vice
so scared that I mistake
the rattle of my thermos ice
for the angry rattlesnake?
I've started when a pine twig broke
or found I'd only been afraid
of some broken branch of dead live-oak
zig-zagged with sun and shade.
But if some barley starts to sway
against the movement of the breeze
and most blades lean the other way
that's when you'd better freeze.
If you've dragged a garden hose
through grass that's one foot tall
that's the way the rattler goes
if you catch a glimpse at all.

I killed snakes once, about a score
in Africa and in Brazil
yet they filled me with such awe
it seemed gross sacrilege to kill.
Once with matchet and domestic broom
I duelled with a hooded snake
with frightened children in the room
and all our lives at stake.
The snake and I swayed to and fro.
I swung the broom. Her thick hood spread.
I jabbed the broom. She rode the blow
and I hacked off her hooded head.
Then I lopped this 'laithly worm'
and sliced the creature into nine
reptilian lengths that I saw squirm
as if still one connected spine.
The gaps between the bits I'd lopped
seemed supple snake though made of air
so that I wondered where life stopped
and if death started, where?
Since that time I've never killed
any snake that's come my way
between the wild land and the tilled
where I walk every day
towards my woodland writing shed,
my heart mysteriously stirred
if I get a glimpse of tail or head
or think its rattle's what I heard
when it's only a cicada's chirr
that grates on my cocked ear
not the hidden it/him/her
it so scares me to hear.
I've tried at last to come to terms
and deal only through my craft
with this laithliest of laithly worms
with poison fore, grim music aft

that makes my heart jam up my throat
and fills me with fear and wonder
as at the sound made when *Der Tod*
(in Strasbourg) *schlägt die Stunde.*
The sainted heroes of the Church
beheaded serpents who stood for
the Mother whose name they had to smirch
to get their own foot in the door.
We had to fight you to survive:
Darkness versus Light!
Now I want you on my land alive
and I don't want to fight.
Smitten by Jehovah's curses:
On thy belly thou must go!
I don't think Light is what you're versus
though the Bible tells me so.
I've seen you basking in the sun.
I've seen you entering the earth.
Darkness and Light to you are one.
You link together death and birth.
The Bible has another fable
that almost puts us on a par,
how God smote low ambitious Babel
for trying to reach too far.
From being once your mortal foe
and wanting all your kind to die
because the Bible told me so,
I now almost identify.
So, snake, old rhyming slang's
equivalent for looking glass,
when I walk here draw back your fangs
and let your unlikely ally pass.
I'm walking to my shed to write
and work out how they're linked
what's called the Darkness and the Light
before we all become extinct.

Laithly, maybe, but Earth-lover,
unmolested, let me go.
so my struggles might discover
what you already know.
As the low-flying fire-patrol
makes the slash and live-oaks sway
I go past the deep-dug gopher hole
where I hope my snake will stay
and stay forever if it likes.
I swear no one on this land will kill
the rattlesnake unless it strikes
then, I give my word, I will.
This fire-gap we trim with care
and mow short twice a year
is where we sometimes spot a hare,
a polecat, snake or deer.
They're off so fast one scarcely sees
retreating scut or tail
before they're lost among the trees
and they've thrown you off their trail.
But there's one who doesn't make
quick dashes for the undergrowth
nor bolts for the barley, that's the snake
whose length can bridge them both.
I've seen it span the fire-gap,
its whole six feet stretched out,
the wild touched by its rattle tip,
the tilled field by its snout.
Stretched out where the scrub's been mown
the rattler's lordly manner
treats the earth as all its own,
gap, cereals, savannah.
Best keep to my land if you're wise.
Once you cross my boundary line
the Bible-belters exorcize
all traces of the serpentine,

from Satan plain to demon drink
the flesh you're blamed for keeping hot,
all earth-embracing snakes that slink
whether poisonous or not,
the fairy, pacifist, the Red,
maybe somebody who loves the Muse
are all forms of the serpent's head
their God tells them to bruise,

the God invoked in Titusville
on last night's local news
against the enemies they'd kill
with the blessed and baptized Cruise.

I fear they're not the sort to see,
these Christians of the South,
the only real eternity
is a tale (like your tail) in the mouth.

The Lords of Life

The snake our cracker neighbour had to scotch
was black and white and beautiful to watch.
I'd watched it shift its length, stay still, sashay,
shunting its flesh on shuffled vertebrae
for days before, and thought of it as 'mine'
so long had I wondered at its pliant spine.
My neighbour thinks it queer my sense of loss.
He took a branch festooned with Spanish moss,
at the cooler end of one long afternoon,
and pestled my oaksnake's head into a spoon
he flourished laughing at his dogs, then slung
the slack ladle of its life to where it hung
snagged on a branch for buzzards till, stripped bare,
it trailed like a Chinese kite-string in the air.
Waal! he exclaimed, *if ahda knowed you guys*
liked *snakes on your land* . . . he turns and sighs
at such greenhornery. I'd half a mind
to say I'd checked the snake's a harmless kind
in *two* encyclopaedias but knew the looks
I'd get from him for 'talking books'. –
There's something fairy (I can hear him say)
about a guy that watches *snakes all goddam day!*
The wife he bullies says: *O Bill, let be!*
There's doers and there's watchers, maybe he . . .
Ain't no doer, says he, *that's plain to see!*
I seed him sit out on their porch and read
some goddam great Encyclopaed-
ia, yeah, read! *What does the fairy DO?*
O Bill! she says, *not everyone's like you.*
And you'd be the first man to stand up and say
that people living in the USA
have every right to live the way they please. –
Yeah! But those guys look too young for retirees!
Nothing that I did made any sense
but I think he offered me as recompense

for battering my snake the chance to see
the alligators on his property.

Each Sunday his riding mower wouldn't stop
till every blade of grass had had its crop,
so that the bald, burned earth showed through the green
but any snake that trespassed was soon seen.
That was the front, but out there in the back
he hadn't even hacked a proper track
down to the swampy lake, his own retreat
kept as wild as the front part was kept neat.
This was his wilderness, his very own
left just as it was, rank, overgrown,
and into this he went with guns and beer
to wallow in his dreams of the frontier
and shot the gators we were seeing glide
with egrets on their backs from side to side.
The egrets ride in threes their gator skiffs,
Pharaohs' sarcophagi with hieroglyphs!
He offered me his rifle: *Wanna try?*
Go for the big ones not the smaller fry!
They've taken gators off the Endangered List.
I took aim and, deliberately, missed.
He blasted three egrets like a fairground shy
and then the gator they were ferried by.
Then we sat down at his fire and watched the day,
now reddened at the edges, drain away.
This hissing of damp logs and ringpull *Bud*
drunk from the can, his seal of brotherhood
(the sort where I'd play Abel and him Cain!)
I can't stand his beer but don't complain
as he flings them across the fire for me to catch:
round 1: the shooting, 2: the boozing match!
Each dead can he crushed flat and tossed aside.
(When I was safe back home I also tried
and found, to my great chagrin, aluminum
crushable with pressure from one thumb!)

We stare into his cookout and exchange
neighbourly nothings, gators still in range.
Liberal with his beer-cans he provokes
his gator-watching guest with racist jokes.
Did you know, sir, that gators only eat
dogs and niggers, darker sortsa meat?
But you can eat him if he won't eat you.
I'll give you a gator steak to barbecue.
(He knew that cooking's something that I *do!*)
He'd watched me cooking, and, done out of doors,
cooking could be classed among male chores.
His suspicions of me as some city loafer
who couldn't gut a mullet or stew gopher
I tried, when I felt him watching, to dispel
by letting him see me working, working well.
I make sure, when he stares over, my swing's true
when I heave the axe like I've seen rednecks do,
both hands well-balanced on the slippery haft,
or make certain that he sees me when I waft
the coals to a fierce glow with my straw hat,
the grill bars spitting goat or gator fat.
If them fireants ain't stopped with gasoline
you can say goodbye to every inch of green.
They say on the TV they'll eat their way,
if we don't check 'em, through the USA!
The 'red peril' 's what we call them bugs down here.
(A hiss for those villains from his seventh beer!)
From this house, you know, we're near enough to see
space launchings live. The wife watched on TV,
then dashed outside, and saw, with her own eyes,
'like a silver pen', she said, 'The Enterprise',
then rushed back for the message from the Prez
who'd just been wounded by some nut. He says:
We feel like giants again! *Taking over space*
has made Goliaths of the human race.
Me, I was in the rowboat, trying to relax.
I'd gotten me some chicken, 2 or 3 6-packs

like relaxing, *and I zoomed out of a snooze*
with a sudden start, the way you do with booze,
and saw our spaceship, clear as I see you,
like a bullet disappearing in the blue.
I must say that it made me mighty proud.
I sang God Bless America *out loud*
to those goddam alligators then I got
the biggest of the brutes with one sharp shot.
(But a man might get, say, lovesick, then he shoots
not one of your unendangered gator brutes
that glide so gracefully through silver ooze
and gladden gourmets in those Cross Creek stews,
and instead of potting dumb beasts like your gators
shoots the most acknowledged of all legislators,
on whose scaled back as corpse and cortège glide
the egret of the soul bums its last ride!)

Stuck goat fat's spitting from my still hot grill.
I've eaten very well, and drunk my fill,
and slip my *Early Times*, and to and fro
rock in the rocker watching ashes blow
off the white-haired charcoals and away
into the darkness of the USA.
Higher than the fireflies, not as high as stars,
the sparks fly up between the red hot bars.
I want no truck myself with outer space
except to gaze on from some earthly place
very much like this one in the South,
the taste of *Early Times* warm in my mouth.
Popping meals in pills in zero G
's not the dining that would do for me.
I'm feeling too composed to break the spell
when mosquitoes probe the veins of mine that swell
like blue earthworms. A head with sting
burrows in the blue, starts syphoning.
Let be! the watcher in me says, *Let be!*
but suddenly the doer side of me

(though my cracker neighbour couldn't, though he'd tried,
fathom if I'd got a doer side!)
swats the bastard and its legs like hair
sprout from my drop of blood on the cane chair.
The day's heat rolls away to make night thunder.
I look at the clouded planets and I wonder
if the God who blessed America's keen eye,
when He looked on that launching, chanced to spy,
in this shrinking world with far too many men,
either the cock-pecked wife who saw a pen . . .

(If I'd seen it going I'd've said
it was my snake sprayed silver, whose black head
my neighbour battered concave like a spoon,
pointing its harmless nose towards the moon,
lacquered in rigor mortis and not bent
into eternity's encirclement,
curled in a circle, sucking its own tail,
the formed continuum of female/male,
time that devours and endlessly renews,
time the open maw and what it chews,
the way it had mine chewed down here on earth,
the emblem of continuous rebirth
a bleached spine like one strand of Spanish moss –
for all the above *vide sub* Ouroboros!
All this is booktalk, buddy, more En-
cyclopaedia know-how, not for men!) . . .

either the cock-pecked wife who saw a pen,
or the lurching rowboat where a red-faced man's
sprawled beside his shotgun and crushed cans,
who saw a bullet streak off on its trek,
and to that watching God was a mere speck,
the human mite, his rowboat lapped with blood,
the giant gator hunter killing BUD!

Following Pine

I

When a plumber glues some lengths of PVC
that pipe our cold spring water from its source,
or a carpenter fits porch-posts, and they see,
from below or from above, the heartwood floors
made from virgin lumber, such men say,
as if they'd taught each other the same line:
Boards like them boards don't exist today!
then maybe add: *Now everything's new pine.*

Though the house is in a scant surviving wood
that has black walnut, hackberry, pecan
and moss-festooned live-oaks that have withstood
centuries more of bad news than a man,
sometimes we can drive an hour or more
and see nothing but dense pine trees on both sides
and no glimpse of the timbers for such floors
from virgin forest laid for virgin brides.

The feller/buncher and delimber groans,
grappling the grovelling pines, and dozing flat
a whole stand to a mess of stumps and stones
like some Goliath gorged on them, then shat
what was no use to him back on the land.
The sun and moon are sharing the same sky
as we drive by this totally depleted stand
marked down for GP planks and layer-peeled ply.

We'd set off early but shrill loggers' saws
were already shrieking in the stands of pines.
Fresh-felled, lopped slash pine tree-trunks in their scores
were being bull-dozed into ordered lines

waiting for the trucks in long convoy.
The trimmed-off branches were already burning.
The quiet, early road we'd wanted to enjoy
we did, but met the timber trucks returning.

Our early start was so that we could get
the trees we'd gone to buy into the ground,
watered and well-mulched, before sunset,
and not be digging in the dark with snakes around.
So with fig-trees, vines, and apples in the back,
wilting and losing their *Tree Garden* sheen,
we see on the road ahead a sky half black
and half as brilliantly blue as it had been.

The fast track was all wet, the crawler lane
we'd driven in most of the morning, dry.
The west side was in sun, the east in rain.
The east had black, the west had bright blue sky.
Armadillo blood, on the one side, 's washed away,
and, on the other, further on, sun-dried,
according as the car-crushed creature lay
on the highway's wet or sunny side.

Killed by traffic flowing through the night,
armadillos, rats, snake, dog, racoon,
dead on both road verges, left and right,
are scavenged on and half-decayed by noon,
and browsed over with hummed hubbub by blowfly
like loud necklaces, beads gone berserk,
that, whatever the day's weather, wet or dry,
stay a high-gloss green and do their work.

And as we accelerated fast and overtook,
moving on the rain side as we did,
first one and then another timber truck,
the sudden wet road made me scared we'd skid.

My heart leaped instantly into my mouth
till we seemed safe between two loads of pine,
part of that convoy travelling due South
with east lane raining, and west side fine.

Was it the danger that made me hold my breath,
the quick injection of adrenalin,
the vision of our simultaneous death
and the crushed Toyota we were riding in,
or the giant raindrops that were pelting
onto the windshield and shot through with sun,
that made it seem the two of us were melting
and in a radiant decay becoming one?

Good job with such visions going on
that you were driving and you kept your head,
or that sense of fleshly glory would be gone
with the visionary who sensed it, and you, dead,
as dead as the armadillo, possum or racoon
killed by the nighttime traffic and well
advanced into decay by afternoon
and already giving off a putrid smell.

At least the storm cleaned love-bugs off the car
and washed the windscreen glass so you could drive.
When they copulate in swarms you can't see far.
They'd sooner fuck their brains out than survive.
They hit the car, embracing, and, squashed flat,
their twinned remains are merged into one mess.
It is just the crushed canoodling gnat
that needs for its Nirvana nothingness?

Flattened in airborne couples as they fucked
their squashed millions would make the windscreen dark
if the wipers didn't constantly conduct
the dead to sectors round the dozed-clear arc.

Choked radiators, speckled bumper bars
splattered with love-bugs, two by two,
camouflage the colour of parked cars
pulled up at *Chiang's Mongolian Barbecue*.

From then on we were well and truly stuck
and anxious to get back to plant our trees
behind the huge pine-loaded lumber truck,
its red flag flapping in its slipstream breeze.
Because the lashed lopped slash was newly cut
the pungency of pine filled all the air.
We have to drive with all the windows shut,
the smell of pine too powerful to bear.

Now quite impossible to overtake
the convoy crawls up Highway 26.
Your foot keeps hovering above the brake
behind future coffin lids and cocktail sticks.
Our impatience at the slowness of the road
was not repugnance at the smell of pine,
however pungent, but worry for our load
of apple, pear, and fig, and muscadine.

Pine's the lingering perfume newly-weds
in just-built houses smell off panelling,
off squeaky floorboards, off their platform beds,
that cows smell when their rheumy nostrils sting
and tingle on electric pasture fences,
of the USA's best-selling bathroom spray
spritzed against those stinks that shock the senses,
shit, decomposition, and decay.

This is the smell in Walden that Thoreau's
cabin-builder's hands gave to his lunch,
the resinous pitch that prickled in his nose
whenever he took a sandwich out to munch,

and, maybe, thinking morosely as he chews
how woodlands mostly end up wooden goods,
the wrapping of his butties, week-old news,
was also nature once, and someone's woods.

In some sub-Walden worlds his dream survives
though these dreams of independence are nightmares
where retiree DIYers save their lives
while everyone around them 's losing theirs.
Spacemen go one way, these pioneers
mole down into the earth to find a place
to weather out the days, weeks, even years
that may well, but for these, kill off our race.

Considering their years it's maybe kinder
when they burrow in the ground like gophers do
not to offer them the sobering reminder
that rattlesnakes use gopher burrows too.
However layered with rocks and earth the roof,
however stocked with freeze-drieds (praise the Lord!)
however broad the door, how bullet proof,
no matter how much water they have stored,

until the radiation count all-clear
broadcast (they don't say how) on radio,
when they can, but cautiously, then reappear,
death got there before them, though they grow
by battery-powered Mazda lightbulb beams
alfalfa sprouts, damp blotting pads of cress,
while nations torn apart by common dreams
are united in a state of Nothingness.

Being neither newly-weds nor retirees
today we bought five figs, a pear, a vine,
and still have some belief in planting trees
with lifespans more than three times yours and mine.

Most of my life I've wanted to believe
those words of Luther that I've half-endorsed
about planting an apple tree the very eve
of the Apocalypse; or the Holocaust.

Every time my bags of red goat leather
are lying labelled England in the hall
and we take our last stroll round the land together
whether it's winter, summer, spring or fall,
there's always one last job I find to do,
pruned branches that I need to burn,
one last load of needles left to strew –
it's a way of guaranteeing my return.

A neighbour learns the skills they call 'survival'
living wild off sabal palm and game
killed by various means, knife, bow, or rifle,
even by throttling; me, I've learned to name
and know the subtle differences between
what once was only 'woods', or was before
mere nameless leaves of slightly varied green
but is now, say, persimmon or possumhaw.

Who lives for the future, who for now?
What good's the *cigale*'s way or the *fourmi*'s
if both end up as nothing anyhow
unless they look at life like Socrates
who wished, at the very end, to learn to play
a new air on his novice lyre. *Why?*
said his teacher, *this is your last day.*
To know it before I die, was the reply.

II

Chill, sterile, waterless, inert,
but full, the moon illuminates the night
enough for us to dig the still warm dirt
and plant the trees we've brought home by its light.
That globe above so different from here,
where no one lives and nothing ever grows,
no soil, no moisture and no atmosphere
to culture kumquats in or grow a rose.

From that great plain of death, inert and chill,
light may rebound but life will never come.
Those so-called seas are sterile, dry and still,
Mare Serenitatis, Sinus Iridum.
And yet, I thought, and yet, where would we be
without these light beams bounced off that dead land,
without these ungrassed dunes and lifeless sea
shedding their pallor on my scooping hand?

Light from a surface so cold and so dead
was the one we planted our new fruit-trees by,
the one that casts its glow now on our bed,
the one I find reflected in your eye.
Is not extinction with its eerie light
the appropriate presider when one swears
to sustain each other through the world of night
we've both decided is 'best born in pairs'?

We see all that we need to by a light
beamed off a barrenness of pits and plain,
off the '69 Apollo landing site
where planted flag and giant step remain.
That place, some men aspire to, discovers,
with light reflected from plains pocked with pits,
plantlife, a yellow house, a pair of lovers,
uniting in their love deep opposites.

This Earth, and this Earth's sterile satellite
won't always be, like life and death, apart,
if Man's destructive mind with Nature's might
leaves the planet a pitted lunar chart
with no one here to name its barren craters
after rainbows, or discoverers, or peace,
though there'll be peace when Earth's worst agitators
find in final dissolution their release.

Despite barricaded bolt-holes deep below
it's often said that what will come off best
once, step by step, we've reached All-Systems-Go,
of all life on this Earth, 's the lowliest:
these bugs tonight like high-roast coffee beans
that fling themselves at flames and self-destruct,
that blue wasp juicing bugs like tangerines,
fat bucking locusts jockeyed on and sucked,

these trawling spiders that have rigged their nets
halfway between our porchlamps and the night,
their dawn webs threaded with dew jewelettes
and hauls of flies caught lurching for our light.
A blundering beetle with black lacquered back
that dialled its liquidation to the spider's limb,
embalmed in abseil/bell-pull, a stored snack
swathed in white cerements of sticky scrim.

Phoning that zero gets the spider quick.
Each leg's in touch with 45 degrees
of laddered circle where the insects stick
on tacky wires their weaver walks with ease.
Even the love-bugs, randy and ridiculous,
coupling regardless of death close behind
could still be fucking after all of us
are merged in the molten mess made of Mankind.

Falling asleep to loud cicada chirrs,
to scuttling cockroach, crashing carapace,
the noises that I hear are our inheritors
who'll know the Earth both B. and A. our race.
And underneath those floorboards of good heart
I think I hear the slither of a snake
and then the rodent prey the snake makes start.
Let's forget about the world until we wake!

III

Each board of 'tongue in groove' 's scored by a line
I measure insect movements by from bed.
A spider crossing long since scentless pine
racks its nightcatch on a slender thread.
The blowfly's hawsered body still looks wet
though all night it's been suspended in the dry.
It spins round, flashing, in the spider's net
with shredded cockroach wings and antennae.

I knew I'd wake today and find you gone
and look out of the window, knowing where
you'd be so early, still with nothing on,
watering our new plants with drowsy care.
The night, already stripped of half its dark,
now with the rest sloughed off, 's revealed as day,
and the sun already makes small rainbows arc
out of the hose's nozzle drizzling spray.

Crunching the rusted needles that I strew
to stunt the weed growth on the paths we hacked
I come towards you and am naked too,
and, being naked, feel my nerves react
to the pliant give and snap of spider thread,
snagged on a nipple, sliding on my sweat,
pinged on a whisker, snapped against my head –
the night survivor loosened from the net.

Though impossible to hear I sense each ping
as of an instrument too tautly strung
with notes too high for human voice to sing
and, in any case, not heard if ever sung,
and maybe like that air of Socrates,
I hope he played at least once with some skill,
transposed beyond our ken into high keys
I can't hear now, and know I never will.

For all that unseen threads break on my face,
for all these cordons of cobweb caress
I walk towards you and don't change my pace
feeling each broken thread one stricture less
against my passage to the world of day.
I can only know the last one when it breaks.
You can't see them ahead, and anyway,
I have to scan the ground for rattlesnakes.

I wonder as I walk still half awake
if the trees that baked a bit long in the boot
and we'd planted in the dark would ever take
and if we'd ever taste their hoped-for fruit.
I pass what's become in 12 months gut-high pine
planted last summer in a long close row
as our few acres' demarcation line
and I will what's still a hedge to grow less slow,

and be tall enough to mask the present view
of you watering the saplings as you spray
rainbows at fig-trees planted 2-1-2
and both of us still nude at break of day.
A morning incense smokes off well-doused ground.
Everywhere you water rainbows shine.
This private haven that we two have found
might be the more so when enclosed with pine.

Cypress & Cedar

A smell comes off my pencil as I write
in the margins of a sacred Sanskrit text.
By just sufficient candlelight I skim
these scriptures sceptically from hymn to hymn.
The bits I read aloud to you I've Xed
for the little clues they offer to life's light.

I sit in mine, and you sit in your chair.
A sweetness hangs round yours; a foul smell mine.
Though the house still has no windows and no doors
and the tin roof's roughly propped with 4 × 4s
that any gale could jolt, our chairs are fine
and both scents battle for the same night air.

Near Chiefland just off US 129,
from the clapboard abattoir about a mile,
the local sawyer Bob displays his wares:
porch swings, picnic tables, lounging chairs,
rough sawn and nailed together 'cracker' style.
The hand I shake leaves powerful smells on mine.

Beside two piles of shavings, white and red,
one fragrant as a perfume, and one rank
and malodorous from its swampland ooze,
Bob displayed that week's work's chairs for me to choose.
I chose one that was sweet, and one that stank,
and thought about the sweet wood for a bed.

To quote the carpenter he 'stinks o' shite'
and his wife won't sleep with him on cypress days,
but after a day of cedar, so he said,
she comes back eagerly into his bed,
and, as long as he works cedar, there she stays.
Sometimes he scorns the red wood and works white!

Today I've laboured with my hands for hours
sawing fenceposts up for winter; one tough knot
jolted the chainsaw at my face and sprayed
a beetroot cedar dust off the bucked blade,
along with damp earth with its smell of rot,
hurtling beetles, termites in shocked showers.

To get one gatepost free I had to tug
for half an hour, but dragged up from its hole
it smelled, down even to the last four feet
rammed in the ground, still beautifully sweet
as if the grave had given life parole
and left the sour earth perfumed where I'd dug.

Bob gave me a cedar buckle for my belt,
and after the whole day cutting, stacking wood,
damp denim, genitals, 'genuine hide leather'
all these fragrances were bound together
by cedar, and together they smelled good.
It was wonderful the way my trousers smelled.

I can't help but suppose flesh-famished Phèdre
would have swept that prissy, epicene,
big-game hunting stepson Hippolyte,
led by his nose to cedar, off his feet,
and left no play at all for poor Racine,
if she'd soaped her breasts with *Bois de Cèdre*.

If in doubt ask Bob the sawyer's wife!
Pet lovers who can't stand the stink of cat
buy sacks of litter that's been 'cedarized'
and from ancient times the odour's been much prized.
Though not a Pharaoh I too favour that
for freighting my rank remains out of this life.

Why not two cedar chairs? Why go and buy
a reeking cypress chair as a reminder,
as if one's needed, or primeval ooze,

like swamps near Suwannee backroads, or bayous,
stagnation Mother Nature left behind her
hauling Mankind up from mononuclei?

Cypress still has roots in that old stew
paddling its origins in protozoa,
the stew where consciousness that writes and reads
grew its first squat tail from slimy seeds.
I'd've used it for the Ark if I'd been Noah,
though cedar, I know you'll say, would also do.

This place not in the *Blue Guide* or in *Fodor*
between the Suwannee River and the Styx
named by some homesick English classicist
who loved such puns, loathed swamps, and, lonely, pissed
his livelihood away with redneck hicks
and never once enjoyed the cedar's odour,

or put its smoke to snake-deterrent use
prescribed by Virgil in his *Georgics* III
with *chelydrus* here in the US South
construed as the diamondback or cottonmouth
which freed him, some said, from his misery.
Others said liquor, and others still a noose.

And, evenings, he, who'd been an avid reader
of the *Odyssey* and *Iliad* in Greek,
became an even avider verandah drinker
believing sourmash made a Stoic thinker
though stuck with no paddle up Phlegethon's creek,
and had no wife with clothes chest of sweet cedar.

But you bought one at Bob's place and you keep
your cotton frocks in it, your underwear,
and such a fragrance comes from your doffed bras
as comes from uncorked phials in hot bazaars,
and when you take your clothes off and lie bare
your body breathes out cedar while you sleep.

That lonely English exile named the river,
though it could have been someone like me, for whom,
though most evenings on the porch I read and write,
there's often such uneasiness in night
it creates despair in me, or drinker's gloom
that could send later twinges through the liver.

Tonight so far 's been peaceful with no lightning.
The pecan trees and hophornbeams are still.
The storm's held off, the candleflame's quite straight,
the fire and wick united in one fate.
Though this quietness that can, one moment, fill
the heart with peace, can, the next, be frightening –

A hog gets gelded with a gruesome squeal
that skids across the quietness of night
to where we're sitting on our dodgy porch.
I reach for Seth Tooke's shotgun and the torch
then realize its 'farmwork' so all right
but my flesh also flinches from the steel.

Peace like a lily pad on swamps of pain –
floating's its only way of being linked.
This consciousness of ours that reads and writes
drifts on a darkness deeper than the night's.
Above that blackness, buoyed on the extinct,
peace, pure-white, floats flowering in the brain,

and fades, as finally the nenuphar
we found on a pewter swamp where two roads ended
was also bound to fade. The head and heart
are neither of them too much good apart
and peace comes in the moments that they're blended
as cypress and cedar at this moment are.

My love, as prone as I am to despair,
I think the world of night's best born in pairs,

one half we'll call the female, one the male,
though neither essence need, in love, prevail.
We sit here in distinctly scented chairs
you, love, in the cedar, me the cypress chair.

Though tomorrow night I might well sit in yours
and you in mine, the blended scent's the same
since I pushed my chair close to your chair
and we read by the one calm candle that we share
in this wilderness that might take years to tame,
this house still with no windows and no doors.

Let the candle cliché come out of the chill –
'the flickering candle on a vast dark plain'
of one lone voice against the state machine,
or Mimi's on cold stairs aren't what I mean
but moments like this now when heart and brain
seem one sole flame that's bright and straight and still.

If it's in Levy County that I die
(though fearing I'd feel homesick as I died
I'd sooner croak in Yorkshire if I could)
I'll have my coffin made of cedar wood
to balance the smell like cypress from inside
and hope the smoke of both blends in the sky,

as both scents from our porch chairs do tonight.
'Tvashti', says this Indian Rig Veda,
'hewed the world out of one tree,' but doesn't tell,
since for durability both do as well,
if the world he made was cypress wood; or cedar
the smell coming off my pencil as I write.

V.

'My father still reads the dictionary every day. He says your life depends on your power to master words.'

(Arthur Scargill, *Sunday Times*, 10 January 1982)

Next millennium you'll have to search quite hard
to find my slab behind the family dead,
butcher, publican, and baker, now me, bard
adding poetry to their beef, beer and bread.

With Byron three graves on I'll not go short
of company, and Wordsworth's opposite.
That's two peers already, of a sort,
and we'll all be thrown together if the pit,

whose galleries once ran beneath this plot,
causes the distinguished dead to drop
into the rabblement of bone and rot,
shored slack, crushed shale, smashed prop.

Wordsworth built church organs, Byron tanned
luggage cowhide in the age of steam,
and knew their place of rest before the land
caves in on the lowest worked-out seam.

This graveyard on the brink of Beeston Hill's
the place I may well rest if there's a spot
under the rose roots and the daffodils
by which dad dignified the family plot.

If buried ashes saw then I'd survey
the places I learned Latin, and learned Greek,
and left, the ground where Leeds United play
but disappoint their fans week after week,

which makes them lose their sense of self-esteem
and taking a short cut home through these graves here
they reassert the glory of their team
by spraying words on tombstones, pissed on beer.

This graveyard stands above a worked-out pit.
Subsidence makes the obelisks all list.
One leaning left's marked FUCK, one right's marked SHIT
sprayed by some peeved supporter who was pissed.

Far-sighted for his family's future dead,
but for his wife, this banker's still alone
on his long obelisk, and doomed to head
a blackened dynasty of unclaimed stone,

now graffitied with a crude four-letter word.
His children and grand-children went away
and never came back home to be interred,
so left a lot of space for skins to spray.

The language of this graveyard ranges from
a bit of Latin for a former Mayor
or those who laid their lives down at the Somme,
the hymnal fragments and the gilded prayer,

how people 'fell asleep in the Good Lord',
brief chisellable bits from the good book
and rhymes whatever length they could afford,
to CUNT, PISS, SHIT and (mostly) FUCK!

Or, more expansively, there's LEEDS v.
the opponent of last week, this week, or next,
and a repertoire of blunt four-letter curses
on the team or race that makes the sprayer vexed.

Then, pushed for time, or fleeing some observer,
dodging between tall family vaults and trees
like his team's best ever winger, dribbler, swerver,
fills every space he finds with versus Vs.

Vs sprayed on the run at such a lick,
the sprayer master of his flourished tool,
get short-armed on the left like that red tick
they never marked his work much with at school.

Half this skinhead's age but with approval
I helped whitewash a V on a brick wall.
No one clamoured in the press for its removal
or thought the sign, in wartime, rude at all.

These Vs are all the versuses of life
from LEEDS v. DERBY, Black/White
and (as I've known to my cost) man v. wife,
Communist v. Fascist, Left v. Right,

class v. class as bitter as before,
the unending violence of US and THEM,
personified in 1984
by Coal Board MacGregor and the NUM,

Hindu/Sikh, soul/body, heart v. mind,
East/West, male/female, and the ground
these fixtures are fought out on 's Man, resigned
to hope from his future what his past never found.

The prospects for the present aren't too grand
when a swastika with NF (National Front) 's
sprayed on a grave, to which another hand
has added, in a reddish colour, CUNTS.

Which is, I grant, the word that springs to mind,
when going to clear the weeds and rubbish thrown
on the family plot by football fans, I find
UNITED graffitied on my parents' stone.

How many British graveyards now this May
are strewn with rubbish and choked up with weeds
since families and friends have gone away
for work or fuller lives, like me from Leeds?

When I first came here 40 years ago
with my dad to 'see my grandma' I was 7.
I helped dad with the flowers. He let me know
she'd gone to join my grandad up in Heaven.

My dad who came each week to bring fresh flowers
came home with clay stains on his trouser knees.
Since my parents' deaths I've spent 2 hours
made up of odd 10 minutes such as these.

Flying visits once or twice a year,
and though I'm horrified just who's to blame
that I find instead of flowers cans of beer
and more than one grave sprayed with some skin's name?

Where there were flower urns and troughs of water
and mesh receptacles for withered flowers
are the HARP tins of some skinhead Leeds supporter.
It isn't all his fault though. Much is ours.

5 kids, with one in goal, play 2-a-side.
When the ball bangs on the hawthorn that's one post
and petals fall they hum *Here Comes the Bride*
though not so loud they'd want to rouse a ghost.

They boot the ball on purpose at the trunk
and make the tree shed showers of shrivelled may.
I look at this word graffitied by some drunk
and I'm in half a mind to let it stay.

(Though honesty demands that I say *if*
I'd wanted to take the necessary pains
to scrub the skin's inscription off
I only had an hour between trains.

So the feelings that I had as I stood gazing
and the significance I saw could be a sham,
mere excuses for not patiently erasing
the word sprayed on the grave of dad and mam.)

This pen's all I have of magic wand.
I know this world's so torn but want no other
except for dad who'd hoped from 'the beyond'
a better life than this one, *with* my mother.

Though I don't believe in afterlife at all
and know it's cheating it's hard *not* to make
a sort of furtive prayer from this skin's scrawl,
his UNITED mean 'in Heaven' for their sake,

an accident of meaning to redeem
an act intended as mere desecration
and make the thoughtless spraying of his team
apply to higher things, and to the nation.

Some, where kids use aerosols, use giant signs
to let the people know who's forged their fetters
like PRI CE O WALES above West Yorkshire mines
(no prizes for who nicked the missing letters!)

The big blue star for booze, tobacco ads,
the magnet's monogram, the royal crest,
insignia in neon dwarf the lads
who spray a few odd FUCKS when they're depressed.

Letters of transparent tubes and gas
in Düsseldorf are blue and flash out KRUPP.
Arms are hoisted for the British ruling class
and clandestine, genteel aggro keeps them up.

And there's HARRISON on some Leeds building sites
I've taken in fun as blazoning my name,
which I've also seen on books, in Broadway lights,
so why can't skins with spraycans do the same?

But why inscribe these *graves* with CUNT and SHIT?
Why choose neglected tombstones to disfigure?
This pitman's of last century daubed PAKI GIT,
this grocer Broadbent's aerosolled with NIGGER?

They're there to shock the living not arouse
the dead from their deep peace to lend support
for the causes skinhead spraycans could espouse.
The dead would want their desecrators caught!

Jobless though they are how can these kids,
even though their team's lost one more game,
believe that the 'Pakis', 'Niggers', even 'Yids'
sprayed on the tombstones here should bear the blame?

What is it that these crude words are revealing?
What is it that this aggro act implies?
Giving the dead their xenophobic feeling
or just a *cri-de-coeur* because man dies?

So what's a cri-de-coeur, cunt? Can't you speak
the language that yer mam spoke. Think of 'er!
Can yer only get yer tongue round fucking Greek?
Go and fuck yerself with cri-de-coeur!

'She didn't talk like you do for a start!'
I shouted, turning where I thought the voice had been.
She didn't understand yer fucking 'art'!
She thought yer fucking poetry obscene!

I wish on this skin's word deep aspirations,
first the prayer for my parents I can't make
then a call to Britain and to all the nations
made in the name of love for peace's sake.

Aspirations, cunt! Folk on t'fucking dole
'ave got about as much scope to aspire
above the shit they're dumped in, cunt, as coal
aspires to be chucked on t'fucking fire.

OK, forget the aspirations. Look, I know
United's losing gets you fans incensed
and how far the HARP inside you makes you go
but *all* these Vs: against! against! against!

Ah'll tell yer then what really riles a bloke.
It's reading on their graves the jobs they did –
butcher, publican and baker. Me, I'll croak
doing t'same nowt ah do now as a kid.

'ard birth ah wor, mi mam says, almost killed 'er.
Death after life on t'dole won't seem as 'ard!
Look at this cunt, Wordsworth, organ builder,
this fucking 'aberdasher Appleyard!

If mi mam's up there, don't want to meet 'er
listening to me list mi dirty deeds,
and 'ave to pipe up to St fucking Peter
ah've been on t'dole all mi life in fucking Leeds!

Then t' Alleluias stick in t' angels' gobs.
When dole-wallahs fuck off to the void
what'll t'mason carve up for their jobs?
The cunts who lieth 'ere wor unemployed?

This lot worked at one job all life through.
Byron, 'Tanner', 'Lieth 'ere interred'
They'll chisel fucking poet when they do you
and that, yer cunt, 's a crude four-letter word.

'Listen, cunt!' I said, 'before you start your jeering
the reason why I want this in a book
's to give ungrateful cunts like you a hearing!'
A book, yer stupid cunt, 's not worth a fuck!

'The only reason why I write this poem at all
on yobs like you who do the dirt on death
's to give some higher meaning to your scrawl.'
Don't fucking bother, cunt! Don't waste your breath!

'You piss-artist skinhead cunt, you wouldn't know
and it doesn't fucking matter if you do,
the skin and poet united fucking Rimbaud
but the *autre* that *je est* is fucking you.'

Ah've told yer, no more Greek . . . That's yer last warning!
Ah'll boot yer fucking balls to Kingdom Come.
They'll find yer cold on t'grave tomorrer morning.
So don't speak Greek. Don't treat me like I'm dumb.

'I've done my bits of mindless aggro too
not half a mile from where we're standing now.'
Yeah, ah bet yer wrote a poem, yer wanker you!
'No, shut yer gob a while. Ah'll tell yer 'ow . . .

'Herman Darewski's band played operetta
with a wobbly soprano warbling. Just why
I made my mind up that I'd got to get her
with the fire hose I can't say, but I'll try.

It wasn't just the singing angered me.
At the same time half a crowd was jeering
as the smooth Hugh Gaitskell, our MP,
made promises the other half were cheering.

What I hated in those high soprano ranges
was uplift beyond all reason and control
and in a world where you say nothing changes
it seemed a sort of prick-tease of the soul.

I tell you when I heard high notes that rose
above Hugh Gaitskell's cool electioneering
straight from the warbling throat right up my nose
I had all your aggro in *my* jeering.

And I hit the fire extinguisher ON knob
and covered orchestra and audience with spray.
I could run as fast as you then. A good job!
They yelled "damned vandal" after me that day . . .'

And then yer saw the light and gave up 'eavy!
And knew a man's not how much he can sup . . .
Yer reward for growing up's this super-bevvy,
a meths and champagne punch in t' FA Cup.

Ah've 'eard all that from old farts past their prime.
'ow now yer live wi' all yer once detested . . .
Old farts with not much left 'll give me time.
Fuckers like that get folks like me arrested.

Covet not thy neighbour's wife; thy neighbour's riches.
Vicar and cop who say, to save our souls,
Get thee behind me, Satan, drop their breeches
and get the Devil's dick right up their 'oles!

It was more a working marriage that I'd meant,
a blend of masculine and feminine.
Ignoring me, he started looking, bent
on some more aerosolling, for his tin.

'It was more a working marriage that I mean!'
Fuck, and save mi soul, eh? That suits me.
Then as if I'd egged him on to be obscene
he added a middle slit to one daubed V.

Don't talk to me of fucking representing
the class yer were born into any more.
Yer going to get 'urt and start resenting
it's not poetry we need in this class war.

Yer've given yerself toffee, cunt. Who needs
yer fucking poufy words. Ah write mi own.
Ah've got mi work on show all over Leeds
like this UNITED 'ere on some sod's stone.

'OK!' (thinking I had him trapped) 'OK!'
'If you're so proud of it then sign your name
when next you're full of HARP and armed with spray,
next time you take this short cut from the game.'

He took the can, contemptuous, unhurried
and cleared the nozzle and prepared to sign
the UNITED sprayed where mam and dad were buried.
He aerosolled his name. And it was mine.

The boy footballers bawl *Here Comes the Bride*
and drifting blossoms fall onto my head.
One half of me's alive but one half died
when the skin half sprayed my name among the dead.

Half versus half, the enemies within
the heart that can't be whole till they unite.
As I stoop to grab the crushed HARP lager tin
the day's already dusk, half dark, half light.

That UNITED that I'd wished onto the nation
or as reunion for dead parents soon recedes.
The word's once more a mindless desecration
by some HARPoholic yob supporting Leeds.

Almost the time for ghosts I'd better scram.
Though not given much to fears of spooky scaring
I don't fancy an encounter with my mam
playing Hamlet with me for this swearing.

Though I've a train to catch my step is slow.
I walk on the grass and graves with wary tread
over these subsidences, these shifts below
the life of Leeds supported by the dead.

Further underneath's that cavernous hollow
that makes the gravestones lean towards the town.
A matter of mere time and it will swallow
this place of rest and all the resters down.

I tell myself I've got, say, 30 years.
At 75 this place will suit me fine.
I've never feared the grave but what I fear's
that great worked-out black hollow under mine.

Not train departure time, and not Town Hall
with the great white clock face I can see,
coal, that began, with no man here at all,
as 300 million-year-old plant debris.

5 kids still play at making blossoms fall
and humming as they do *Here Comes the Bride*.
They never seem to tire of their ball
though I hear a woman's voice call one inside.

2 larking boys play bawdy bride and groom.
3 boys in Leeds strip la-la *Lohengrin*.
I hear them as I go through glowing gloom
still years away from being skald or skin.

The ground's carpeted with petals as I throw
the aerosol, the HARP can, the cleared weeds
on top of dad's dead daffodils, then go,
with not one glance behind, away from Leeds.

The bus to the station's still the no. 1
but goes by routes that I don't recognize.
I look out for known landmarks as the sun
reddens the swabs of cloud in darkening skies.

Home, home, home, to my woman as the red
darkens from a fresh blood to a dried.
Home, home to my woman, home to bed
where opposites seem sometimes unified.

A pensioner in turban taps his stick
along the pavement past the corner shop,
that sells samosas now not beer on tick,
to the Kashmir Muslim Club that was the Co-op.

House after house FOR SALE where we'd played cricket
with white roses cut from flour-sacks on our caps,
with stumps chalked on the coal-grate for our wicket,
and every one bought now by 'coloured chaps',

dad's most liberal label as he felt
squeezed by the unfamiliar, and fear
of foreign food and faces, when he smelt
curry in the shop where he'd bought beer.

And growing frailer, 'wobbly on his pins'
the shops he felt familiar with withdrew
which meant much longer tiring treks for tins
that had a label on them that he knew.

And as the shops that stocked his favourites receded
whereas he'd fancied beans and popped next door,
he found that four long treks a week were needed
till he wondered what he bothered eating for.

The supermarket made him feel embarrassed.
Where people bought whole lambs for family freezers
he bought baked beans from check-out girls too harassed
to smile or swap a joke with sad old geezers.

But when he bought his cigs he'd have a chat,
his week's one conversation, truth to tell,
but time also came and put a stop to that
when old Wattsy got bought out by M. Patel.

And there, 'Time like an ever rolling stream' 's
what I once trilled behind that boarded front.
A 1,000 ages made coal-bearing seams
and even more the hand that sprayed this CUNT

on both Methodist and C of E billboards
once divided in their fight for local souls.
Whichever house more truly was the Lord's
both's pews are filled with cut-price toilet rolls.

Home, home to my woman, never to return
till sexton or survivor has to cram
the bits of clinker scooped out of my urn
down through the rose-roots to my dad and mam.

Home, home to my woman, where the fire's lit
these still chilly mid-May evenings, home to you,
and perished vegetation from the pit
escaping insubstantial up the flue.

Listening to *Lulu*, in our hearth we burn,
as we hear the high Cs rise in stereo,
what was lush swamp club-moss and tree-fern
at least 300 million years ago.

Shilbottle cobbles, Alban Berg high D
lifted from a source that bears your name,
the one we hear decay, the one we see,
the fern from the foetid forest, as brief flame.

This world, with far too many people in,
starts on the TV logo as a taw,
then ping-pong, tennis, football; then one spin
to show us all, then shots of the Gulf War.

As the coal with reddish dust cools in the grate
on the late-night national news we see
police v. pickets at a coke-plant gate,
old violence and old disunity.

The map that's colour-coded Ulster/Eire's
flashed on again as almost every night.
Behind a tiny coffin with two bearers
men in masks with arms show off their might.

The day's last images recede to first a glow
and then a ball that shrinks back to blank screen.
Turning to love, and sleep's oblivion, I know
what the UNITED that the skin sprayed *has* to mean.

Hanging my clothes up, from my parka hood
may and apple petals, browned and creased,
fall onto the carpet and bring back the flood
of feelings their first falling had released.

I hear like ghosts from all Leeds matches humming
with one concerted voice the bride, the bride
I feel united to, *my* bride is coming
into the bedroom, naked, to my side.

The ones we choose to love become our anchor
when the hawser of the blood-tie's hacked, or frays.
But a voice that scorns chorales is yelling: Wanker!
It's the aerosolling skin I met today's.

My *alter ego* wouldn't want to know it,
his aerosol vocab would baulk at LOVE,
the skin's UNITED underwrites the poet,
the measures carved below the ones above.

I doubt if 30 years of bleak Leeds weather
and 30 falls of apple and of may
will erode the UNITED binding us together.
And now it's your decision: does it stay?

Next millennium you'll have to search quite hard
to find out where I'm buried but I'm near
the grave of haberdasher Appleyard,
the pile of HARPs, or some new neonned beer.

Find Byron, Wordsworth, or turn left between
one grave marked Broadbent, one marked Richardson.
Bring some solution with you that can clean
whatever new crude words have been sprayed on.

If love of art, or love, gives you affront
that the grave I'm in's graffitied then, maybe,
erase the more offensive FUCK and CUNT
but leave, with the worn UNITED, one small v.

victory? For vast, slow, coal-creating forces
that hew the body's seams to get the soul.
Will Earth run out of her 'diurnal courses'
before repeating her creation of black coal?

But choose a day like I chose in mid-May
or earlier when apple and hawthorn tree,
no matter if boys boot their ball all day,
cling to their blossoms and won't shake them free.

If, having come this far, somebody reads
these verses, and he/she wants to understand,
face this grave on Beeston Hill, your back to Leeds,
and read the chiselled epitaph I've planned:

Beneath your feet's a poet, then a pit.
Poetry supporter, if you're here to find
how poems can grow from (beat you to it!) *SHIT*
find the beef, the beer, the bread, then look behind.

The Act

for Michael Longley & James Simmons

Newcastle Airport and scarcely 7 a.m.
yet they foot the white line out towards the plane
still reeling (or as if) from last night's FED
or macho marathons in someone's bed.
They scorn the breakfast croissants and drink beer,
and who am I to censure or condemn?
I know oblivion 's a balm for man's poor brain
and once roistered in male packs as bad as them.
These brews stoke their bravado, numb their fear
but anaesthetize all joy along with pain.

To show they had a weekend cunt or two
they walk as if they'd shagged the whole world stiff.
The squaddies' favourite and much-bandied words
for describing what they'd done on leave to birds
as if it were pub-brawl or DIY
seem to be, I quote, 'bang', 'bash', or 'screw',
if they did anything (a biggish if!)
more than the banter boomed now at the crew
as our plane levels off in a blue sky
along with half-scared cracks on catching syph.

They've lit Full Strengths on DA 141
despite NO SMOKING signs and cabin crew's
polite requests; they want to disobey
because they bow to orders every day.
The soldiers travel pretty light and free
as if they left Newcastle for the sun,
in winter with bare arms that show tattoos.
The stewardesses clearly hate this run,
the squaddies' continuous crude repartee
and constant button-pushing for more booze.

I've heard the same crude words and smutty cracks
and seen the same lads on excursion trains
going back via ferry from Stranraer
queuing at breakfast at the BR bar,
cleaning it out of *Tartan* and *Brown Ale*.
With numbered kitbags piled on luggage racks
just after breakfast bombed out of their brains,
they balance their empty cans in wobbly stacks.
An old woman, with indulgence for things male,
smiles at them and says: 'They're nobbut wains!'

Kids, mostly cocky Geordies and rough Jocks
with voices coming straight out of their boots,
the voices heard in newsreels about coal
or dockers newly dumped onto the dole
after which the army's the next stop.
One who's breakfasted on *Brown Ale* cocks
a nail-bitten, nicotined right thumb, and shoots
with loud saliva salvos a red fox
parting the clean green blades of some new crop
planted by farm families with old roots.

A card! The stewardesses almost throw it
into our laps not wanting to come near
to groping soldiers. We write each fact
we're required to enter by 'The Act':
profession; place of birth; purpose of visit.
The rowdy squaddy, though he doesn't know it
(and if he did he'd brand the freak as 'queer')
is sitting next to one who enters 'poet'
where he puts 'Forces'. But what is it?
My purpose? His? *What* are we doing here?

Being a photographer seems bad enough.
God knows the catcalls that a poet would get!
Newcastle-bound for leave the soldiers rag
the press photographer about his bag
and call him Gert or Daisy, and all laugh.
They shout at him in accents they'd dub 'pouf'
Yoo hoo, hinny! Like your handbag, pet!
Though what he's snapped has made him just as tough
and his handbag hardware could well photograph
these laughing features when they're cold and set.

I don't like the thought of these lads manning blocks
but saw them as you drove me to my flight,
now khakied up, not kaylied but alert,
their minds on something else than *Scotch* or skirt,
their elbows bending now to cradle guns.
The road's through deep green fields and wheeling flocks
of lapwings soaring, not the sort of sight
the sentry looks for in his narrow box.
'Cursed be dullards whom no cannon stuns'
I quote. They won't read what we three write.

They occupy NO SMOKING seats and smoke,
commandos free a few days from command
which cries for licence and I watch them cram
anything boozable, *Brown Ale* to *Babycham*
into their hardened innards, and they drain
whisky/lemonade, *Bacardi/Coke*,
double after double, one in either hand,
boys' drinks spirit-spiked for the real *bloke*!
Neither passengers nor cabin crew complain
as the squaddies keep on smoking as we land.

And as the morning Belfast plane descends
on Newcastle and one soldier looks,
with tears, on what he greets as 'Geordie grass'
and rakes the airport terrace for 'wor lass'
and another hollers to his noisy mates
he's going to have before their short leave ends
'firkins of fucking FED, fantastic fucks!'
I wish for you, my Ulster poet friends,
pleasures with no rough strife, no iron gates,
and letter boxes wide enough for books.

Y

'I'm good with curtains.'
     (Mrs Thatcher)

The thing I drink
from above the earth
's by *Technoplastics Inc.*
(Fort Worth)

I hear the chinks
of pukka glass
from what I think 's
called Business Class,

my taste buds impressed
as bustle helps waft
the Premium repast
to the Y Class aft.

Farther fore there's china
and choices for dinner.
The wines get finer,
the glass thinner.

Veuve Cliquot for the man
with a 1st thirst; for me
a tiny ring-pull can
of California Chablis!

From our plastic drinking,
O Ys of all nations,
it's maybe worth thinking
that the one consolation 's:

if the engines fail
and we go into a dive
only Ys in the tail
ever seem to survive!

As the stewardesses serve
first to 1st, last to Y,
I can't fail to observe,
as on earth so in the sky,

that the USA
draws no drapes –
the First Class can pay
while the Y Class gapes

pour encourager . . .
any man can fly
Premium if he can pay
(or his company).

We curtain the classes
while they eat,
the plastics from glasses,
we are so discreet!

And from LHR to JFK
from JFK to LHR
things are going to stay
just as they are.

Summoned by Bells

'The art of letters will come to an end before AD 2000 . . .
I shall survive as a curiosity.'

(Ezra Pound)

O Zeppelins! O Zeppelins!
prayed poet E.P.
any Boche gets 60 pence
to bust this campanolatry!

Doubles, triples, caters, cinques
for corpse or Christmas joys
for him, or anyone who thinks,
may be 'foul nuisance' and mere noise.

Carillons can interfere
and ruin concentration.
I've had it wrecked, my rhythmic ear,
by the new faith of the nation.

So sympathize with E.P.'s plight.
This moment now it's hard to hold
this rhythm in my head and write
while those bloody bells are tolled.

St Mary Abbot's, they're passé.
What gets into my skull
any time of night and day
are the new bells of John Bull,

The new calls to the nation:
Securi-curi-curi-cor!
Join the fight against inflation!
Double-Chubb your door!

'Beat Inflation' adverts call.
Invest in stronger locks!
Display for all on your front wall
the crime-deterrent box.

Almost every day one goes
and the new faith that it rings
is vested in new videos
and the sacredness of things.

I got done once. No piercing peal
alerted neighbourhood or force
but then there's nothing here to steal
bar 'a few battered books', of course.

The poor sneak thief, all he could do
he had so little time to act,
was grab a meagre coin or two
and my bag there ready packed.

What bothers me perhaps the most
is I never heard the thief,
being obsessively engrossed
in rhymes of social grief.

In haste behind the garden wall
he unzipped my bag. Bad luck!
One glance told him that his haul
was 50 copies of one book!

Poems! Poems! All by me!
He dropped the lot and ran
(and who would buy hot poetry
from a poor illiterate man?)

deeply pissed by what he'd found,
dumped books and bag unzipped.
He'd've even ditched an Ezra Pound
Cantos manuscript.

I got my books, he went scot-free,
no summons, gaol or fines.
I used him for such poetry
this alarm leaves in these lines

on 'a botched civilization'
E.P. helped to rebotch
where bells toll for a nation
that's one great Neighbourhood Watch.

Fire & Ice

The dusky, extinct 16 June 1987, Florida

A sprinkler simulates the rain.
A man in Lysolled wellies brings
live larvae to it, crickets, grain,
and the dusky, near extinction, sings.

The dusky in its quarantine 's
the very last there'll ever be.
In a Georgia lab its frozen genes
stay fledged with numb non-entity.

It's mocked up well its habitat.
The meal-supply's well-meaning.
Though there's no mate to warble at
the dusky goes on preening.

So let's be glad that it dropped dead
in that life-affirming mood.
The keeper found its little head
still buried in its food.

The Saxon saw man's spirit fly
like a bird though glowing firelight,
a warmth between two blanks of sky,
a briefly broken night.

Ours could be a dusky clone,
the freezered phoenix of our fate,
that flies, preens, even sings, alone
singed by the sparks from its charred mate.

The Pomegranates of Patmos

'We may be that generation that sees Armageddon.'
(Ronald Reagan, 1980)

My brother, my bright twin, Prochorus,
I think his bright future 's been wrecked.
When we've both got our lives before us
he's gone and joined this weird sect.

He sits in a cave with his guru,
a batty old bugger called John,
and scribbles on scrolls stuff to scare you
while the rabbi goes rabbiting on.

He seems dead to us, does my brother.
He's been so thoroughly brainwashed by John.
'I look in your eyes,' said our mother,
'but the bright boy behind them has gone.'

And the God with gargantuan ΓΡΑΨΟΝ
commanding that crackpot to write
is a Big Daddy bastard who craps on
the Garden of Earthly Delight.

If that sect's idea of a Maker 's
one who'll rid the world of the sea
I'm sitting beside watching breakers
he's the wrong bloody maker for me.

Who believes that their God began it
when he's ready to end it so soon,
the splendours of Patmos, the planet,
and the sea and the stars and the moon?

There'll always be people who'll welcome
the end of the sea and the sky
and wail to their God to make Hell come
and rejoice to hear the damned cry,

a date ringed in red in their diary
when they know that Doomsday will be
sure they'll be safe from the fiery
Gehenna engulfing, among billions, me!

I tell him it's crap, his Apocalypse.
I'm happy here in this world as I am.
I'd sooner wear shorts specked with fig pips
than get all togaed up for the Lamb.

If begged to go up where their Lamb is,
those skyscrapers of chrysolite,
kitted out in a cloud-issue chlamys,
with no darkness, then give me the night,

night with its passion and peril,
Patmos with pomegranates and figs
not towerblocks built out of beryl
and glazed with best sardonyx.

When Prochorus comes back from a session
up the hill in the cave with the saint,
he plunges me straight into depression
and, more than once, has made mother feel faint.

All he sees is immediately made
an emblem, a symbol, a fable,
the visible world a mere preaching aid,
even the food mother lays on the table.

An Apocalyptic cock on his heap,
Prochorus crowed as I tried to dine:
'Awake, ye drunkards, and weep,
and howl, all ye drinkers of wine!'

In one of his scrolls envisioning Hell
where the divine allowed him to delve,
in Joel, son of Pethuel
(he added, the pedant, 1.12!),

he found a quotation that made his day
and he tried to use to mar mine,
how pomegranates would wither away
and shrivelled grapes hang from the vine.

He tried to convince me but didn't succeed,
as I spiked out the vermilion gel
from the pomegranate, that its seed
stood for the sperm of the Future flame-lit from Hell,

an orb of embryos still to be born,
a globe of sperm globules that redden
not with the glow of the Aegean dawn
but the fires of his God's Armageddon.

My orb of nibbleable rubies
packed deliciously side by side
his roes of doom-destined babies
carmine with God's cosmocide.

The pomegranate! If forced to compare,
to claim back what eschatology stole,
what about, once you've licked back the hair,
the glossed moistness of a girl's hole?

He could take a gem-packed pomegranate,
best subjected to kisses and suction,
and somehow make it stand for the planet
destined for fiery destruction.

But in Kadesh in the deserts of Zin,
I asserted, the children of Israel chode
their leader Moses for dumping them in
what they called an *evil* abode.

They called that place evil, and why?
(Ask your divine, he should know!)
Because the deserts of Zin were dry
so that no pomegranates could grow.

They saw no hope of staying alive
without the fruits you'd love to see blighted
(see *Numbers* xx.5 –
not bad for one branded 'benighted'!)

Prochorus wasn't prepared for debate.
He and his sort preferred
pouring out endless sermons of hate
and from us not a dicky bird.

The more he went on about how our isle
would vanish along with its ocean
the more I spat kernels and flashed him a smile
and ate more in provoking slow motion.

And what made my brother really rave
and hiccup and spit 666,
what finally sent him back to his cave
were my suckings and sensual licks.

Each seed I impaled I'd hold up high
as though appraising a turquoise,
then with a satisfied sensual sigh
suck off the gel with a loud noise.

Apoplectic with Apocalypse,
his eyes popped watching me chew,
he frothed at the mouth as I smacked my lips
at the bliss of each nibbled red bijou.

So that verse (*Rev.* XXII.2)
about the fruit tree with 12 different crops
was my brother's addition, if John only knew,
as a revenge for me smacking my chops.

But I knew that I'd never be beaten
by his brayings of blast and of blaze,
and since then, when disheartened, I've eaten
pomegranates to give joy to my days.

And their flowers also are so brave and red,
a redness I've seen intensify
when the storm pressed down and overhead
and darkest clouds massed in the sky.

When the storm clouds bear down their most black,
at the moment the gloom looms most low,
and blown bright balausts bugle back
their chromatic jubilo.

The Doomsday Clock's set at 5 to.
The lovers I follow have time for their stroll
and to let their sensual selves come alive to
the Patmos that gladdens the soul,

the Patmos of figs and pomegranates,
the Patmos of the sea and the shore,
Patmos on earth among planets,
Patmos that's Patmos and no metaphor.

I'm so weary of all metaphorers.
From now on my most pressing ambition 's
to debrainwash all like Prochorus
made Moonies by metaphysicians.

But my poor brother could never respond.
I couldn't undermine his defences.
His brain went before him to the Beyond.
He took all leave of his senses.

My brother's heart was turned to stone.
So my revenge on St John's to instil
in lovers like these, who think they're alone,
the joy John and his ilk want to kill,

and try any charm or trick
to help frightened humans affirm
small moments against the rhetoric
of St Cosmocankerworm.

And I follow them lovingly strolling
by the sea I was always beside
with the breakers that I watched still rolling
though its 2,000 years since I died.

Though the rubbish that's out there floating
shows these days are far distant from mine,
no one should rush into quoting
St John the Doomsday Divine.

Some can't resist the temptation to preach
'The End of the World is Nigh'
when they see the shit on the beach
or white dishes scanning the sky.

And the johnnies jostling for sea room
like the eelskins of very sick eels
Prochorus would see as new signs of doom
and the angels halfway through the seals.

My charms are mere whispers in lovers' ears
against the loud St End-It-All
and Prochorus would say my present career 's
like the Serpent's before the Fall.

I know nipples brushed by fingertips
that mole up out of their mound
may not arrest their Apocalypse
but it brings the senses to ground.

Lover and lover, a man and his wife,
so grounded assert the sheer
absolute thisness of sublunar life
and not the hereafter, the *here*.

And maybe senses so grounded
will not always be straining to hear
the moment the trumpets are sounded
when the end of the world is near.

And so subliminally into their Sony
I'll put words that I've long thought obscene,
a dose of that dismal old Johnny
but more as a *Weltschmerz* vaccine,

a charm against all Holocausters
and the Patmos Apocalypse freak
and give them the joys that life fosters –
they go back to work in a week!

I follow them walking arm in brown arm.
I sit near to them in the taverna
whispering pagan words as a charm
against the blight of this isle's World-Burner.

By the beach that's a little bit shitty
what I'll sow in these lovers' brains
is a pop poemegranatey ditty
with six verses but seven refrains:

1–2–3–4–
5–6–7
their silvery fire
is staying in Heaven.

Seven seals, love,
and it's said they're at six.
We're lucky to live
with starlight and sex.

1–2–3–4–
5–6–7
their silvery fire
is staying in Heaven.

The stars shine. The moon wanes.
Your left hand undoes
my 501s.
I count the Pleiades.

1–2–3–4–
5–6–7
their silvery fire
is staying in Heaven.

To hell with St John's
life-loathing vision
when I feel in my jeans
your fingers go fishing.

1–2–3–4–
5–6–7
their silvery fire
is staying in Heaven.

Your turn to count.
My turn to lick
your moistening cunt
like a fig, fig.

1–2–3–4–
5–6–7
their silvery fire
is staying in Heaven.

No stars are falling,
all the figs ripen,
I have a gut feeling
the World's End won't happen.

1–2–3–4–
5–6–7
their silvery fire
is staying in Heaven.

The stars won't fall
nor will the fig.
Our hearts are so full
as we fuck, fuck.

1–2–3–4–
5–6–7
their silvery fire
is staying in Heaven.

Broadway

A flop is when the star's first-night bouquets
outlast the show itself by several days.

Losing Touch

in memoriam George Cukor, died 24.1.83

I watch a siskin swinging back and forth
on the nut-net, enjoying lunchtime sun
unusual this time of year up North
and listening to the news at five past 1.

As people not in constant contact do
we'd lost touch, but I thought of you, old friend
and sent a postcard now and then. I knew
the sentence starting with your name would end:
'*the Hollywood director, died today*'.

You're leaning forward in your black beret
from the *Times* obituary, and I'd add
the background of Pavlovsk near Leningrad
bathed in summer and good shooting light
where it was taken that July as *I*'m
the one you're leaning forward to address.
I had a black pen poised about to write
and have one now and think back to that time
and feel you lean towards me out of Nothingness.

I rummage for the contacts you sent then:
the one of you that's leaning from *The Times*
and below it one of me with my black pen
listening to you criticize my rhymes,
and, between a millimetre of black band
that now could be ten billion times as much
and none that shows the contact of your hand.
The distance needs adjusting; just a touch!

You were about to tap my knee for emphasis.

It's me who's leaning forward now with this!

The Mother of the Muses

in memoriam Emmanuel Stratas,
born Crete 1903, died Toronto 1987

After I've lit the fire and looked outside
and found us snowbound and the roads all blocked,
anxious to prove my memory's not ossified
and the way into that storehouse still unlocked,
as it's easier to remember poetry,
I try to remember, but soon find it hard,
a speech from *Prometheus* a boy from Greece BC
scratched, to help him learn it, on a shard.

I remember the museum, and I could eke
his scratch marks out, and could complete
the . . . however many lines there were of Greek
and didn't think it then much of a feat.
But now, not that much later, when I find
the verses I once knew beyond recall
I resolve to bring all yesterday to mind,
our visit to your father, each fact, *all*.

Seeing the Home he's in 's made me obsessed
with remembering those verses I once knew
and setting myself this little memory test
I don't think, at the moment, I'll come through.
It's the Memory, Mother of the Muses, bit.
Prometheus, in words I do recall reciting
but can't quote now, and they're so apposite,
claiming he gave Mankind the gift of writing,

along with fire the Gods withheld from men
who'd lived like ants in caves deprived of light
they could well end up living in again
if we let what flesh first roasted on ignite
a Burning of the Books far more extreme
than any screeching Führer could inspire,

the dark side of the proud Promethean dream
our globe enveloped in his gift of fire.

He bequeathed to baker and to bombardier,
to help benighted men develop faster,
two forms of fire, the gentle one in here,
and what the *Luftwaffe* unleashed, *and* the Lancaster.
One beneficial and one baleful form,
the fire I lit a while since in the grate
that's keeping me, as I sit writing, warm
and what gutted Goethestrasse on this date,

beginning yesterday to be precise
and shown on film from forty years ago
in a Home for the Aged almost glazed with ice
and surrounded by obliterating snow.
We had the choice of watching on TV
Dresden destroyed, then watching its rebirth,
or, with the world outside too blizzardful to see,
live, the senile not long for this earth.

Piles of cracked ice tiles where ploughs try to push
the muddied new falls onto shattered slates,
the glittering shrapnel of grey frozen slush,
a blitz debris fresh snow obliterates
along with what was cleared the day before
bringing even the snowploughs to a halt.
And their lives are frozen solid and won't thaw
with no memory to fling its sparks of salt.

The outer world of blur reflects their inner,
these Rest Home denizens who don't quite know
whether they've just had breakfast, lunch, or dinner,
or stare, between three lunches, at the snow.
Long icicles from the low roof meet
the frozen drifts below and block their view
of flurry and blizzard in the snowed-up street
and of a sky that for a month has shown no blue.

Elsie's been her own optometrist,
measuring the daily way her sight declines
into a growing ball of flashing mist.
She trains her failing sight on outside signs:
the church's COME ALIVE IN '85!
the small hand on the *Export A* ad clock,
the flashing neon on the truck-stop dive
pulsing with strobe lights and jukebox rock,

the little red Scottie on the STOOP & SCOOP
but not the cute eye cast towards its rear,
the little rounded pile of heaped red poop
the owners are required to bend and clear.
To imagine herself so stooping is a feat
as hard as that of gymnasts she has seen
lissom in white leotards compete
in trampolining on the TV screen.

There's one with mashed dinner who can't summon
yet again the appetite to smear
the food about the shrunk face of a woman
weeping for death in her 92nd year.
And of the life she lived remembers little
and stares, like someone playing Kim's Game,
at the tray beneath her nose that fills with spittle
whose bubbles fill with faces with no name.

Lilian, whose love made her decide
to check in with her mate who'd had a stroke,
lost all her spryness once her husband died . . .
He had a beautiful . . . all made of oak . . .
silk inside . . . brass handles . . . tries to find
alternatives . . . *that long thing where you lie*
for words like coffin that have slipped her mind
and forgetting, not the funeral, makes her cry.

And Anne, who treats her roommates to her 'news'
though every day her news is just the same
how she'd just come back from *such a lovely cruise*
to that famous island . . . I forget its name . . .
Born before the Boer War, me, and so
I'm too old to remember I suppose . . .
then tries again . . . *the island's called . . . you know . . .*
that place, you know . . . where everybody goes . . .

First Gene had one and then a second cane
and then, in weeks, a walker of cold chrome,
now in a wheelchair wails for the Ukraine,
sobbing in soiled pants for what was home.
Is that horror at what's on the TV screen
or just the way the stroke makes Jock's jaw hang?
Though nobody quite knows what his words mean
they hear Scots diphthongs in the New World twang.

And like the Irish Sea on Blackpool Beach,
where Joan was once the pick of bathing belles,
the Lancashire she once had in her speech
seeps into Canadian as she retells,
whose legs now ooze out water, who can't walk,
how she was 'champion at tap', 'the flower'
(she poises the petals on the now frail stalk)
'of the ballet troupe at Blackpool Tower'.

You won't hear Gene, Eugene, Yevgeny speak
to nurses now, or God, in any other tongue
but his Ukrainian, nor your dad Greek,
all that's left to them of being young.
Life comes full circle when we die.
The circumference is finally complete,
so we shouldn't wonder too much why
his speech went back, a stowaway, to Crete.

Dispersal and displacement, willed or not,
from homeland to the room the three share here,
one Ukrainian, one Cretan, and one Scot
grow less Canadian as death draws near.
Jock sees a boozer in a Glasgow street,
and Eugene glittering icons, candles, prayer,
and for your dad a thorn-thick crag in Crete
with oregano and goat smells in the air.

And home? Where is it now? The olive grove
may well be levelled under folds of tar.
The wooden house made joyful with a stove
has gone the way of Tsar and samovar.
The small house with 8 people to a room
with no privacy for quiet thought or sex
bulldozed in the island's tourist boom
to make way for Big Macs and discothèques.

Beribboned hats and bold embroidered sashes
once helped another émigré forget
that Canada was going to get his ashes
and that Estonia's still Soviet.
But now the last of those old-timers
couldn't tell one folk dance from another
and mistakes in the mists of his Alzheimer's
the nurse who wipes his bottom for his mother.

Some hoard memories as some hoard gold
against that rapidly approaching day
that's all they have to live on, being old,
but find their savings spirited away.
What's the point of having lived at all
in the much-snapped duplex in Etobicoke
if it gets swept away beyond recall,
in spite of all the snapshots, at one stroke?

If we *are* what we remember, what are they
who don't have memories as we have ours,
who, when evening falls, have no recall of day,
or who those people were who'd brought them flowers.
The troubled conscience, though, 's glad to forget.
Oblivion for some 's an inner balm.
They've found some peace of mind, not total yet,
as only death itself brings that much calm.

And those white flashes on the TV screen,
as a child, whose dad plunged into genocide,
remembers Dresden and describes the scene,
are they from the firestorm then, or storm outside?
Crouching in clown's costume (it was *Fasching*)
aged, 40 years ago, as I was, 9
Eva remembers cellar ceiling crashing
and her mother screaming shrilly: *Swine! Swine! Swine!*

The Tiergarten chief with level voice remembered
a hippo disembowelled on its back,
a mother chimp, her charges all dismembered,
and trees bedaubed with zebra flesh and yak.
Flamingos, flocking from burst cages, fly
in a frenzy with their feathers all alight
from fire on the ground to bomb-crammed sky,
their flames fanned that much fiercer by their flight;

the gibbon with no hands he'd had to shoot
as it came towards him with appealing stumps,
the gutless gorilla still clutching fruit
mashed with its bowels into bloody lumps . . .
I was glad as on and on the keeper went
to the last flayed elephant's fire-frantic screech
that the old folk hadn't followed what was meant
by official footage or survivors' speech.

But then they missed the Semper's restoration,
Dresden's lauded effort to restore
one of the treasures of the now halved nation
exactly as it was before the War.
Billions of marks and years of labour
to reproduce the Semper and they play
what they'd played before the bombs fell, Weber,
Der Freischütz, for their reopening today.

Each bleb of blistered paintwork, every flake
of blast-flayed pigment in that dereliction
they analysed in lab flasks to remake
the colours needed for the redepiction
of Poetic Justice on her cloud surmounting
mortal suffering from opera and play,
repainted tales that seem to bear recounting
more often than the facts that mark today:

the dead Cordelia in the lap of Lear,
Lohengrin who pilots his white swan
at cascading lustres of bright chandelier
above the plush this pantheon shattered on,
with Titania's leashed pards in pastiche Titian,
Faust with Mephisto, Joan, Nathan the Wise,
all were blown, on that Allied bombing mission,
out of their painted clouds into the skies.

Repainted, reupholstered, all in place
just as it had been before that fatal night,
but however devilish the leading bass
his demons are outshadowed on this site.
But that's what Dresden wants and so they play
the same score sung by new uplifting voices
and, as opera synopses often say,
'The curtain falls as everyone rejoices.'

Next more TV, devoted to the trial
of Ernst Zundel, who denies the Jews were gassed,
and academics are supporting his denial,
restoring pride by doctoring the past,
and not just Germans but those people who
can't bear to think such things could ever be,
and by disbelieving horrors to be true
hope to put back hope in history.

A nurse comes in to offer us a cot
considering how bad the blizzard's grown
but you kissed your dad, who, as we left, forgot
he'd been anything all day but on his own.
We needed to escape, weep, laugh, and lie
in each other's arms more privately than there,
weigh in the balance all we're heartened by,
so braved the blizzard back, deep in despair.

Feet of snow went sliding off the bonnet
as we pulled onto the road from where we'd parked.
A snowplough tried to help us to stay on it
but localities nearby, once clearly marked,
those named for northern hometowns close to mine,
the Yorks, the Whitbys, and the Scarboroughs,
all seemed one whited-out recurring sign
that could well be 'Where everybody goes . . .'

His goggles bug-eyed from the driven snow,
the balaclavaed salter goes ahead
with half the sower's, half the sandman's throw,
and follows the groaning plough with wary tread.
We keep on losing the blue revolving light
and the sliding salter, and try to keep on track
by making sure we always have in sight
the yellow Day-glo X marked on his back.

The blizzard made our neighbourhood unknown.
We could neither see behind us nor before.
We felt in that white-out world we were alone
looking for landmarks, lost, until we saw
the unmistakable McDonald's M
with its '60 billion served' hamburger count.
Living, we were numbered among them,
and dead, among an incomputable amount . . .

I woke long after noon with you still sleeping
and the windows blocked where all the snow had blown.
Your pillow was still damp from last night's weeping.
In that silent dark I swore I'd make it known,
while the oil of memory feeds the wick of life
and the flame from it's still constant and still bright,
that, come oblivion or not, I loved my wife
in that long thing where we lay with day like night.

Toronto's at a standstill under snow.
Outside there's not much light and not a sound.
Those lines from Aeschylus! How do they go?
It's almost halfway through *Prometheus Bound*.
I think they're coming back. I'm concentrating . . .
μουσομητορ 'εργανην . . . Damn! I forget,
but remembering your dad, I'm celebrating
being in love, not too forgetful, yet.

Country people used to say today's
the day the birds sense spring and choose their mates,
and trapped exotics in the Dresden blaze
were flung together in their flame-fledged fates.
The snow in the street outside 's at least 6ft.
I look for life, and find the only sign 's,
like words left for, or *by*, someone from Crete,
a bird's tracks, like blurred Greek, for Valentine's.

(Toronto, St Valentine's Day)

Initial Illumination

Farne cormorants with catches in their beaks
shower fishscale confetti on the shining sea.
The first bright weather here for many weeks
for my Sunday G-Day train bound for Dundee,
off to St Andrew's to record a reading,
doubtful, in these dark days, what poems can do,
and watching the mists round Lindisfarne receding
my doubt extends to Dark Age Good Book too.
Eadfrith the Saxon scribe/illuminator
incorporated cormorants I'm seeing fly
round the same island thirteen centuries later
into the *In principio*'s initial I.
Billfrith's begemmed and jewelled boards get looted
by raiders gung-ho for booty and berserk,
the sort of soldiery that's still recruited
to do today's dictators' dirty work,
but the initials in St John and in St Mark
graced with local cormorants in ages,
we of a darker still keep calling Dark,
survive in those illuminated pages.
The word of God so beautifully scripted
by Eadfrith and Billfrith the anchorite
Pentagon conners have once again conscripted
to gloss the cross on the precision sight.
Candlepower, steady hand, gold leaf, a brush
were all that Eadfrith had to beautify
the word of God much bandied by George Bush
whose word illuminated midnight sky
and confused the Baghdad cock who was betrayed
by bombs into believing day was dawning
and crowed his heart out at the deadly raid
and didn't live to greet the proper morning.

Now with noonday headlights in Kuwait
and the burial of the blackened in Baghdad
let them remember, all those who celebrate,
that their good news is someone else's bad
or the light will never dawn on poor Mankind.
Is it open-armed at all that victory V,
that insular initial intertwined
with slack-necked cormorants from black laquered sea,
with trumpets bulled and bellicose and blowing
for what men claim as victories in their wars,
with the fire-hailing cock and all those crowing
who don't yet smell the dunghill at their claws?

A Cold Coming

'A cold coming we had of it.'
  (T. S. Eliot, 'Journey of the Magi')

I saw the charred Iraqi lean
towards me from bomb-blasted screen,

his windscreen wiper like a pen
ready to write down thoughts for men,

his windscreen wiper like a quill
he's reaching for to make his will.

I saw the charred Iraqi lean
like someone made of Plasticine

as though he'd stopped to ask the way
and this is what I heard him say:

'Don't be afraid I've picked on you
for this exclusive interview.

Isn't it your sort of poet's task
to find words for this frightening mask?

If that gadget that you've got records
words from such scorched vocal chords,

press RECORD before some dog
devours me mid-monologue.'

So I held the shaking microphone
closer to the crumbling bone:

'I read the news of three wise men
who left their sperm in nitrogen,

three foes of ours, three wise Marines
with sample flasks and magazines,

three wise soldiers from Seattle
who banked their sperm before the battle.

Did No. 1 say: God be thanked
I've got my precious semen banked.

And No. 2: O Praise the Lord
my last best shot is safely stored.

And No. 3: Praise be to God
I left my wife my frozen wad?

So if their fate was to be gassed
at least they thought their name would last,

and though cold corpses in Kuwait
they could by proxy procreate.

Excuse a skull half roast, half bone
for using such a scornful tone.

It may seem out of all proportion
but I wish I'd taken their precaution.

They seemed the masters of their fate
with wisely jarred ejaculate.

Was it a propaganda coup
to make us think they'd cracked death too,

disinformation to defeat us
with no post-mortem millilitres?

Symbolic billions in reserve
made me, for one, lose heart and nerve.

On Saddam's pay we can't afford
to go and get our semen stored.

Sad to say that such high tech's
uncommon here. We're stuck with sex.

If you can conjure up and stretch
your imagination (and not retch)

the image of me beside my wife,
closely clasped creating life . . .

(I let the unfleshed skull unfold
a story I'd been already told,

and idly tried to calculate
the content of ejaculate:

the sperm in one ejaculation
equals the whole Iraqi nation

times, roughly, let's say, 12.5
though that .5's not now alive.

Let's say the sperms were an amount
so many times the body count,

2,500 times at least
(but let's wait till the toll's released!).

Whichever way Death seems outflanked
by one tube of cold bloblings banked.

Poor bloblings, maybe you've been blessed
with, of all fates possible, the best

according to Sophocles i.e.
'the best of fates is not to be'

a philosophy that's maybe bleak
for any but an ancient Greek

but difficult these days to escape
when spoken to by such a shape.

When you see men brought to such states
who wouldn't want that 'best of fates'

or in the world of Cruise and Scud
not go kryonic if he could,

spared the normal human doom
of having made it through the womb?)

He heard my thoughts and stopped the spool:
'I never thought life futile, fool!

Though all Hell began to drop
I never wanted life to stop.

I was filled with such a yearning
to stay in life as I was burning,

such a longing to be beside
my wife in bed before I died,

and, most, to have engendered there
a child untouched by war's despair.

So press RECORD! I want to reach
the warring nations with my speech.

Don't look away! I know it's hard
to keep regarding one so charred,

so disfigured by unfriendly fire
and think it once burned with desire.

Though fire has flayed off half my features
they once were like my fellow creatures',

till some screen-gazing crop-haired boy
from Iowa or Illinois,

equipped by ingenious technophile
put paid to my paternal smile

and made the face you see today
an armature half-patched with clay,

an icon framed, a looking glass
for devotees of "kicking ass",

a mirror that returns the gaze
of victors on their victory days

and in the end stares out the watcher
who ducks behind his headline: GOTCHA!

or behind the flag-bedecked page 1
of the true to bold-type-setting SUN!

I doubt victorious Greeks let Hector
join their feast as spoiling spectre,

and who'd want to sour the children's joy
in Iowa or Illinois

or ageing mothers overjoyed
to find their babies weren't destroyed?

But cabs beflagged with SUN front pages
don't help peace in future ages.

Stars and Stripes in sticky paws
may sow the seeds for future wars.

Each Union Jack the kids now wave
may lead them later to the grave.

But praise the Lord and raise the banner
(excuse a skull's sarcastic manner!)

Desert Rat and Desert Stormer
without scars and (maybe) trauma,

the semen-bankers are all back
to sire their children in their sack.

With seed sown straight from the sower
dump second-hand spermatozoa!

Lie that you saw me and I smiled
to see the soldier hug his child.

Lie and pretend that I excuse
my bombing by B52s,

pretend I pardon and forgive
that they still do and I don't live,

pretend they have the burnt man's blessing
and then, maybe, I'm spared confessing

that only fire burnt out the shame
of things I'd done in Saddam's name,

the deaths, the torture and the plunder
the black clouds all of us are under.

Say that I'm smiling and excuse
the Scuds we launched against the Jews.

Pretend I've got the imagination
to see the world beyond one nation.

That's your job, poet, to pretend
I want my foe to be my friend.

It's easier to find such words
for this dumb mask like baked dogturds.

So lie and say the charred man smiled
to see the soldier hug his child.

This gaping rictus once made glad
a few old hearts back in Baghdad,

hearts growing older by the minute
as each truck comes without me in it.

I've met you though, and had my say
which you've got taped. Now go away.'

I gazed at him and he gazed back
staring right through me to Iraq.

Facing the way the charred man faced
I saw the frozen phial of waste,

a test-tube frozen in the dark,
crib and Kaaba, sacred Ark,

a pilgrimage of Cross and Crescent
the chilled suspension of the Present.

Rainbows seven shades of black
curved from Kuwait back to Iraq,

and instead of gold the frozen crock's
crammed with Mankind on the rocks,

the congealed geni who won't thaw
until the World renounces War,

cold spunk meticulously jarred
never to be charrer or the charred,

a bottled Bethlehem of this come-
curdling Cruise/Scud-cursed millennium.

I went. I pressed REWIND and PLAY
and I heard the charred man say:

A Celebratory Ode on the Abdication of King Charles III

It's not surprising that the Muse
has had to bypass Laureate Hughes
and chooses me to be the bard
to hymn the close of this charade,
and hymn the Crown's demise I will
with this black goose-feather quill
I've saved for ages just to write:
Goodbye! Good riddance, Divine Right!
and anything that still pretends
divinity shapes human ends.
No *Fidei Defensor* now can guard
the worn-out Church from knacker's yard.

First with its feather end I'll dust
the eyeballs of the Milton bust
I've kept as a constant inspiration
towards a now maturer nation,
Milton, whose Latin justified
to Europe Britain's regicide,
with his blind and marble eyes
sheds no tears for this demise.
We only weep we had to wait
so long to have an adult state.
Why has it taken all this while
desceptring 'this sceptred isle'?

Between Charles I and II
Britain had a chance she blew.
Britain blew her biggest chance
to be a grown-up girl like France
but history has cried FINIS
and drawn a line at King Charles III.
Britain's watched as waves have swept her

last King with his crown and sceptre
into the tides of change Canute
saw lapping at his well-licked boot.
Though later kings chose to ignore
the breakers crashing on the shore
that leave poor Charles's ermine sodden
with the momentum of the modern.

More democratic, more adult
with no mystique of monarch cult,
let's begin by hauling down
the Rs in names that mean the Crown,
the R from every acronym
that's lost its use along with him.
Remove that R that's everywhere!
First, you, my friend (Sir?) Richard Eyre
take that R from RNT
always a sore point with me
so I'm the first to shout hurrah
that the National's free to drop its R.
They claimed the added R would raise
much needed cash much more than plays.
'It gave us dignity abroad'
according to Chairman Rayne (now Lord!)
I beg to differ, *au contraire*,
we just seem backward everywhere.
All that bowing to the Royal Box
just makes us into laughing stocks.
From now on let our stage creation
be simply offered to the nation
and none of us need now be forced
to be so royally endorsed.
Now work should seem its own reward
to every would-be Sir or Lord
and all those former Sirs and Dames
will be content with simple names

without a prefix or a suf-.
In a republic work's enough.
Hopefully the day is dawning
when Britons lose their taste for fawning
on Lords and Ladies, Dames and Knights
dubbed by bepurpled parasites
and will demand a Bill of Rights.
A UK with a prefix 'Former'
sends tiaras into trauma
but *King*-dom's nothing when the King
's been taken under history's wing.
It's probably just British luck
the acronym comes out as FUK!

Now finally we've cast aside
the monarch without regicide.
It's 'off with his crown' instead
of, as before, 'off with his head'!
And he's agreed all by himself
to put the crown on to the shelf
where it must for ever stay
except for V&A display.

If Britain goes back where she was
and Republicans all flee to Oz
and there's a new ode to be written
to welcome King Charles back to Britain
I rather fear the Royal Muse
will have to go to Laureate Hughes.
An 'Ode on Monarchy Restored'
could make a Laureate a Lord.

Deathwatch Danceathon

Six centuries of insect sex
make hallowed rafters hollow wrecks,
the high and holy upheld by
oak-beams gnawed to casks of ply,
and their *Totentanz* tattoos
percussive in half-empty pews
are sex-sex-sex, the tapping crown
of cruising bug brings churches down.

How many houses for the Lord
has the knock-for-nooky squatter gnawed?
Carved escutcheon, scuncheon-squatters
more bug cloggies than gavotters,
rafter-feasters, roodscreen-wreckers
send morse-a-mate from mite maracas.
In oak as old as Robin Hood
the midnight maters knock on wood.

The male bug's tappings telegraph to
every female in the rafter,
11 times per second beat
the insect 42nd St
and oak-feasters' Easter Parade's
booming in old balustrades,
and the sick man in the bed below
hears the knock-tease to and fro.

The mortal patient in the bed
hears their mating call with dread.
He hears the termite dancers tapping
tattoos that terminate in tupping,
the Deathwatch Beetle like Blind Pew
groping towards his rendezvous
and that dry staccato sound
brings old institutions to the ground.

Beetle bonkers in the beams
spell the end of old regimes.
Down come beams and joists and doors
to the foreplay of the xylovores,
ancient truss and cruck
cracked by fronsaphonic fuck.
Bluntly put the bugger's fucked yer
entire infested infrastructure.

Devourers of dead wood supports
of mansions, palaces and courts,
each fat white grub will have gnawed a
good few yards of Old World Order.
The rat-a-tat-tat of rafter roaches
tapping their sexual approaches,
a frolic of phallic infestation
expected in a monarch nation.

Old palaces, old churches, courts
with rotting tap-schools for supports,
sex-mad rafter-hopping hordes
in chapel panel, west-wing boards.
In the end the bug brings down
the bedpost carved with shield and crown
and goes on dining and makes fall
the portrait-laden palace wall.

Other lives get nourished by
the sick man who's about to die.
On Ilka Moor Baht 'at
declares: man's himself a habitat
where worm and duck and fellow Tyke'll
help complete the foodchain cycle.
So don't imagine it's all gloom
to hear the deathwatch in the room.

The mortal summons in the wall's
some other creature's mating calls,
sending a rhythm along the beams
the spells the end of old regimes.
And the fruitful female bears
a future horde of new Astaires,
each a tuneful tapping trouper
part Gene Kelly, part Gene Krupa.

Gilt cherubs once with chubby cheeks
look down now like noseless freaks.
Like stuffing from a teddy bear
their wooden innards fill the air,
little motes of carven oak
with brief puffs of a golden smoke,
golden *putti* tiny specks
of oak confetti for mite sex.

The wooden saintling wondreth whither
cometh the knock-knock-knock come-hither,
from his brain or from his heart
or from some other uncarved part.
Sawdust created by no saw
but sexaphonic xylovore,
their friable physique now floats
as dancing, dull or golden motes.

The momentum of this very verse
drums up the stretcher and the hearse,
a beat that comes from long before
the King-beheading Civil War
divided still divided Britain
and Andrew Marvell's poem got written
(though now he'd say that at his back
trotted ghost-writer Pasternak!).

So 'never send' and 'had we but'
and such like thoughts sublimely put
by poets who've used the tolling bell
to cast an otherworldly spell,
or 'time's winged chariot' as a ploy
to make a mistress act less coy.
Put less ornately 'we're soon dead,
my sweetest darling, come to bed!'

So lovers lie, listening to taps,
part copulation, part collapse,
the mortal summons in the wall
that's just some creature's mating call –
Eros/Thanatos a pair
like Ginger Rogers/Fred Astaire,
one figure fleshless and one full,
the dancing duo, cheek to skull.

The very verse the poet employed
to make the virgin see the void
and be thus vertiginously sped
into Andrew Marvell's bed,
is the beat whose very ictus
turns smiling kiss to smirking rictus,
the urgent beat that wipes away
the urgency of what poems say.

Like the car and house alarms
that lovers in each other's arms
hear going off and left to bleep
the neighbourhood from love and sleep,
piercing, pulsating throbbers
disturbing everyone but robbers.
Everywhere there is a measure
heard or unheard of our pleasure.

Two pulses slightly out of synch,
flexi-phials of coursing *Quink*,
the metred couplet with its rhyme
revels in and coasts on time
we haven't got enough of – there
beneath the gently lifted hair
the artery that keeps repeating
life and its ending in one beating.

And in a palace's four-poster where
deathwatch dustmotes fill the air
in the densest dancing cloud
the beetle's drumming is most loud.
In Kensington he makes a killing,
the Deathwatch Beetle, drumming, drilling,
head in and out the polished oak
leaves one last prick-hole as they poke –

Their 'grubby' passion, his and hers,
spurned, pampered Princess, squire in spurs,
and as four-poster bedposts rock
we hear the deathwatch: knock . . . knock . . . knock . . .
and though too gentle for the axe
quicker than Anna Pasternak's,
I think, with Andrew Marvell, I can hear
the gavel of the auctioneer . . .

(The Deathwatch geigering for fucks
leaves the book worm to the books!)

Laureate's Block

for Queen Elizabeth

I'm appalled to see newspapers use my name
as 'widely tipped' for a job I'd never seek.
Swans come in Domestic, Mute, and Tame
and no swan-upper's going to nick my beak.

I'm particularly vexed that it occurred
in those same Guardian *pages where I'd written*
on the abdication of King Charles III
in the hope of a republic in Great Britain.

I wrote the above last night but what comes next
I wrote the day that Ted Hughes, sadly, died
and to exit from the lists I've faxed the text
for inclusion in the Guardian *(op.ed side?):*

No doubt inspired by the lunchtime news
the salesman, passing volumes by myself,
was selecting all the second-hand Ted Hughes
to move to the window from the poetry shelf.

A poet's death fills other poets with dread,
timor mortis like Dunbar's, and of the fate
of being remaindered, and not ever read,
but this bookshop window's got *Crow* laid in state,

with front cover showing now not just the spine.
At least they get your books out on display.
I'm doubting that they'll bother much with mine,
as I buy an old 4-volume Thomas Gray.

It was in this Stratford bookshop that I heard
Ted died, and needed my lover, stuck on stage
as Queen Elizabeth in *Richard III*,
to help me not to brood I'm near Ted's age.

While she ran the gauntlet of gut-curdling guile
child murder, mayhem, lust for monarchy
I walked by the swollen Avon for a while.
The plastic bag with Gray in banged my knee.

The swans' feet were slapping on deep towpath mud.
They wouldn't venture on the Avon out of fear
of the overflowing river in full flood
and getting their necks wrung dragged into the weir.

While my lover had to do two *Richard III*'s
I went to bed and read from front to back
all those four vols of Gray and found these words:
the saponaceous qualities of sack

in a letter that I think's worth perusal
especially by unversed journalists
who speculate which poet after Hughes'll
get a post Gray wouldn't credit still exists.

Though I could, because I've practised, paraphrase
in his *Elegy*'s quatrains if I so chose,
the following remarks of Thomas Gray's.
I'll quote them as he wrote them in plain prose:

Though I very well know the bland emollient saponaceous quali-
ties of sack and silver, yet if any great man would say to me 'I
make you rat-catcher to his Majesty, with a salary of £300 a
year and two butts of the best Malaga; and though it has been
usual to catch a mouse or two, for form's sake, in public once a
year, yet to you, sir, we shall not stand upon these things' I
cannot say I should jump at it, nay, if they would drop the very
name of the office, and call me Sinecure to the King's Majesty, I
should still feel a little awkward, and think everybody I saw
smelt a rat about me . . .

The office itself has always humbled the professor hitherto

(even in an age when kings were somebody), if he were a poor
writer by making him more conspicuous, and if he were a good
one by setting him at war with the little fry of his own profession,
for there are poets little enough to envy even a poet laureat.

(Dec 19, 1757)

That's Gray 2 centuries and more ago
with sentiments I find quite close to my mine.
And anyone who knew my work would know
which words of Thomas Gray I'd underline.

And the new rat-catcher to our present Queen,
who must have palace rodents sleek and fat,
though he/she washes after catches and keeps clean,
still sports retainer's raiment rank with rat.

There should be no successor to Ted Hughes.
'The saponaceous qualities of sack'
are purest poison if paid poets lose
their freedom as PM's or monarch's hack.

Nor should Prince Charles succeed our present Queen
and spare us some toad's ode on coronation.
I'd like all suchlike odes there've ever been
binned by a truly democratic nation.

Are there poets who are monarchists who'll try?
They might well get a Garter for their guts.
You'll never hear me heave an envious sigh.
I'd sooner be a free man with no butts,

free not to have to puff some prince's wedding,
free to say up yours to Tony Blair,
to write an ode on Charles I's beheading
and regret the restoration of his heir

*(I'd hoped last week that would-be royal hacks
that self-promoting sycophantic flock
would whet their talents on the headman's axe
but it seems like a bad case of laureate's block –*

*30 January 1649
though it's hard to use the date for self-promotion
the anniversary's gone by with not a line
from toadies like Di-deifying Motion),*

free to write what I think should be written,
free to scatter scorn on Number 10,
free to blast and bollock Blairite Britain
(and alliterate outrageously like then!)

free to write exactly as I choose
and heed both Thomas Gray's and Milton's ghost.
It's not for Laureate poems we'll miss Ted Hughes
nor any past pretender to the post.

And free, once Richard's off and Richmond's on
the battered throne with hacked crown on his head
and widowed women wan and woebegone,
when my unpainted queen's back in our bed,

to kiss my dedication, hot with scenes
of regal wrath, rage, wrangle, kiss away,
as we kiss equals and do not kiss queens,
the bitter taste of Shakespeare's bloody play.

A poet's death fills other poets with dread,
a king's death kings, but under my duvet
is Queen Elizabeth, and off our bed
slide these quatrains and all of Thomas Gray.

Legal Ruling

Our future King *de jure* may be dunked
into his spouse's cunt no more his whore's.
O let Law make this monarch as defunct
as Camilla's tampon after menopause.

[untitled]

for Richard Eyre

You'd so brilliantly directed what I wrote
with our anti-royal ranter centre-stage
that I re-read *The Prince's Play* to find a quote
to gloss my mugshot on the facing page,
but, reluctantly, decided in the end
that the lines that I liked most weren't any use –

How could I shower my newly knighted friend
with all that deeply felt republican abuse?

English Opera

Sir Harry
Sir Gawain
Surtitles!

Three Poems from Bosnia

1. *The Cycles of Donji Vakuf*

We take *Emerald* to Bugojno, then the *Opal* route
to Donji Vakuf where Kalashnikovs still shoot
at retreating Serbs or at the sky
to drum up the leaden beat of victory.
Once more, though this time Serbian, homes
get pounded to façades like honeycombs.
This time it's the Bosnian Muslims' turn
to 'cleanse' a taken town, to loot, and burn.
Donji Vakuf fell last night at 11.
Victory's signalled by firing rounds to Heaven
and for the god to whom their victory's owed.
We see some victors cycling down the road
on bikes that they're too big for. They feel so tall
as victors, all conveyances seem small,
but one, whose knees keep bumping on his chin,
rides a kid's cycle, with a mandolin,
also childish size, strapped to the saddle,
jogging against him as he tries to pedal.
His machine gun and the mandolin impede
his furious pedalling, and slow down the speed
appropriate to victors, huge-limbed and big-booted,
and he's defeated by the small bike that he's looted.

The luckiest looters come down dragging cattle,
two and three apiece they've won in battle.
A goat whose udder seems about to burst
squirts her milk to quench a victor's thirst
which others quench with a shared beer, as a cow,
who's no idea she's a Muslim's now,
sprays a triumphal arch of piss across
the path of her new happy Bosnian boss.

Another struggles with stuffed rucksack, gun, and bike,
small and red, he knows his kid will like,
and he hands me his Kalashnikov to hold
to free his hands. Rain makes it wet and cold.
When he's balanced his booty, he makes off,
for a moment forgetting his Kalashnikov,
which he slings with all his looted load
on to his shoulder, and trudges down the road
where a solitary reaper passes by,
scythe on his shoulder, wanting fields to dry,
hoping, listening to the thunder, that the day
will brighten up enough to cut his hay.

And tonight some small boy will be glad
he's got the present of a bike from soldier dad,
who braved the Serb artillery and fire
to bring back a scuffed red bike with one flat tyre.
And among the thousands fleeing north, another
with all his gladness gutted, with his mother,
knowing the nightmare they are cycling in,
will miss the music of his mandolin.

(Donji Vakuf, 14 September 1995)

2. *The Bright Lights of Sarajevo*

After the hours that Sarajevans pass
queuing with empty canisters of gas
to get the refills they wheel home in prams,
or queuing for the precious meagre grams
of bread they're rationed to each day,
and often dodging snipers on the way,
or struggling up sometimes eleven flights
of stairs with water, then you'd think that the nights
of Sarajevo would be totally devoid
of people walking streets Serb shells destroyed,
but tonight in Sarajevo that's just not the case –

The young go walking at a stroller's pace,
black shapes impossible to mark
as Muslim, Serb or Croat in such dark.
In unlit streets you can't distinguish who
calls bread *hjleb* or *hleb* or calls it *kruh*.
All take the evening air with stroller's stride,
no torches guide them but they don't collide
except as one of the flirtatious ploys
when a girl's dark shape is fancied by some boy's.

Then the tender radar of the tone of voice
shows by its signals she approves his choice.
Then match or lighter to a cigarette
to check in her eyes if he's made progress yet.

And I see a pair who've certainly progressed
beyond the tone of voice and match-flare test
and he's about, I think, to take her hand
and lead her away from where they stand
on two shell splash scars, where in '92
Serb mortars massacred the breadshop queue

and blood-dunked crusts of shredded bread
lay on the pavement with the broken dead.
And at their feet in holes made by the mortar
that caused the massacre, now full of water
from the rain that's poured down half the day,
though now even the smallest clouds have cleared away,
leaving the Sarajevo star-filled evening sky
ideally bright and clear for bomber's eye,
in those two rain-full shell-holes the boy sees
fragments of the splintered Pleiades,
sprinkled on those death-deep, death-dark wells
splashed on the pavement by Serb mortar shells.

The dark boy shape leads dark girl shape away
to share one coffee in a candlelit café
until the curfew, and he holds her hand
behind AID flour sacks refilled with sand.

(Sarajevo, 20 September 1995)

3. *Essentials*

(Conversation with a Croat)

'I looked at my Shakespeares and said NO!
I looked at my Sartres, which I often read
by candlelight, and couldn't let them go
even at this time of direst need.

Because he was a Fascist like our *Chetnik* foes
I lingered for a while at my Célines . . .
but he's such a serious stylist, so I chose
Das Kapital to cook my AID canned beans!'

(Sarajevo, 20 September 1995)

Two Poems for My Son in his Sickness

1. Rice-Paper Man

(i)

Anything, or almost, 's worth at least a try.
Lifelong rationalists, afraid to die,
shuffle shiftily to 'healers', often lurch
from chemotherapy back to the church.
When, if I fall ill, things get that bad,
I'll try to stand by reason. As a dad,
I have to say, there've been times when I've done
deeds I hate confessing, for my son.
I never pray; I scorn religious quacks
but do things I despise, for my son, Max,
out of unbearable panic at his pain:
like light a candle in a church in Spain.

(ii)

On either side were grim *memento mori*
by Valdes Leal: *The End of the World's Glory*,
and Death with a scythe: *In Ictu Oculi*
(English: *In the Twinkling of an Eye*),
that blink that makes smooth bishops and rough bums
lie clasped in the charnel like close bosom chums.
Here Death glides by as if on rollerblades
over disarrays of books, maps, red brocades,
unplucked violas, and goes on to spin
a globe with now 6 billion people in.
The monarch *esqueletto* squats
on piles of skulls ten billion times Pol Pot's.

(iii)

The church is near the bullring and *olés*
keep breaking in on my despairing daze.
In Ictu Oculi! I hear crowd roars
at *torero*'s coup de grâce or *toro*'s gores.

In Ictu Oculi! Each loud *olé*
cheers scything *esqueletto* on his way,
a match for both the bull and brave bullfighter,
casual crusher of crozier and mitre,
serial suffocator, who can snuff
the most brilliant suit of lights with just one puff.
Death trashes all. The minute that we're born's
the moment *toro Tod* dips his honed horns.

(iv)
Dereliction, death, decay, *olé! olé!*
images designed to make you pray.
I light a candle. The paintings say we die,
but don't recover 'in the twinkling of an eye'.
All that Death in triumph can induce
a taste for lighting candles. No excuse!
And it gets worse. The next thing was the day
at Bran I flung my loose Romanian *lei*
into Vlad the Impaler's castle well,
and made a wish: *please free Max from his hell.*
Asking Dracula! How slippery the slope
when a despairing man runs out of hope.

(v)
The third thing was this last year in Japan
trying a temple shrine's rice-paper man.
From bad to worse. The third thing that I've done,
so desperate and despairing for my son,
is drop 200 yen into a box and buy
a small rice-paper man to give a try.
You scribble the sickness on the mannikin
on whatever part the pain or trouble's in
and drop it in the temple pail. With me
it'd be my chronic shoulder or arthritic knee,
or heartache. For his specific form of pain
the word's too big to write across its brain.

(vi)

One rice-paper man! I'd have to scrawl
his sickness on hundreds if I wrote it all,
without the skills of Signor Cossovel
who micrographically wrote Dante's *Hell*,
and *Purgatory* AND *Paradise*,
not on a mannikin made out of rice,
but (I've *seen* it in Ravenna!) on one sheet
of A3 paper in 1888.
The shock of seeing his wee *figlio* die
left him with hyperaesthesia of the eye,
which condition allowed him to condense,
the entire *Commedia* without a lens.

(vii)

So I write the diagnosis and that's all –
schizophrenia's hard to fit in even small.
It started with the head that bowed and curled
to hide from the constant terrors of the world.
The head rolls downwards like a curling leaf,
the whole brain foetal in its fall of grief.
The dissolving man in pain's now like a worm,
then dull slug trail and, last, like cloudy sperm,
come in a loo bowl that won't ever know
the tragedy of man and all his woe.
Once the paper man's dissolved no eye could tell,
say, my arthritis from his mental hell.

(viii)

Circles of hell and *Haliperidol*
Cossovel wouldn't cram in one fat vol
let alone on one rice-paper man
the desperate put their faith in in Japan.
Cossovel got his skill when his wee lad,
his *figlioletto*, died. And mine's gone mad.

Though the terror didn't traumatize my sight,
the shock, like Cossovel's, forced me to write.
You may have other props but this is mine.
Follow me down the stairway, line by line,
solidarity in darkness, writer/reader,
tu mi segui, e io sarò tua guida.

(ix)

A serene young monk in saffron silk
takes all the water suffering's made milk
or more opaque than milk, a spermy goo,
and swills it down a drain of dry bamboo,
then takes clear water from a dragon spout
that spews spring water not spit fire out,
and, waiting with bowed shaven head, refills
the bamboo bucket for tomorrow's ills.
Each little floating scapegoat's pain tattoo
will sink the swimmer that it bends in two.
And tomorrow there'll be new queues with their yen
loading their hopes on frail rice-paper men.

(x)

When all you want to do's sit down and cry
anything, or almost, 's worth at least a try,
from Dracula's deep well in Castle Bran
to the temple pail I tried out in Japan.
Or is it, was it, when I have at my command
my mind, my heart, my guts, my writing hand?
My pen's no wand, and I'm no Prospero,
but poems are the one redemption that I know.
Anything with God in is the worst.
This last resort I should have fled to first.
Somewhere I always have to draw the line.
You have your own props and poetry's mine –

(xi)

Poetry wasn't first because I go
to poetry whenever I feel low,
but by resorting to it O so many times
I've built up an immunity to rhymes.
My deliverance, the drive to shape,
that throws up no solutions nor escape,
that drive to shape, 's my son's destroyer,
the just as well wrought urn of paranoia.
Other poets' sons and daughters, Joyce's,
Frost's and Victor Hugo's, all heard voices.
Is what tears our offsprings' minds apart
the shaping spirit of poetic art?

(xii)

First came the hour-long candle in Seville,
with loud *olés*, that left my son still ill,
second the silly well in Castle Bran
and last a bamboo bucket in Japan.
Great remedies! But not the last resort
which might have more in common than I thought
with those superstitious nonsenses above,
springing as all do from fear and love,
the last resort is these words, that you read,
possibly yourself in desperate need.
I've tried to keep out all false hope, and lies,
that kill those quack concoctions I despise.

(xiii)

We're all subject to the Cossovellian rule:
a loved one's pain makes epics minuscule,
and not just epics, I imagine his changed eyes
reduced all man esteems to micro size.
In Ictu Oculi, one little blink,
one little death makes even Dante shrink.

In Ictu Oculi! But just suppose,
in another sort of trauma, Dante grows
into manuscript constructed by Brunel,
alphabet bulk blocks bridging Earth and Hell,
one's reductionist, and neither use
the true proportions of the human Muse.

(xiv)
Poetry's neither vast nor micro size.
I've shown you things I've done that I despise,
desperate for my son. I can't excuse
betraying my true, my truth-tormented Muse
who moves this poem that's coming to a close.
And what the hell 's its use in all our woes?
The question is: Do you think poetry,
specifically *this* poem, was worth a try?
If not, and you found no comfort, not one phrase
to brave *memento mori* and *olés*,
or redeem doomed spermatozoa, drive
a stake through this undead art and you'll survive.

2. *Sugaring the Pill*

In Africa I'd give you *Paludrine*
with guava jam to hide its tart taste in.

I poised above you in your netted pram
with malaria prophylactic mashed in jam.

I put the spoon near my mouth, said *yum-yum*
to persuade you that some treat's about to come.

Even so tiny, after once or twice, you knew
the performance of smacked lips just wasn't true.

The nets are down; our roles have been reversed
you take the bitterest pill and taste it first.

No malaria then, but later much, much worse
too full of gall to swallow even mashed in verse.

Four Poems for Jonathan Silver in his Sickness

1. *Auroras*

You gave me your *Aurora* pen,
something I'd never buy.
It had scented lilac ink in then,
now that lilac ink 's run dry.

That scented lilac ink 's run dry,
my *Aurora* 's filled with black,
though today I won't deny
I'd like some lilac back.

Aurora (as you know) means dawn
and you've ordered a new one.
May the shining gold get worn
with greeting each day's sun.

I hear the *Aurora* you gave me
scratch across the page
desperate to write some poetry
you can re-read in old age.

Not only do I love its flow,
its gold Greek key motif,
the *Aurora* 's the only way I know
to reach beyond our grief.

Let's both pick up *Auroras*
(with permanent black or nay)
and write that what's before us
is another dawning day,

when sometimes the gold nib will glow
and sometimes will look dull,
but either way our *Auroras* flow
because days are so full.

(20 January 1997)

2. *Marie Mastat*

Painted *Marimastat* fore and aft,
the *Marimastat* is your craft.
The *Marimastat* was a yacht
that Marie Mastat sailed a lot.
Marie Mastat, Balkan diva,
walking with her black retriever
that, on the cliff edge, wags its tail
to see the *Marimastat* sail.
And the sea song that you'll hear
is Marie Mastat's whose career
burgeoned first in Bucharest
and *every*body knows the rest –
the legendary vocal chords
vibrating as the world applauds!
She gave the yacht her name because,
her voice not being what it was,
she said that 'given the right breeze'
she still could venture on high Cs.

They also named a sweet brown wine
Marie Mastat (a Murfatlar vine
found near the Danube and Black Sea)
the diva passes off as tea
as she lolls in her *conservatoire*,
Marie Mastat, Balkan star,
smoking a black cigarette
among mementos of the Met,
and each smoke ring that she blows
turns into a Yorkshire rose
she tosses at her dearest fan,
a venturer called Jonathan,
who with the rose between his teeth
and the *Marimastat*'s deck beneath,

sails towards the next Aurora
with Marie's ghost as his wine-pourer.
And on the high seas Marie's ghost
pours *Marie Mastat* for a toast
to Jonathan, who her ghost guides
through the night-times and the tides.
The label peeling off the bottle
shows the diva in full throttle,
the mouth wide, about to pour a
cascade of high Cs for Aurora.

The *Marimastat* spreads her sails.
Marie's ghost goes through her scales,
and, when storms brew or when night falls,
sings arias through dark and squalls,
and her voice will summon from the shore a
lifeboat with the name: AURORA.

(2 February 1997)

Note. Marimastat was a new drug in trials for cancer treatment.

3. *Valetudinous Valentine*

for Jonathan and Maggie

Better than red roses and red hearts,
today a new tradition starts.
Every Valentine's from now
we'll all of us remember how
Jonathan Silver of Salts Mill,
when popping his first small pink pill
discovered the right course to follow
to guarantee long life is swallow
the initial dosage of the drug
with Aurora-toasting vintage KRUG.

(14 February 1997)

4. *Border Honey*

She tends her border hives and sings.
   She gives me honey wax to chew
   to stave off hunger till we're through
and dabs vinegar on my five stings.
She yelled the price in *lev* and *lei*
   over the deep hum of the swarm
   and poured the honey thick and warm
into this bottle that I bring today,
to sweeten your sustaining tea.
   The border I brought it from took hours
   crossing, but both the states' sunflowers
stretched as far as the eye could see.

Both sides the tailback border bees
   through yellow, dwarfing most of us,
   first browse Romania's then buzz
Bulgaria's with stateless ease.
When David H. feared you might die
   he painted sunflowers for you
   'for hope and joy' when you came through
and brought the canvas still not dry.
So that, when they wheeled you back
   from cancer surgery, you'd get
   the sunflowers he brought them wet
with petals printed on his mac.

A Bulgarian barrier blocks the way
   and for guards to let the cursing queue,
   cars, trucks, and bullock wagons, through
took almost the whole bloody day,
with time at least to sleep and rest
   and time to sense the moving sun
   turn millions of heads as one

by slow degrees towards the West.
I queued and took snap after snap
    but the guard, with nothing else to do,
    ripped the new roll from my μ
to show he was a macho chap.

But the roll the guard did not destroy
    I laser-copied to A4
    and, like David's painted ones before,
bring *Sunflowers for Hope and Joy*,
to show how sweetness brought through
    more borders after those have come
    from flowers David's cadmium
under skies Matisse's blue.
And when it waits to cross, your soul,
    may border honey, from free bees
    browsing both states' flowers, ease
your passage through control.

That viaticum from border hive,
    the photographs I took for you,
    brilliant yellow and bright blue,
you saw and tasted still alive.
On this side still how sad I am
    this poem that went with them's late.
    Because my verses imitate
the metre of In Memoriam,
they seemed too much an omen then
    so I never gave the poem I'd penned
    for hope and joy for my lost friend
with my (once his) Aurora *pen.*

(*in memoriam* Jonathan Silver, 21.10.49–25.9.97)

Fruitility

What a glorious gift from Gaia
raspberries piled on papaya,
which as a ruse to lift my soul
I serve up in my breakfast bowl,
and, contemplating, celebrate
nature's fruit, and man's air-freight
speeding my fruit breakfast here
through tropo- and through stratosphere.
I praise papaya and celebrate
the man who packed it in its crate,
the worker or Hawaiian grower
in Kipahula or Pahoa,
the worried cultivator who
scans the sky from Honomu,
with global warming getting higher
than is good for his papaya;
worries I myself had known
when, in Nigeria, I'd grown
what we called pawpaws of my own;
picked, deseeded, served fridge-fresh
I fed my kids their orange flesh.
I gave my kids fruit to repeat
the way I once got fruit to eat,
not so exotic but the start
of all my wonder and my art.
My mother taught me to adore
the fruit she scrounged us in the War,
scarce, and marred with pock and wart
nonetheless the fruit she brought
taught me, very young, to savour
the gift of fruit, its flesh and flavour.
Adoring apples I've linked Eve's
with my mother's ripe James Grieves

no God could ever sour with sin
or jinx the juice all down my chin.
Still in my dreams my mother comes
her pinafore full of ripe plums,
Victorias, with amber ooze
round their stalks, and says: Choose! Choose!
Now so much older, I,
more aware I've got to die,
use such ruses, I derive
from my mother, to survive.
Last week I saw here at the Met
a 'Wheel of Life' made in Tibet
where 'Man Picking Fruit' 's used to depict,
in both the picker and the picked,
ultimate futility. Such dismal crap'll
never spoil my mother's apple.
Fuck philosophy that sees
life itself as some disease
we sicken with until released,
supervised by Pope or priest,
into a dry defruited zone
where no James Grieves were ever grown.
I'd barter nebulous Nirvanas
for carambolas or bananas.
I need to neologize to find
the fruit in futile humankind,
and *fruitility* is what I call
the fate which falls upon us all.
Meaningless our lives may be
but blessed with deep fruitility.
It could take pages if I list
all the joys of the fruitilitist:
retsina and grilled squid in Greece,
that death-bed cut-out of Matisse
I chanced on on a trip to Dallas,
Sempre libera sung by Callas,

love-making in the afternoon,
the ripe papaya on this spoon
lingered over as my way
of starting on a fruitile day,
where 73rd and Broadway meet.
Even now the morning heat
brings the piss smells off the street,
Dobermann's and man's piss soars
as far as us, and we're eight floors.
This breakfasting's my Zensual ruse
to counteract such Broadway views
as those below, where homeless spread
the books and mags to earn their bread
and, after bread, if not before,
the rocks of crack some value more.
I read titles with my opera glasses:
Opera News and *Chunky Asses*,
Honcho, *Ramrod*, *Newsweek*, *Time*,
stiff from showers 2 a dime,
but, if like new, then 4 a dollar,
Bush, the Pope, the Ayatollah,
Noriega, Gorbachev,
and other ones with covers off,
a *danse macabre*, a *Vanitas*
of big cheeses, and the chunky ass.
Diva-adoring gays peruse
the laid-out rows of *Opera News*.
Spectacles of temporal flux,
sidewalk piles of grubby books,
30 copies of one play
billed a great hit in its day,
and some still supposed to be
a dollar each, or 4 for 3.
And there's a neighbour off to buy
the opera discs that help him die.

He's young but shuffles with a cane
but will only use CDs for pain.
His father, who won't meet him, mails
his sick son clothes from car-boot sales,
but Pa and Ma don't realize
AIDS makes their son a smaller size.
They've never talked of death or sex
but occasionally Pa sends him cheques
to buy AZT, as AZT's
one drug that slows down the disease.
I saw him in the lobby:
                              Hi,
Pa sent me some more cash to buy
AZT, but I bought these!
and showed me scores of new CDs.
My pa would think it such a waste
me and my opera ain't his taste.
Got all of Callas's CDs
to comfort me through this disease.
It's Puccini next when Pa sends more,
and he got off at the 7th floor . . .

There's someone wanting to be Mayor
haranguing winos in the square,
under Verdi's statue who presides
over crack-heads, crooks and suicides.
Verdi with his vision blurred
by birdshit stares from 73rd
down at Dante at the Met
where Verdi helps some to forget.
But when they leave or enter there
there's no avoiding Dante's stare,
nor what's beneath his constant gaze
and stays there, while the opera plays,
and pizza cartons three feet square
leave mouth-watering hot blasts of air,

a phantom mozzarella trail,
for carton dwellers to inhale
in lungfuls, hungry and alone
beyond the pale of *Pizzaphone*.
A claret goblet and WITH CARE
that housed video or frigidaire
now packages a shoeless man
who rummages the garbage can
already rummaged countless times
for cans you can redeem for dimes.
Shops redeem the empty can
but not the can-redeeming man,
nor that woman who's got business sense
so beds down where machines dispense
24hr cash, and men, when pissed,
might leave five dollars in her fist.
One night I saw a famous diva
stop her limo there and leave her
scores of fresh fan-flung bouquets
to wake to from her wino haze.
And when she woke they say she cried
with rage and terror, horrified
the morning sun should wake her
laid out for the undertaker.
Death was all these blooms could mean,
these tributes she was stretched between,
beneath the bank's cashpoint machine.
Once aware she wasn't dead
she flogged the star's bouquets for bread,
well, pretzels; those posh bouquets
kept her in booze for several days.

I dread the moment, while I muse
on all my fruitile 8th floor views,
I hear the answerphone replay
the dark side of the fruitile day:

message one, a Scottish friend,
sick, insomniac, half round the bend,
drying out in St Luke's, lying
all tubed-up, detoxifying.
His message goes as follows: *Hi!*
just checking in before I die!
The trolleyphone's beside his bed.
I call him back. He isn't dead.
Thought you were dying.
                              I am! I am!
Fucking dying for a dram!

Another friend made mad by AIDS
leaves night-time answerphone tirades.
It wakes us when the tape records
his rabid ravings from the wards.
First his operatic repertoire
that made him a TV bar star:
Sempre libera, in falsetto,
voice corseted as Violetta,
Sempre libera, always free,
he from AIDS and she TB.
In sigmoidoscopy he'd brag:
I am the world's most buggered fag.
Your rooter's nothing, every dick
I've ever had's ten times as thick!
After the aria and the pause
while he curtsies to applause
and clasps flung posies to his heart
the mad Munchausen stories start
and I hear a new bass voice begin:

Those things like wine-stains on my skin
those fucking things like spilled Merlot
they ain't what you guys think you know.
They came, these scars like fucking Claret

from the forest of the flame-flayed parrot.
They're burns! They're burns! I tried to seize
the cure for AIDS from blazing trees.
I was in Brazil, Manaus, where I gave
my Violetta. And did Manaus rave!
They adore me, darlings, in Brazil.
They think I was just acting ill.
Brava! brava! on and on
beside the steaming Amazon.
If I chose I could earn millions
from brava-bravaing Brazilians!
(Were you aware the rubber trade's
booming again because of AIDS?
You see the stripe-gashed cauchos oozing
condoms I never packed when cruising!)
I went up-river in a cute caique
from Manaus with the urge to seek
the cure for what afflicts our kind
and the sights up-river blew my mind –
I saw pink dolphins, pink!
and I hadn't had a drop to drink!
and no Colombia up my nose –
dolphins pink as any fan-flung rose!
I'd gone in costume. It was better
trekking dressed as Violetta.
Those creepers with sharp thorns don't snag
my depilated legs in drag.
And where the forest was ablaze,
brave Violetta, on behalf of gays,
in corsets botanizing raced
through dense forest now laid waste,
charcoal gallows, charcoal glades
of gutted antidotes for AIDS,
the canopy deserted by
the roasted birds that used to fly.

And there were cures. They've gone. They've gone
in the bonfires of the Amazon.
Some creeper, bud, some bitter seed
might be the breakthrough doctors need.
All September it's been blazing
to give more future Big Macs *grazing.*
Even now the forest flames
are burning cures that have no names.
In the ash of Amazonian oak
the cure for AIDS went up in smoke . . .

All this gabble seems quite graphic
though culled from *National Geographic*
bought at the sidewalk mag bazaar
with covers of the passé star
or politician laid between
Butt Lust 'Seat Meat' magazine
and iron-pumping *Bulkritude*
both with pages wanker-glued.
Then his falsetto ends the story:

Cessarono gli spasimi del dolore . . .

The sun sets here while it's rising
on countries just industrializing
and day ends in a dying fire
hued like my rasps piled on papaya,
Broadway windows with glossed sheen
of cranberry and carotene,
sunset as the turning planet
paints New York in pomegranate,
with chemicals that now pollute
the skies to look like too ripe fruit.

The spoon-scraped limp papaya skin
goes first into the garbage bin,
then a big black trash bag, later
down the chute to the incinerator,
and the flotsam of time's fleeting flux
goes into dawn's first garbage trucks.
I'll hear them grinding as it's time
again for papaya spritzed with lime.
Tomorrow's rasps piled on papaya
chilled, ready for the life-denier,
tomorrow when my heart says *Yea*
to darkness ripening into day,
remembering my mother whose
gifts of fruit taught me this ruse,
whose wartime wisdom would embrace
both good and grotty with sweet grace,
she who always used to say:
Never wish your life away!
Of all my muses it was she
first taught me to love fruitility.

Toasting Jocelyn

A Toast on the 80th birthday of Jocelyn Herbert

I'm getting up today to make a toast
to the person in my life I've toasted most,
and can't propose this toast unless I list
(and I *don't* mean all the times that we got pissed!)
those many toasts I've made when I've felt blessed
to know and work with someone who's the best.
And so before I raise this glass, dear Jocelyn,
these are some wines that you've been toasted in:

The first toast though was not in wine but beer
and the toast I made you then you didn't hear.
Long before our paths were, happily, to cross
I saw Ionesco's *Chairs* designed by Joc.
This play, some twenty years before we met,
was the first I'd seen in London, her first set.
Thrilled and elated by what I saw,
with half of bitter in the pub next door,
inspired, I made a silent toast, and thought:
Here's to George and Jocelyn and the Court!

How could I know then we had before us
the *Oresteia* that we played in Epidaurus.
And from that time there've been more than a few
magic moments when I've toasted you:

With five sheep roasting on a charcoal fire
in barrel retsina for the *Oresteia*.
What else? What else? Let's see! Let's see . . .
that strange Arachova rosé with *kokkoretsi*,
that strange Parnassus resinous rosé
in which I thanked you for our satyr play.

And by the Danube when the nightingale
sang for our satyrs after violent hail
flooded our whole set and you and I,
with a garden roller, rolled our desert dry,
then later when the stars began to shine
toasted each other in *Dreikaiserwein*.

Dreikaiserwein was once again the brew
in which I toasted all I owed to you,
when we mounted in Carnuntum such a sight
that still gives Viennese a sleepless night,
and I don't just mean the lions, tigers, bears,
prowling beneath the seating and the stairs,
but something far more scary and horrendous –
Barrie Rutter, in silk stockings and suspenders!
Or getting a taxi to Slovakia to have a
stroll round medieval Bratislava
and, with herby *Becherovka* and weak tea,
I toasted you in Slovak: *Nazdravi!*

Retsina, *Dreikaiserwein* and *Becherovka* . . . Shit!
(Excuse me!) I forgot the *Aquavit*
in Copenhagen when on tour with *Trackers*,
toasting our collaboration, and Lord Bacchus.

But in case you think us both obsessed with booze
I ought to say we've pledged the Tragic Muse
and Comic Muse, Melpomene and Thalia,
in the purest crystal waters of Castalia,
and when I dip my scooping palm and drink
at Castalia with Jocelyn I think
that she's been more inspiring than the Muse
and deserves from me a million ιασους.
And mostly I remember toasting you
in my favourite toast of all, the Greek ιασου!

And ιασου comes from one who can't be here
all the way to London from Itea.
Tsaros who catches and then cooks our favourite dish
γαριδες σαγανακι sends his birthday wish
and told me to say 'Come soon' and say a
loud ιασου from the Silenus of Itea.
Also Dionissis Fotopoulos
asked me to tell you that he loves you, Joc.
And is sending you, via Hermes, a bouquet
of herbs, picked in Delphi, on this very day.

This glass is the memory of those toasts
I've made on Greece's mountains and her coasts,
and the happiness of glasses still to raise
in all our future recces, films and plays.
For the toasting won't by any means stop here,
we've another big adventure on this year,
when I think that toasts will have to be
in Romanian *tuica* and Bulgarian *raki*,
until we'll end up saying ιασου in retsina
at that taverna by the docks in Elefsina.
So this glass I toast you with I poise
between all the work we've done and all the joys
and all the work and joys we've still to do
and say with all my heart: ιασου, ιασου!

It's impossible to make such heartfelt toasts
and not invite the most beloved of ghosts,
and as present here this evening as I am
are George and Lindsay, Tony, Ron, John, Sam . . .
and they're all here to do what we'll all do,
raise our glasses and thank God for you.
And now in (What's this wine?) . . . *Viña Mayor*
(don't think I've toasted you in this before) . . .

This glass of wine we all have in our hands
is from the fertile vine of love, and stands
for all the wines you've been and will be toasted in –

I love you, and I toast you: JOCELYN!

(22 February 1997)

Leavings

I think that's the last one gone behind the sink!

Though after every meal we wipe and sweep,
though every crack's sealed up, the kitchen clean,
no matter how particular we've been,
the cockroaches emerge once we're asleep,
and waking in the night to get a drink
I switch on the kitchen light and see them run
from their catches and (for them) rich hoards
behind the oven and the skirting boards,
all safe for another night-hunt; but for one.

Caught also by the suddenness of light
my dream attempts to scuttle back to sleep,
scatters in all directions, but part stays
betrayed by its hunger for its yesterdays
into futures with a blunted appetite
for tomorrows that are fresh but do not keep.
Love strews its leavings where the lean nights feed.
The scavengers we keep at bay with care,
those night-thoughts that gnaw days with manic greed,
at death, are going to gorge on all they need
from memory's disconnected frigidaire.

The mind skates round its own transparent walls,
though that restraints exist it's unaware,
thinking because it sees there's nothing there
between what we once were and what we are,
and, feasting on old love, too gorged to climb
the slithering steep slopes of see-through time,
I feel the full heart gets so far, then falls,
like this cockroach skidding in the cookie jar.

Rubbish

All my rubbish is discreetly bagged,
some heavy with indulgence, some lightweight.
Some sail through the air, and some get dragged,
clinking, down to the gap that was the gate.

I didn't move when roofers fixed my tiles
or when the builder came to point the wall;
with the window cleaner I swap nods and smiles
and don't budge from my littered desk at all,
so why, when two men cross my threadbare lawn
each Monday morning emptying my bins,
as if my refuse was exposed to scorn,
my garbage a glaring index to my sins,
do I bolt from my study and go hide?

I think the reason is I can't abide
being caught pen in hand as gloved men chuck
black plastic sacks of old drafts on their truck.

Passer

His knuckle tattoos say: *Nothing* and *Futile*:

I'll kick in his knackers, boot straight to his bollocks.
I'll twist his tackle, he'll not toss off tomorrow!
His nob'll be naff for wanking for weeks!

Sigurd of sickbursts, brew-belcher, *Brown Aler*,
What *lot* or *dom* do such dickheads lust after?
Spewdom for starters, the Sat'day excesses
lack and lacunae in lad-lore and lager,
livid at life, lashing out in lads' lingo,
Newky Nirvanas, the nightly negations,
the doubled-up drunkard heaving his *humous*.

But soaks' slop 's sustaining to the spuggy survivor:
the spuggy picks over the piss-artist's spew,
the *passer* picks over the piss-artist's puke,
unsqueamish in Corfu at squid-rings in sick slosh,
never nauseous on North roads at Niagaras of *Newky*,
slices of carrot in school crayon sunbursts,
Tandoori and *Tennants*, late nosh and *Newky*
devoured in the dawnlight, sluiced on to sidewalks,
kebab bits and *Carlsberg* gob-cacked, cataracted,
slivers of sleevers from last midnight's mêlée
tested for taste just in case they were juicy.
There's no lust for poison in the spuggy's spare spirit.
It's flight-feather fodder, spew is for spuggies.

Over boulders of gneiss, the bust kneecaps of Lenin,
the star-gazing eyes of horizontaled old Stalins,
pecking places for the *passer* (posh Latin for spuggy)
berries that bounce off the cracked busts and bronzes,
red hawthorn, pyracantha, the fruits of the May.

Look there, though, the spuggy, Bede's old soul symbol,
dodging the juggernauts to banquet on boke-bits.
The spuggy's the spirit Bede saw in brief transit
from darkness to darkness via being as banquet.
The scrabbled Cyrillic spuggies leave with birdclawfeet
's nowt spirit-lifting, but nowt nay-saying neither.
Spuggies sing as the light lifts, serenade the sun's sinking.

All meadhalls are measured by men at their margins,
the glee by the gloomfast, the song by the silence,
Sprechgesang by splutterings, Strad string by stranglers,
Puccini by punch-ups, *Tosca* by torture,
Callas by cattleprods, kilowatts to the cunt,
violins by the violence, cellos by the chokings,
the cabaret by the carton, built in the Bull Ring,
the paean by piss-artists, the beercan berserker
barracking the bardic, putting the boot in,
cornflakes or kippers by cranking the rack cogs,
snap crackle pop with the same in some cellar,
Gloucester's eyes acted by such deeds done daily,
curtain calls by kids kipping on kerbsides.
The *scop* scours the ruins for scraps of lost rhythms.
He once wrote *The Ruin* but on his returning
The Ruin is ruined, the writing has rotted,
the penmanship perished in fungoids or flamemarks.
There's no going back to piece it together
he looks through the lacunae to see Leeds and London,
the sacked scriptoria marked Stasi – Top Secret.
The *scop* of *The Ruin* felt like the *passer*
scop, spuggy, *passer*, the sorrowful sparrow
condemned to rewriting the gaps in *The Ruin*.

The willow herb waves once more on the wallstones.
The scop's messy mss. slashed with lacunae,
rubbler hyphen rebuilder, a walker of wallstones,
the *Wreacca-scop* walking Rome's empire in ruins,

pig troughs inscribed IMPERATOR or DIVUS,
cannibalized columns from Corbridge now Christian
upholding church masonry not a Mithraeum.
You might well bewail, in the wattle/daub era,
the giants have built, but their buildings are broken.
If such great constructions should come to the ground,
barracks and bath-house go for a Burton,
it buttered the Brits up to crave their conversion,
made all things regarded vain, vanishing, frail.
Now Socialist strongholds collapse into commerce,
sold at streetmarkets collected as kitsch,
military medals a marketed mêlée.

Canta mihi aliquid. Nescio, inquit, cantare.

Now ask that Caedmon to sing the collapses,
the megaliths ruined like the Romans before them,

The *Wreacca* met Caedmon and said: Fuck off, Caedmon!
Now Caedmon couldn't say: Cunt! back, now could he?

Bridlington

Sitting for David Hockney

Him drawing those lines me composing these,
our breathing inside louder than the sea's.
Yorks*sshhh*ire . . . *ssshhh* . . . Yorks*shhh*ire . . . *ssshhh* they say
the whispering waves of this last day of May.

Pebbles skimmed by two school-skiving kids
bounce on bulky waves that dawdle on to Brid's
bare beaches where a man shouts, 'Stay!'
to his disobedient dog who runs away,
the studio clock with its metallic tick,
the craftblade scratching on the charcoal stick,
the gulls' cries and the crows' dry caws
as I compose, stock-still, and David draws,
and Brid's grey ocean, lisping and then lush
shuffles into one long silent *ssshhh!*

Doncaster

I've noticed Donny's bridal gownshop's lights
are only on, in winter, Saturday nights.
Though window shopping for white wedding gear
's not done this coldest, darkest time of year,
maybe, the owner reckons, as they pass
those near-nude girls, reflected in the glass,
might remember his window's lacy white,
if they get pregnant from their date tonight.

In Donny at the *Danum* all alone
hearing the coal trucks on the railway line,
the pit to power station wagons beat
a metre as my eye moves down to *Sweet*
on the menu that I've studied countless times,
my head on coal trucks and on coupled rhymes,
and, there, added in purple print, I find
a mouthful of assonance to tempt my mind,
but not my tastebuds, knowing that only
the leisurely, the literary, or the lonely
or some passing, half-pissed plaiting of all three,
Saturday in Donny, and tonight that's me,
notice, of all things in the hopping town
with disco birds and desolate bridal gown,
the Union flag garrotting the flagstaff,
cracking crosses over girl gangs, frozen stiff,
but cackling and cramming the jam-packed pub
or past the bouncers to the throbbing club,
with midriffs, thighs and shoulders, bare and blue,

or Chef's special: melon balls in *Malibu*.

Suspensions

The heave and rattle of the freezer trucks
hauling their rot-prone loads across the Tyne.
That black mid-river is in its state of flux
Durham/Northumberland's dividing line.

No boundaries seem fixed. It's all in flow.
From bed we hear the bridges' constant hum.
I count from out of night's continuum
the FRIGOSCANDIA and FRIGORIFICO
from Tarragona or from Bergen docks.
My eyesight's still not bad. You're quite impressed.
I also see both church and Customs clocks,
give or take five minutes, say get dressed.

I wind both windows of my taxi down
to let your smell blow off me down the quays.
I trail your fragrance through the drunken town.

Tonight your essences are on the breeze
suspended in the smells of river slime,
brewery, tarworks, Baltic Flour Mill,
caught in this fixed place, this measured time.

The rushing night air makes my body chill.
My life's one taut suspension, one blind arc!

My semen in your body's not yet dried.
My wife sleeps warm and naked by my side –

my bones, cold girders cast across the dark.

Mouthfuls

The *Kourtaki* retsina that I buy
from *Kwiksave* costs 2.99.
It helps my nostalgia for Greek sky
when I'm gloomy on the Tyne.

My dad's tastebuds in my head
they've never gone away
and though he's been a longtime dead
he's got to have his say.

Even at 2.99,
he doesn't like retsina
Tastes like bloody turpentine!
Or bloody carpet cleaner!

I quaff it out of barrels though
back where *Kourtaki*'s made
in the Attic town Markopoulo
where they bake a biscuit braid.

This bakery's my dad's ghost's treat.
In Greece he liked this most
though I no longer like things sweet
I go to gratify his ghost.

My father's tastebuds like to go
tasting biscuits I resist
so when I'm in Markopoulo
this bakehouse can't be missed.

The biscuit's got a braided form
made from cinnamon and must
you pick them from the trays still warm
and white with icing dust.

His tongue-tied tastebuds help me speak
in a workplace like his own,
all the proper words in Greek,
words he never could have known.

'They're μουστοκουλουρακια,* Dad.'
Nay! Gerraway!
Bloody mouthful for a biscuit, lad!
We both taste one, and I say:

'Cinnamon!' He says: *Too much for me!*
For a foreign biscuit, though, not bad!
In that Markopoulo bakery
I was close to my dead dad.

I dream of him, his spirit comes
from the cold Leeds earth below
spouting μουστοκουλουρακια crumbs
in warm Markopoulo.

Though tarts and stuff are in my blood
the sweetest thing I ever eat
is fruit and never cake or pud
when Dad's tastebuds crave for sweet.

His tastebuds always go AWOL
and leave mine on their own to try
'that cocktail stuff wi' a parasol
to keep all t'bloody ice cubes dry.'

And they'd always go on strike
when I've worked in Japan.
Raw? Nay, lad, tha knows ah like
mi fish from t'frying pan.

* moustokoulourakia

I like his tastebuds in my gob
when sampling posh 'cuisine'
then I'm glad they do their job
of saying what they mean.

'All satisfactory, sir, I trust?'
I hear the waiter bray.
Dad's tastebuds have the sauces sussed
and force my tongue to grumble: *Nay!*

But so often now I feel them shrink
in a kind of sad defeat
when I neither eat nor drink
anything that's sweet.

Exasperated once I yelled,
'Try something else for pity's sake.
It's time that your baker's tooth rebelled
against craving for sweet cake.'

It's nowt to do wi't'job ah 'ad.
Ah'm bloody glad not to be slaving
ovver t'ovens like ah had to, lad,
but nowt'll stop this craving.

When you go near to summat sweet
it's like a geni's got released.
One crumb of cream-cake you might eat
to me's like a great feast.

Then in a measured and grave tone,
Tha'll soon enough know t'simple truth:
when tha's lying under t'ground alone
Death'll give yer us sweet-tooth.

The Pen and the Gun

There's never a time I use this fountain pen
without I'm haunted by a pigeon's pain.

This pen scrats out the panic that it felt.
It took almost two days dying. All my fault.

My friend Pinhead got an airgun once
and what we did with it still makes me wince.

His mam bought him it when his dad died.
She thought it'd help him not to miss his dad.

It was the thing that Pinhead wanted most.
He had the first few goes, and always missed

the pigeon on his chimney, nowhere near,
so wide the bird stayed basking, unaware.

Then I tried and got, beginner's luck, a hit,
of sorts, with my first ever shot.

It fell in the gutter out of reach and sight
but for its claws that scraped against the slate

and scratched all day, all night, and not until
teatime the next day were those claws still.

I was young enough to cry. Never again
did I show any interest in a gun

I grew to think the pen far mightier than
though the scraped claw sound still haunts me from back then.

This pen scratching like its slowly blunting claw
has haunted me for fifty years or more.

Wordsworth's Stone

Where silent zephyrs sported with the dust
Of the Bastile I sate in the open sun
And from the rubbish gathered up a stone,
And pocketed the relic in the guise
Of an enthusiast . . .
The Prelude (1805), IX 67–70

I wonder if that bit of stone
that Wordsworth had from the Bastille
ever got itself rethrown
against repressive steel,

or was it tossed into a lake,
the poet watching from the bank,
seeing what ripples it would make
and go on making while it sank?

Was it that sacred relic's fate
to scatter minnows in a moonlit pond
and for a moment help create
the golden whorls of the Beyond?

Noah's Sacrifice

'Il sacrificio di Noè dopo il diluvio'
(Sinibaldo Scorza, 1589–1631, Genova)

Too much Ligurian light has left it bleached
but Sinibaldo's rainbow, now a shade of grey,
shines over blue/black bodies freshly beached.

Spared pairs start their mating straightaway
among the washed-up corpses of the drowned,
coupling while the dead start to decay.

The sinners of the Flood lie all around
coop-crazy couples deArked copulating
on still marshy but emerging flood-free ground,

and there's Noah and his family celebrating,
burning a sacrifice, one of who knows what
now mateless pair while all the fauna's mating.

On the craggy upper slopes of Ararat,
spared herdsman's prod, for now, and hunter's dart,
bull mates with cow, ram ewe, and rat fucks rat.

And the sacrifice to mark Mankind's new start
puffs a black smokecloud in the air
forcing two Flood-spared birds to pull apart –

or cope with their fear of fire before they pair.

Hotlines

Samaritans, Drug Abuse, Rape, Homicide,
the moonrock and the crack ODs,
a man in Florida misdialled and died
reaching the hotline for *Tagged Manatees.*

Measures

Time that's seen my shirt-size swell
from S to M and now to L
won't see it shrink back to petite
until my shirt 's my winding sheet.

Reconnected

Years later, with a desperate need, I phone
and almost pull the flex out of the wall
when the younger voice that answers me 's my own:

Sorry we're not here to take your call.

Realism

What happens when the theatre shuns the word
and an actor strains to show us that he's shitting
's that, strain though he might, from where I'm sitting
I can neither see nor smell a single turd.

Fire & Poetry

The *shakuhachi*'s shattered, the *tatami*'s torn,
the besom's ashes on the scorched moss lawn,
the temple's maples smoking stumps now, but
Basho's ink-stick's made from soot.

Wine & Poetry

(i)

I only drink white wine, no spirits and no beer.
There've been all told, two wines I couldn't drink
and after just one sip poured down the sink:
one called *President*, the other *Poesia*!

No, sorry, three! A sparkling wine, and Greek,
and called *Lord Byron* but it made me puke!

(ii)

One glass and no refill
is life for men,
so keep on pouring till
Death says *when*.

(after Amphis, fourth century BC)

Fig on the Tyne

for Siani, on her birthday

My life and garden, both transforming,
thanks to you, and global warming,
started today to intertwine
tasting my first fig on the Tyne.

When I heard scientists predict
there'd be apricots and peaches picked
in Britain's South, and *pinot noir*
where the rhubarb fields of Yorkshire are,
the pithill *pinot* from lush vines
ripening on demolished mines,
a Rossington *viognier*,
Sheffield *shiraz*, Grimethorpe *gamay*,
fancy made a sun-kissed fiction:
Dionysus redeeming dereliction.
Dionysus! Wishful thinking,
sitting in Doncaster drinking
in Southern sun that lasts all day
a local Donny *vin du pays*.
No sommelier worth his salt 'll spurn
Gewürztraminer from Wath-on-Dearne!
No longer would we need to traipse
through airports to the lands of grapes.
No more queuing at Heathrow
when we grow all they used to grow.
There'll come a day no Loiner needs
to go beyond the *caves* of Leeds
to sup champagne that's bottled where
they throw their empties in the Aire.
The South creeps Northwards, some say sweeps,
swapping *Beaujolais nouveau* for neaps.
This vision of Yorkshire by the Med
no doubt won't come till I'm long dead.

Torridity in Tyne and Wear
won't come till I'm no longer here.
Predictions for this land of plenty
start, at the soonest, 2020,
which is cutting it a wee bit fine
if I'm to bask beside the Tyne.
Sometimes I have to fantasize
I'm living under bluer skies,
but today I had a little sign
here in Newcastle-upon-Tyne.
Not just that this year's birds are late
leaving the North-East to migrate,
they linger, O they're welcome, they
still sing for me at break of day.
Some prophets that I've read believe
there'll come a day the birds don't leave.
The sign I mean was true but small
and grown against my garden wall.
If the scientists' prediction
isn't all just wishful fiction,
I thought once, why, if Leeds grows wine,
can't I grow a fig tree on the Tyne?
Why not, if the River Aire's
going to wind through wine hectares,
assume the scientists really know
and plant something that needs sun to grow,
more sun than usually comes its way
in Newcastle or Whitley Bay,
and here, on Tyneside, I'll install
a fig on my least sun-starved wall,
and wait for global warming to produce
figs oozing with full taste and juice.
'Fig trees don't grow in my native land'
wrote Lawrence, when his work was banned.
The climate 's changing, figs do grow
(and franker paintings go on show!)

though not like San Gervasio,
where the starved Midlander Brit
found figs as 'fissure', 'yoni', 'slit'.
All those eyesores and black spots
bulldozed flat in his native Notts,
wait the creeping South's advance
to metamorphose into France.
The climate he was restless for
would come up to his own front door.
I tell him now, the man who grew
one Northern fig, that it's not true:
If you want figs, stay put in Notts,
trust global warming, you'll have lots.
In parts of Europe blessed with sun
I've picked hundreds. Now, here, one.
I've roamed about in similar fashion
seeking Southern fruit and passion.
His restlessness fed into mine
though I've always come back to the Tyne.
Though my life 's been a different story.
I've been 'ο ποιητης' and 'Il Signore'.
Places where he used to go,
Italy, New Mexico,
I've also been to, half-inclined
to leave everything at home behind,
then on Guatavita's shores I found
gold everywhere just on the ground.
I come to El Dorado and I find
exactly what I'd left behind!
Too busy being Pissarro
ever to let my garden grow
anything but those tough weeds
I've known in Newcastle or Leeds,
this gold I came to look upon
with an 'O my America' of Donne,

this El Dorado in my head,
when I found it, only led,
after all the searches I got high on
to the El Dorado dandelion.
That was my discovery,
poet/Pissarro of the *piss-en-lit*!
All that we search for when we roam
is nowhere if not here at home.
I picked one for you, and pressed the head
of that Andean piss-a-bed,
and now this one fig I discover
I want to share with you, my lover.
I never thought that it would grow
when I planted it ten years ago.
I decided this was what I'd do
about the same time I'd met you.
I watched it grow and much away
feared it'd die, but now, today,
September 20, '99,
your birthday, love, here on the Tyne,
not flooded yet in Grecian sun,
I picked one fig from it, just one!
I picked the first fig that I'd grown
but tasted its sweet flesh alone,
when I'd wanted, O so much, to share
the fig with one who wasn't there,
you with whom I hope to see
years of figs from that same tree,
I'd wanted here to cut in two
one half for me, one half for you,
to celebrate the first sweet sign
of global ripening on the Tyne
and with the first of my Tyne figs
celebrate you're 46!

I never thought the tree would root
let alone produce a fruit,
I've seen it, like our love, survive
from when you were only 35.
That's almost the length of time it took
to pick this first ripe fig to suck.
My heart too has felt the South,
that puts this fig into my mouth,
warm my heart's North at a time
life's forecast as a colder clime,
and, in the heart's depths, it renewed
love in life's last latitude.
And now today you're 46
and far from the first of our sweet figs.
I've watched it ripen from where I sit
at the kitchen table candle-lit.
I've watched it ripen at each meal.
Facing the autumn now I feel,
as reflected candle on the wall 's
flickering, licking the fig, like you my balls,
so lost without you, that I've plucked
the sweetest fig I've ever sucked.
Such flavour, sweetness! Half 's a feast
though ripened in the chill North-East
ripened through gales and CFCs
warming the globe a few degrees,
and by the shredded ozone layer
and, I confess, my loving care.
(Because my fig tree 's far from Greece
I protect it now with garden fleece.)

I ate my half and then thought yours,
like kids leave cake for Santa Claus,
should be left out on a plate all night
with the half-burnt candle left alight,

so tomorrow, when I woke, I'd know
you'd come to me from Tokyo,
where, as I picked, you'd been performing
among typhoons born of global warming
Goneril in Shakespeare's *Lear*.
But I know you won't be here,
to share the fig picked from my wall
with a ripeness that we know is all.
But so it wouldn't go to waste,
and longing for my favourite taste,
just as Kent said his *Alack*
(Act V, scene iii) I ate the black/
deep ruby bit I'd left for you
just as your corpse came into view.
May the both halves that I've eaten,
like 'an ounce of civet', sweeten
my imagination when I brood
alone on this bleak latitude,
trying to make my simple rhyme
obey the weight of this sad time,
but honour, too, rare days of joy
that death or distance can't destroy.
In Japan your curtain falls
and all the corpses take their calls.
Happy Birthday! I'd raise a glass,
if those prophecies had come to pass,
of Bradford bubbly or Leeds *Mumm*,
though unhappy that you couldn't come,
being borne with Regan on a bier
as the deaths piled up in *Lear*,
to the sweetest woman that I've known
most welcome to the figs I've grown.
Next September if you're freer,
and raised from the corpse-pile of *King Lear*
we'll celebrate your birthday here

with storm-ripened fruit. 46
leaves life enough for future figs,
and I still hope to suck a few
though this year I turned 62!
May whatever 's left in yours and mine
bring figs like my first fig on the Tyne.

The Krieg Anthology

I. *The Hearts and Minds Operation*
'Decapitation' to win minds and hearts,
a bombing bruited surgical, humane, 's
only partially successful when its start 's
a small child's shrapnelled scalp scooped of its brains.

II. *Mirror Image*
Forced indoors with shining sun outside,
a child of seven who should have peace to play
on a swing, a roundabout, a slide
slid out on a chilled morgue metal tray.

III. *Comforter*
Maybe she was teething up to her last day!
The dummy with smeared honey on its tip 's
to soothe the fretful babe till USA
grab life and plastic nipple from her lips.

IV. *Rice Paddy*
'US Airborne 's not there to escort
kids to school,' snorts Condoleeza.
'No, not to school,' I counter-snort,
'but to the mortuary freezer.'

V. *The Body Re-count*
Dead Iraqis vote BUSH after all!
Florida's Bushibboleth 's become Baghdad's.
He's re-elected by them as they fall
with flayed-off human flesh like hanging chads.

VI. *Rose Parade*
Sorry they're shrivelled, your liberators' petals!
There's no water here to keep the flowers fresh
though your laser-guided shower of shattering metal 's
sown these damp red roses in our flesh.

VII. *Shake, Pardner!*
Bush, who dragged him into this mad folly
though shown flag and painted V and warning flare,
will, like the A10 'cowboy on a jolly',
with friendly fire, finish Tony Blair.

VIII. *Favours*
The friendly fire from George Bush and his pards
rains on Tony Blair who shrieks *et tu!*,
like so many open wounds from bomblet shards
spattered party rosettes, blue on blue.

IX. *Baghdad Lullaby*
Sshhh! Ssshhh! though now shrapnel makes you shriek
and deformities in future may brand you as a freak,
you'll see, one day, disablement 's a blessing and a boon
sent in baby-seeking bomblets by benefactor Hoon.

X. *Illinois Elegy*
My son's remains come back for me to grieve.
They'd've brought me more to bury if they could.
They went to so much trouble to retrieve
the DNA smear on this cotton bud.

XI. *Holy Tony's Prayer*
Why is it, Lord, although I'm right
I find it hard to sleep at night?
Sometimes I wake up in a sweat
they've not found WMDs yet!
The thought that preys most on my mind,
is the only arms they'll ever find
(unless somehow I get MI6
to plant them to be found by Blix,
that's *if* the UN sneaks back in)
are Ali's in the surgeon's bin.
Ali Ismail Abbas who
is a sick Iraqi PR coup.

Lord, Thou must divinely care
for Thy servant Tony Blair
since Thou decreed I was created
morally more elevated
and by Thy grace created blessed
with clearer conscience than the rest.
When little children squeal in pain
my conscience, Lord, 's without a stain.
Thou knowest that my conscience, Lord,
for all the bloodflow stays unflawed.
I unleash terror without taint
a sort of (dare one say it?) saint!
Miraculous! No moral mire
soils my immaculate attire.
None of the blood and shit of war
ever clogs a single pore.
What a good boy am I, Jack Horner
self-cleansing in his moral sauna.
At Camp David dinner I say grace
with my most holy parson's face.
Though brother George requires no prod
to bring your name up often, God,
fact is I competed with my host
to see who can mention Thee the most.
Lord, buff now my halo's sheen
dimmed now that the nation 's seen
Ali Ismail Abbas who
is a sick Iraqi PR coup,
the bandaged forehead to enhance
the pathos of his helpless glance.
Poor Cherie's throat gets a small lump
when Ali waves his bandaged stump.
It made me think, Lord, that they'd win
if we can't contrive some counterspin
against this winsome amputee
specially created for TV.

They held a country-wide audition
to undermine the coalition.
Let 's hint that vile Iraqi guile
chooses a boy with eyes and smile
that melt the heart, then (how I hate
such callous brutes!) amputate
both his arms with blunt axe hack.
The British 'll buy that from Iraq!
I need a spokesman, Hoon for choice,
he 's got the gall and boring voice,
someone like Geoff Hoon to say
how Ali's mother will one day
(oops, can't, sorry I forgot
our bomb, apart from Ali, killed the lot)
mothers 'll draw comfort from
the coalition cluster bomb.
Then once hostilities soon stop
there'll be a brilliant photo op
outside with me at number 10
(yes, I'll still be PM then!)
outside number 10 with me,
once every Saddam statue 's downed,
Ali with prosthetic V!
(Twist his wrist the right way round.)

XII. *Epilogue to* The Recruiting Officer *of Mr Farquhar*

spoken by MR REDGRAVE from the stage of the Garrick Theatre,
Lichfield, September 2003

You might consider me more brazen if I doff
my feathered hat, and bluff persona off,
and as my brazen self stand up and say
what else our Farquhar might put in his play.
I tell you that our playwright Mr Farquhar
could have made your evening a lot darker
and made our play uncomfortably black
by showing you recruiting for Iraq,

and war management in Tony Blair's UK,
the doctored facts, the dodgy dossier,
that sent deluded soldiers overseas
on the strength of spurious WMDs.
Suckers fell for our recruiters' tricks
and took the shilling in 1706,
now they are conned, the suckers of our times,
when Brazen Blair doles out George Bush's dimes.
Seek recruiters in our cast you won't find any,
not Neve, Harry, Brendan, Harley, Petra, Penny,
and the recruiter's job is absolutely foreign
to Owen and to James, and to me, Corin.
As Kite and Plume and Brazen we'd dragoon
the deluded and the duped for Mr Hoon,
but as ourselves we'd damn Hoon, Blair and Straw
and drum up people to condemn their war.
We're resisters not recruiters, anti- not pro-wars.
Pray show which you prefer by your applause.
Hats on, recruiters!
                          Off, resisters!
                                    Pro-?
                                          Or anti-wars?
Pray show which you prefer by your applause!

XIII. *Off the Scent*
Thank God (the PM's pal) he's not resigned
and still here to lead his party from behind.
Though not actually voting he was there
in spirit to spare the fox, our caring Blair
whose far far shriller view halloos
set off packs of Tomahawks and Cruise,
Blair in his Iraq-hued hunting coat,
whose cheeks with Bush-brush daubings bloat
when he blows hard on Herod's hunting horn
to cluster-bomb the cradle-culled newborn,
whose taste for dismemberment 's more amputees
hunted by helicopters and Humvees.

Species Barrier

An Afghan mega food-aid drop
this plump cow banquet, but no parachute,
not carved up into packs of steak and chop,
or some collaterally slaughtered brute?

Or is it a whole cow colony of spores
with no rushed R & D to 'weaponize',
an FMD carcass with raw sores,
the staggers stampeding from the skies?

Not aid-drop mega-feast, not germ warfare
though it's pregnant with explosive, putrid gas,
this maggot Mecca crescendoing with prayer
will never feed the hungry folk who pass.

An Afghan's total herd like some gunned stray
from culled Cumbria dumped on Kabul,
the colluding cabinet of the hooked UK
still committing its 'contiguous cull'.

Ales Stenar

for Lasse Söderborg

From the smokery a whole eel, a
piece of birch-browned Baltic halibut.

And the vision? The vulva of Valhalla
always open, always shut.

Amazon

At the watery border
of three countries
(one eliminated early,
two still in the running),
tethered to thick trees
the floating house
with foundations of gators
strains on its moorings
so the satellite rocks
and the football flickers.

Swinging in hammocks
watching the World Cup
on dodgy reception
with six macaws
feathered in fan strip,
blue, yellow, red,
Colombia's colours,
swigging shots of cane-hooch
men shout at the screen,
when Colombia scores,
and *gol! gol! gol!*
yell the loyal macaws.

Outside on the verandah
the world's biggest rat
the pig-size *chiguero*'s
almost wholly devoured
the national team calendar,
and a black boy in blonde wig,
El Pibe Valderrama's curls,
balanced on felled floating timber
on currents full of piranhas
boots his World Cup ball

from his log to his sister's
who gets her own yellow wig
under her brilliant header
of the, till then dry, ball into the flood
of the Amazon where it swirls
and bobs from Colombia to Peru
past pink dolphins and sawmill
through rubber trees on to Brazil
and the downstream fish-market
where a black-scaled fish just sliced
in six still writhing slices
bloods the white marble and a priest
makes grunting gourmet noises
under a glass Parisian roof
where non-fan flocks of parrots,
untrained for the touchline,
fly like a curtain over the glazing,
team jerseys shredded to pixels
showering from shouted-at screens,
a cloudburst of dazzle and hue
over Colombia, Brazil, Peru.

The Gifts of Aphrodite

These figs missed the picker
moved to pluck tokens
of love or welcome to strangers,
missed bird, missed casual snacker,
so are burst and outspread
as red as hibiscus,
scuffed pistil opera plush,
carmine mite-view velveteen
the pile of posh bath robes.

The carob pods clatter,
as the woman rattles
her long pole in the tree,
down through the branches
to the roadside ditch
from which she picks a handful
as we pass her: 'Take, sweet
as honey. Eat! Eat!'
All Eve's kin and as kind
with their sweet temptations
nuts, ripe figs, pears,
a fragrant herb to smell,
thyme, basil, oregano . . .
a red pomegranate flower
a sprig of white jasmine.

Then as we walked, hot and thirsty,
a groaning green truck
laden with leafy oranges
driven by a black-clad priest
drove past us. 'Catch!' he cried.
The flung rogue orange
rolled down the dusty hill
till stopped by a wicket

of three roadside asphodels
that went on gently vibrating
the chord of thankful receivers.
I held the fruit high
in greeting and gratitude
at the retreating truck,
a sunburst reflected
then eclipsed in the cassock.

At the Baths of Aphrodite
where bathing 's forbidden
a first fig leaf falls
yellowing into the pool
with shed off-white dove fluff
startling the basking eel
suppler than asphodels
into two brief shudders
from an I to an S
and back, twice:
IS it spells IS
the be all and end all
settling to a still I.

At dawn we swim the sun up
over blue/purple mountains
as the swordfish flotilla
heads back to harbour and docks,
tonight's feast aboard
in fresh bloody slices.

11 September 2001

for Alfie in Cyprus

Turquoise, indigo, the water
I teach my grandson to love,
who now chews his octopus
swirled in oil and oregano
an inch of tentacle gnawed
and another, savouring the strange,
oil dribbles over his belly,
laughing at everything
was at birth not even a kilo,
so premature he only just made it,
and whose little heart racing
I saw slow down the first time
out of his tent in his mother's arms
the monitor's red digits decreasing,
so he needs no lessons in loving the life
he scarcely scraped into,
but today I made a wish
that all the gifts of this morning,
clear comforting water
so joyfully splashed in,
his octopus, *Sprite*,
pomegranate in yoghurt,
at a beach not that far from
British Army manoeuvres,
and wild forest and mountains,
in an island divided
by bankrupt religions
both bred in the desert,
is all Alfie will ever crave
of Paradise.

Cremation Eclogue

Pig pyres are crackling in the snow-flecked fields,
dawn bonfires next to cleaned-out byres and folds.
I know my taxi driver. FMD,
the tragic traincrash (ten dead) yesterday
are what we talk about: Heddon-on-the-Wall
may be infected from untreated swill,
the micro virus and the cattle plague
that could cross borders between bloc and bloc
when the world was so divided, let alone
unpatrolled farm fences, ditch and lane.
The taxi's heater's fierce, we discuss
the icicles hanging from the underpass,
this zero morning as we track the Tyne
and follow the STATION signposts towards town.

I was in what was then Leningrad
I say (as we rattle over a cattle grid
and then squelch across a disinfectant mat,
not the first this morning that we've met)
a falling icicle caused the death
of a man who was walking underneath,
pole-axed as he sauntered with his wife,
right through his fur hat of sleek grey wolf,
the sharp tip with its glossy shine
sticking through his badly shaven chin.
In Leningrad you couldn't buy a blade
you'd get a decent shave from and not bleed.

An ice-bolt from malicious gods
could chill the skull and slice the vocal chords
of this Geordie smoker here, under threat
getting quick drags of smoke into his throat
banished the bank so many times a day
increasing the odds that maybe he will die

this ostracized, cold, street-drag Damocles
under the half-thawed bank roof icicles.
The frozen, furtive smoker in shirt sleeves
under icicle-hung gutterings and eves
puffs fast on his cupped fag and quickly stubs
half out among the scattered kerbside tabs.

I enter Dobson's elegant colonnade,
its Railway Age proportions just renewed,
aware of risk and how a roof-slate slid,
only two days ago, a heavy slate,
off my front roof and cut the garden seat
where normally on warm days I'd've sat
and almost did that first bright day of March
when the sun woke up a solitary midge.
If the temperature had been two more degrees
I might have sat there and not cut my grass
so that the tile that weeks of gale winds loosed
missed me by metres and my skull's unsliced.
Yesterday ten passengers on this route died
which makes today's predictably subdued
like me, who's thinking did fate choose to spare
me from slate, and collision, as a kind of spur,
to go on doing what I do, that's look and write
as I've done since the sixties on this route?

I remember all the great books that I've read
I'd never 've started if I'd gone by road,
the poems, like this one, that I've written
some passable, and published, most though rotten.
I used to know the landmarks on this route
the industries of Britain left and right.
Once I'd know exactly where we were
from the shapes of spoil heaps and from winding gear
spinning their spokes and winching down a shift
miles deep into this sealed and filled-in shaft

and which bits of field you'd see a score
of rabbits in the passing train would scare,
which Yorkshire coal-dust-lacquered black lagoon
had crested grebes on once but now long gone,
but once my own slack-blackened Hippocrene,
though the Pegasus would be more like that crane,
raising a replica of this coach, ripped and crushed
when yesterday's Newcastle–King's Cross crashed,
I see from a jerkily slow, jinxed British train
through snow, cremation smoke-clouds, quarantine.

If you still could get them open then I'd throw
these pages I've been scribbling, 1–2–3,
out of the window. All I've done so far
of *Cremation Eclogue* floats towards the fire,
where choking piles of stiff-legged Friesians blaze
their piebald blending, poem into place.

Queuing for Charon

Cretans still can't stand 'the Krauts'
but don't turn them away,
gaga ex-Nazis, lager louts,
cramming Crete on holiday.
Fifty odd years of so-called peace
fill beaches with old foes.
Northern Europe flocks to Greece
to warm its frozen toes.
And my old carcass likes these coasts,
archaeology and joy,
but even in Greek sun the ghosts
come back to haunt the boy.
Underneath the skin that's tanned
these Krauts are frail and ill
but once they served the Fatherland
with more than time to kill.
This museum that they shuffle round
groggy from too much sun
has finds out of the Cretan ground
once trampled by the Hun.
Of an age to have yelled *Zieg Heils*,
worn jackboots, marched like geese,
they stagger round with vacant smiles
smeared with anti-UV grease.
A few years younger I'd only seen
Belsen on newsreels but the sight
I saw at eight on that big screen
fell on me like a blight.
It clouded all my childish fun.
My voice, before it got its bass,
squeaked against the humbled Hun
and murderous Master Race.

Younger than these Krauts on Crete
my old Hun-hatred flares.
They've come in to escape the heat
and dodder up the stairs.

These dodderers I demonize
aren't garbed in SS might
but kit that bares their flabby thighs
and blistered cellulite.
An hour to kill till their lamb stew
then I can be left alone
to keep my promised rendezvous
with a laureate of bone.

II

A dolphin dominates the room
caught at the zenith of its arc
leaping inside an ancient tomb
from mortality's deep dark.
Once the painting had been done
it was hidden from the light
sealed with a lid that weighed a ton
and seamlessly sun-tight.
Do dolphins soar out of the deep
and, soaring, seem to pack
all joy there is into the leap
because they're going back?
I'd sooner see them live at sea
but this corpse's private view
shows the surface of mortality
their leaps keep breaking through.
The Germans think the dolphin's *schön*;
more comfort than the coffin quilt
cushioning them when it's their turn
to attempt a leap from guilt.

I saw a dolphin diver/flyer
from a ferry Lesbos bound
to where the floating head and lyre
of Orpheus ran aground.
And here's a skull with golden wreath
a sort of Orpheus but
songless for ever and his teeth
clamped permanently shut.
One jovial elder cracks a joke
that's meant to keep at bay
the thought that even *Herrenvolk*
end up as skulls one day.
It makes the old girls all guffaw,
but their laughter quickly dies
faced with the skull I stand before
whose sockets hold my eyes.
The Germans crowd me at the case
where the poet's skull's displayed.
It's fleshed by my reflected face
and when I leave reflayed.
The Gerriatrics quieten down
at the case where I am now,
a poet's skull with laurel crown
still on its bony brow.
What strikes me dumb is that I spy
the obol put inside his cheek
to pay his fare 's still there, but why?
Did the ferry bar this Greek?
Why the coin still with the skull?
Was it, as in these old folks' day,
that Charon's stiff-skiff was chock full
and the bard was turned away?
And turned away because art fails
when violence is rife
and doesn't help to tip the scales
towards the claims of life?

Are hearts touched by your great gifts
or softened just a jot?
Since I'm working double shifts
they're obviously not!
If any poems or piddling odes
can be shown (a monstrous if)
ever to have lightened my huge loads
I'll scull you in my skiff.
Charon said: 'Piss off, I'm full!
At least to poets I am.'
That's why the obol's with the skull
all bards get told to scram.

And poets' obols are still leaning
against their fleshless jaw
because they failed to give a meaning
to all those ghosts of War.
I think for poets the moral 's
when they reach those Styx bank queues
they should ditch their golden laurels
and stand behind the queuing Jews
until the last one's safely crossed,
then poets might have their say.
Poetry since the Holocaust
's a Stygian stowaway.

III
Charon can't work any quicker
to clear the endless line
and the rear is getting thicker
with new blood from Palestine.
The bards are crowding on the banks
of this slithery nearer shore
with zlotys, kroner, pennies, francs
tucked inside their jaw,

and all of them doomed to repeat,
whatever tongue they speak,
the stutters of the skull of Crete
choking on his Greek.
The bards hope Charon won't capsize
with loads who 've lost their tongue
for what these Germans' shaded eyes
looked on when they were young,
these burned who leave to board their bus,
the red bus that reads Bonn,
making a gentle, gallant fuss
of sleeveless ladies they help on.
So the dumb poet with the wreath of gold
has he taught them any lesson?
Live every moment when you're old?
The bus moves. Next stop: *Essen!*
They'll leave the island in a week
and take the ferry back from Crete
with peppermints inside their cheek
to keep their short breath sweet.
From the ferry rail they scan the waves
and keep their weak eyes peeled
for dolphins that can leap from graves
before their lids are sealed.

WW

He wanders lonely as a cloud
to watch the cattle being culled.

I see the well-soled boot
of William's ghost on walkabout

dent the disinfectant mat.
He was declaiming when we met,

and all at once his eyes beheld
dead sheep bleeding in the field,

no stirring but wind-ruffled fleece
and rats and crows and worms and lice.

And the bard's iambic bursts by coughs
caused by smoking cows and calves.

The victims in these MAFF culls
outnumbering the daffodils;

a JCB 's their mass-grave hearse
now rendered into smoke and verse.

über al

Uns hat der Winter geschadet über al . . .

Winter's done his worst all round,
leafless trees, and lifeless ground,
silence where birdsong used to sound.
I want summer back with girls at play
and birds that sing at break of day.

Till the birds bring back their song
I'd like to sleep all Winter long
while his stranglehold 's still strong.
But once May weakens Winter's powers
from this frostbound ground I'll pick you flowers.

(Walther von der Vogelweide, 1170–1230)

A Question of Sentences

(Nuremberg, 1946)

One Nazi 's tongue-tied, and one's tongue 's loose.
Speer lives to see his fluent *Memoirs* toasted.
One gets twenty years, and one the noose.
Sauckel's *Life* could only have been ghosted.

Speer enunciates, and Sauckel mutters.
Speer looks them in the eye. His *Deutsch* is *Hoch* –

Sauckel's heels go click! The whole man stutters,
strung up, a lifetime's words he never spoke.

Eggshells

One year in Washington DC
 a girl I got to know
said she came from Germany.
She looked quite like Bardot.

And her first name was Brigitte
(rhymes with bitter not with sweet)
and though things turned out bitter
we met for walks, for drinks, to eat.

In a little while she let me see
her total tan, breasts, belly, legs.
And that Easter Sunday in DC
she brought me Easter eggs.

She'd painted all the eggs by hand
with folk-style whorls and flowers
in the manner of her fatherland.
It took her hours and hours.

Daddy took my hand to guide
the brush's gleaming tip
and held it firm when fuss outside
might make me smudge or slip . . .

I stuck out my tongue like this
(I knew that tongue quite well)
to master all that artifice
we both lavished on the shell.

The eggs in an ashtray by my bed
with their gay patterns made me glad
but, on our next date, Brigitte said
I should know more about her dad.

Before you get too fond of me
I've got something to confess,
she said that April in DC
in her Yves St Laurent dress.

If her face said it was bad,
when the words came it was worse.
My Washington bedfellow's dad,
she said, was Rudolf Hoess.

Though I hugged her when we said goodbye
I couldn't face her after that.
Though I still admired the artistry
I squashed the frail eggs flat.

In Poland I saw where she was shown
to make yellow out of onion peel
and they'd decorate the eggs he'd blown,
the Kommandant, with cochineal.

Delicate execution learned,
helped by sticking out her tongue,
where millions were gassed and burned
and egg-dyeing Dad was hung.

No doubt she still tops up the tan
on bronzed belly, breasts and legs,
and dreams one day she'll find a man
who won't smash her Easter eggs.

The Grilling

I'd just walked up and down Vesuvio
as Goethe did two centuries ago.
At the bottom with a bottle of white wine
I heard the great poet talking to Tischbein:

Vesuvio puffing smoke out not far off
flavours this fine vino that we quaff.
That force that belches forth its molten mass
has poured this tinkling gold in my raised glass.
Devastation, Tischbein, ancient waste
gives this Vesuvial vintage its fine taste.
While we're drinking let's remember hope's
what goes with hoe in hand to smoking slopes,
ploughs blistering cinders into ashy fields
knowing the fine vines cooled lava yields.
Before the hoers came and earth showed green
singed Satyrs would be first back on the scene,
as before spectators' tears have time to dry
the Satyrs enter with their cock-tips high.
After the mask, with always opened eyes
seeing the worst, the phallus of gross size.
When lust for life is bankrupt, head and heart
get bridging loans from that exuberant part.
I think of the Satyrs dancing on the coals
and celebrating life with blistered soles,
or, if seen as half-horse, hooves, not feet,
gelatinous from jigging on that heat,
and they dance more featly, fleeter, faster
because their dancefloor's on the site of a disaster.
Does their acrobatic goat/horse/man gavotte
come from the ground they jig on being hot?
All I'm suggesting is we might enquire
if the dancing is dependent on the fire.

Tragedies, extinctions and the night
trodden by dancing into draughts of light.
The world's unjust to Satyrs. They enact
a valetudinous Walpurgisnacht.

(I'm pretending not to notice, but I see
Tischbein, all this while, 's been sketching me!)
Goethe's in full flow. I see him glug
two great draughts of wine straight from the jug
I knew he liked to drink. His favourite wine
came from Würzburg's vineyards on the Main.
I felt like saying it's OK for you –
your cut-off point is 1832!
Between then and my own day
there've been far worse disasters than Pompeii . . .

Once he's glugged his wine I hear him say:

Martial, that poet of Priapus, remembers
love's green haunts beneath the glowing embers,
a dappling of grape pattern where sun shone
on slopes ash scoria now slither on.
It's this ash-strewn, bleak volcano, this
that Marcus Valerius Martialis
makes so vine-clad and beloved of Bacchus,
those oozing wine vats, madidos lacus,
and this, black as it looks today, the Satyrs
dedicated to Dionysian matters.
I've never been particularly partial
to the rather puerile epigrams of Martial,
but his poem, particularly the last line,
rather tolls the knell of the divine.
More wine! More figs! And while I pour
read me Epigrams iv.xliv.
Thank God for real figs, not those charred
Pompeian relics carbonized and hard.

Tischbein looks it up, and line by line
reads it for Goethe's benefit. And mine:

Hic est pampineis viridis modo Vesuvius umbris
*   presserat hic madidos nobilis uva lacus*
haec iuga, quam Nysae colles plus Bacchus amavit;
*   hoc nuper Satyri monte dedere choros;*
haec Veneris sedes, Lacedaemone gratior illi;
*   hic locus Herculeo numine clarus erat.*
cuncta iacent flammis et tristi mersa favilla
*   nec superi vollent hoc licuisse sibi.*

They improvised translations and sipped wine.
Here's Thomas May's then Addison's then mine:

Vesuvius, shaded once with greenest vines
Where pressed grapes did yield the noblest wines;
Which hill far more than Nysa Bacchus lov'd,
Where Satyrs once in mirthful dances mov'd,
Where Venus dwelt, and better lov'd the place
Than Sparta where Alcides temple was,
Is now burnt downe, rak'd up in ashes sad.
The gods are grill'd that such great power they had.
    (Thomas May, 1595–1650)

(*grill* as in to grieve to hurt, give pain,
grill as in 'The grones of sir Gawayne
does my heart grille'. But *grill* as well has heat
and whatever gods there were have blistered feet.)

'Vesuvius cover'd with the fruitful vine,
Here flourish'd once, and ran with floods of wine:
Here Bacchus oft to the cool shades retired,
And his own native Nysa less admired:
Oft to the mountain's airy tops advanced,
The frisking Satyrs on the summits danced:

Alcides here, here Venus, graced the shore,
Nor loved her favourite Lacedaemon more.
Now piles of ashes, spreading all around
In undistinguish'd heaps, deform the ground:
The gods themselves the ruin'd seats bemoan,
And blame the mischiefs that themselves have done.'
        (Joseph Addison, 1672–1719)

Vesuvius, green yesterday with shady vine,
    where the crushed grape gushed vast vats of wine,
ridges, Bacchus loved and put before
    his birthplace Nysa, Venus favoured more
than Lacedaemon, and where Satyrs stomped
    till now, and Herculaneum, all swamped,
engulfed by cinders in a flood of fire:

power like this not even gods desire.
        Martial IV.44
        (Tony Harrison, 1937–   )

Goethe dashed his own off, and his wine
in which he tasted AD 79,
then spoke to my portraitist Tischbein:

The gods are grilled to have such dreadful powers.
But what gods' hands let go of ends in ours.
What Martial's gods say no to, Man says yes;
his cold palm weighs the orb of Nothingness.
Gods refuse the powers and late Man weighs
like a regent the recentest of days.
Drink!

        There is no danger of the thing erupting?

Excuse me, *Meine Herren*, excuse my interrupting . . .
I've just been listening to your conversation
about wine tasting of old devastation.

Vesuvio, vine-enricher and crop killer
spouting fatal/fertile hot *favilla*.
In Santorini vines from cliffs of clinker
give, even to the life-affirming drinker,
an old extinction in its strange bouquet
the Knossos catastrophe haunts that wine today.
Pompeian figs turned carbon in their bowl
can only, if you'd crunch them, taste of coal
figs from the cinders now can still taste sweet
but the wine still has the tang of rubbled Crete.
How does the *vino* here compare to wine
you're said to have drunk so much of from the Main
Not under the volcano the vines there
but in '45 our fire rained from the air.
Not volcanic wine but since we bombed it flat
disaster goes with grapes into the vat.
If you drank those Main wines now you'd taste
Würzburg and its vintages laid waste,
Würzburg where you bought 'goat's scrota' from
was levelled by the British *Fire Bomb*,
bodies in the poses of Pompeii
9000 filled the rubbled streets next day.

(Wine in glass *Bocksbeuteln* (goats' scrota)
from Würzurg was the *Lieblingstrank* of Goethe.)
and all the glass goats' scrota popped
and fused together when the bombs were dropped.
From that molten mass of glass like boiling glue
Riesling steam clouds rose into the blue.
Does that *Stein Wein*, you guzzled taste the same
after the vineyards passed through fire-storm flame?
Würzburg vintners always quote the line
your *gewohnter Lieblingstrank Frankischer Wein*
your, at least reputed, yearly quota
of *sehr gut* gluggable 'goats' scrota'

was 900 litres – well, I suppose
colleagues in Weimar quaffed some of those.

Entschuldigung, Herr Goethe, Herr Tischbein,
I didn't want to spoil lunch with my story.
Let me at least replenish your white wine:

Cameriere, Vesuvio bianco per le signori!

Signori? Questi? Dove? you OK?
Sit there, talk to self all bloody day.

But Tischbein had torn his sketch out of his book
me, half finished with a haunted look.
Behind me smudged with spilled Vesuvial wine
a cloud from the crater shaped like Pliny's pine.
I picked it up but in one blinding flash
it erupted into flame and turned to ash.
On one frail flake the outline of an eye
went floating on the heat into the sky.

Reading the Rolls: An Arse-Verse

Note: arse-verse: West Yorkshire: a spell on a house to ward off fire.
ars > ardere Lat; burn, as in *arson.*

'quin etiam passim nostris in versibus ipsis
multa elementa vides multis communia verbis,
cum tamen inter se versus ac verba necessest
confiteare et re et sonitu distare sonanti.
tantum elementa queunt permutato ordine solo.'
(Lucretius, *De Rerum Natura,* 1.823–827)

I

The Pythia on her rock seat
inhaling rot learned to recite
before Homer's age the very first
hexameters a human voiced.
Full of reek, dead dragon slouch,
the reptile on its rocky ledge,
the putrid serpent, was the true
inspirer of pure poetry.

With thoughts like these I'd reconcile
those years of writing with the smell
of leaking gas and fantasized
of serpents when the gas-fire hissed.
It helped me concentrate, the hiss
like that of the clobbered Pythoness
Apollo clubbed to one long bruise,
a serpent pelt the champion's prize,
clobbered so Apollo could
be Delphi's one presiding god.
He clubbed his way to serpent's lair
then swapped flesh-coated club for lyre,
but still rank bits of snake-gut fly
when the god's in full lyre-maestro flow.
The Muse who did his manicure
forgot to clean his nails of gore.

So when Apollo plucks the strings
pure music comes with serpent stinks.

Through over thirty years of writing
miasma from the monster's rotting,
seeping through pine and carpet wool,
was the inspiration I'd inhale.
I've tolerated that vague whiff
but now they've turned my gas taps off . . .
rank reptile guts, bad gas escapes
from my dodgy cracked lead pipes.
Not old gas now, thank God! – CO 's
what the suicidal mostly chose
(and once when I tried to choose which
gas came joint top with Tyne Bridge).
It's long been North Sea I hear hiss
like the sleeping Delphi Pythoness
whose crusted viscera and bones
they've just dumped in my rubbish bins.
with all my fires though I pleaded –

You're lucky none of 'em exploded.

Commotion over such a smell
I can recall when very small.
There's summat snuffed it under t'floor
granpa said *Get Freddy Flea.*
Fred, for fifty years, had toured
with his flea circus. Now retired
he'd get called in to help pinpoint
where rats had died and earn a pint.
Fred's kennel of winged tracker dogs
were bluebottles in a *Lifeboat* box.
Fred let them out, that's all he did
to find out where the rat had died.

They buzzed and settled. Once Fred knew
the spot where all his trackers flew
he raised a floorboard to reveal a
rotting rat *voilà, voilà!*
Fred's trackers got their own reward.
My first lesson as the rat's devoured
how what's alive thrives on what's not.
Then Fred caught them in a little net
and pushed their bright blue faience backs
back into the *Lifeboat* box.

II

I'm aware today the earliest verse
I ever mumbled wiped my arse,
enjoyed for what they were, not judged,
torn off the roll, and used, and flushed.
No poems now on toilet paper
(imagine slim flat-packs from Faber,
but not the sort of verse one reads
and harder on the haemorrhoids!).
But then when I was just gone four
and in the second year of war,
I unrolled poems to recite
precarious on the toilet seat,
some bright quatrain not epic saga
to be consigned to the cloaca.
Those moments I communed with metre
set me on course to be a writer.
From those rough sheets I learned to read
verses in the smell of rot,
dumped dactyl, and turd-smeared trochee
primed the prosodics of decay.

I can't recite the sort of ditty
I remember reading in the netty.

I remember rhythms not the words
that went with war-time infant turds,
but I do remember one
that pitched poetics at the Hun,
the raving loo-roll Hitler
bull's-eyed by the childish piddler.
The flush-churned *Führer* screams
and below him in red writhing rhymes:

Hitler now screams with impatience
Our good health is proving a strain
May he and his Axis relations
Soon find themselves right down the drain . . .

Lord Chesterfield's advice
to his son was Latin verse,
not lengthy epics like Lucretius
dangerous and irreligious,
but shorter poems like Horace *Odes*
construed while extruding turds,
a page per shit for the beginner
before consigned to Cloacina.
Lise, Ragueneau,
the baker's wife in *Cyrano*
wrapped brioche and quiche and tart
in poems by the baker/bard.
Poor old Heine dreamed his *Lieder*
made baccy wrap or fire lighter.
Two centuries ago
Drury Lane made storms of snow
from the shredded pages of the plays
of poets who had failed to please.
Shred me for snow, I'd like these pages
drifting down while Lear rages.
Or feel free in need to use these verses,
if not too rough, to wipe your arses.

(but there is no perforation here
continue sitting do not tear . . .)

III
(If you've not yet wiped your arse
it's either 1. because my verse,
more captivating than reputed,
grips you, or 2. you're constipated!)

A Philodemus poem's apt:
(could be read three times while you crapped)
*life's a papyrus being ripped
column by column as it's read*
and no one ever can re-read.
Apter though, I think, by far
is this charred roll as metaphor.
Poetry and the human soul.
A carbonized papyrus scroll
taking months to read an inch
unwound on the rack-cum-winch
contraption of Piaggio
who daily sketched Vesuvio
over two centuries ago.
Tightening the silk rack's screw
black syllables slide into view.
Each day another millimetre
made visible to that rare reader
whose eye could con such text and crack
the secrets of black script on black.
What's this illegible black writing
on carbonized papyrus hiding?
Tilting it this way and then that
reveals a radiant alphabet.
The black on black is not a blank.
Light flashes from the lamp-soot ink,
words in iridescent lustre

like the nacre of the oyster,
a lustre like black mackerel scales
or like the peacock coal of Wales.
What iridesces is philosophy
that aims to free the mind from fear
and put the old gods out to grass
and live life in the moment's grace.
The philosopher is infamous
as the poet Philodemus
Cicero called a Greekling creep
whose fawning poetry was crap,
who flattered Piso, one of Rome's
known layabouts, in tacky rhymes.
He brown-nosed Piso and got lodged
and looked on while his patron leched,
luxuriated, lounged and lauded
the Epicurus he diluted
especially for Piso's taste:
all life boiled down to getting pissed,
the *diem carpe*ed in good booze
(Chian, of course!), eels, turbot; boys.
Though it's claimed that Xanthippe,
his wife, kept Philodemus happy,
it's Flora's blazoned boobs and arse
that bob up often in his verse
addressed and undressed with the O's
Epicureans always use.
O, poetry's fundamental core,
chrysanthemums in Zen haiku.
To begin with put down eight
like a beauty queen parade.
ω ω ω ω ω ω ω ω
8 omegas all in a row,
all loose and ready to apply
wherever lust or wonder blow.

Though omega stands for what's last,
in his poems of love and lust
you'll see Philodemus add
that letter of the alphabet
as *blason anatomique*,
an O or exclamation mark
before or after all the bits
a sensual lover celebrates:
ω γλουτων, ω κτενος, ω λαγονων.
O plus the lingered-over noun
from cunt with little comb-like fringe
to kissing (definitely French!)
foot, shoulders, breasts, all get
the last letter of the alphabet –
ω ω ω ω

Omegas are O's not Ah's
Its sound is O, its shape an arse,
a 42nd St chorine's,
a 50s swimsuit beauty queen's.
John Donne's 'O my America!'
works like the Greek poet's omega,
Flora's shoulders! breasts! neck! thighs!
to add O to or apostrophize,
apostrophizing buttocks, cunt
and how she moves them: *'If she can't
recite a Sapphic ode OK!
So she's called Flora I don't care!
her name is Flora from the sticks
she's a real star when she fucks.'*

This is philosphy reduced
to loving flesh that turns to dust
entropy's attractive butt
before the O-hailed flesh or fruit,
as though the grasped IS IS IS IS

is balanced on a precipice.
Colours intensify, not fade
against annihilating void.
But all it needs to do that O
as we *carpe diem* is to grow
and we'll go straight into its maw.
Once it gets out of control
it swallows all we're praising whole.
The O we use to mark our joy
needs but to widen to destroy,
to suck fellators and their O's
down the void's vast vacuum hose.

Life is atoms and the void
of which we shouldn't be afraid,
says Titus Lucretius Carus,
poet/follower of Epicurus,
in scrolls still buried from the doom
that fell on Herculaneum.
Carbonized in 79
their iridescence now may drown.
Still interred unlike the Greek
papyri we've begun to crack,
packed *capsae* of papyri fated
to be flooded if unexcavated.
Maybe the *De Rerum Natura*
made accessibly much clearer
on how the chemistry that recombines
the consonants of verbs and nouns
is like the void where atoms dance,
alliteration, assonance,
the voiced and voiceless counterparts
used in *cynghanedd* by Welsh bards,
p/b k/g s/z t/d
pairs in disparate unity
which makes the listener or reader

through a great O-sweeping radar
aware of bright life *and* life's undertow
of chaos tugging from below.
In a charred Lucretius each new clue
needs lacunae and the black to glow.
And from each alphabetic spark
work out the letters left in dark
Bright *g* . . . bright *d* . . . or *n* . . . bright *o*
with void around brings vertigo,
but iridescences deciphered claim
all radiance enhanced by gloom,
and knowing this the soul is freed
from what before made it afraid.

The soul goes with cloacal matters
as much as tragedy with satyrs,
so, If you're still sitting on the loo
where your ω fits in an O,
peruse these prosodics from my pen,
then use, and flush them down the pan.

(Though perhaps for average shits
I've given you too many sheets.)

Shrapnel

A summer day with all the windows wide
when suddenly a storm-presaging breeze
makes the scribbled papers that I'm sorting slide
onto the floor. They're these you're reading, these.
I rummage through my many paperweights,
grandad's knuckleduster, this one from Corfu –
a rosette from the Kaiser's palace gates,
and shrapnel from an air-raid I lived through.

Down in our cellar, listening to that raid,
those whistles, those great shudders, death seemed near,
my mother, me, my sister, all afraid
though my mother showed us kids no sign of fear.
Maybe the blackout made the ground too dark
for the aimer to see the target for his load
but all the bombs fell onto Cross Flatts Park
and not onto our house in Tempest Road.

And not onto our school, Cross Flatts CP.
A hit would mean no school and I'd be spared
old 'Corky' Cawthorne persecuting me.
If he'd've copped a bomb would I have cared?
'Don't talk like that!' I heard my mother chide
though she didn't know that Corky used to tell
her frightened little son that when he died,
because not christened, he would go to hell.

On the rare occasions that I chose to speak
in Corky's RI class I'd make him mad,
trying out bits of calculated cheek
and end up being called 'a wicked lad'.
Sir, if you've had your legs off, sir, like say
poor Mr Lovelock down Maude Avenue
will you get 'em back on Judgement Day?
Does God go round and stick 'em back wi' glue?

Corky Cawthorne's cruel and crude RI
put me off God for life. I swore I'd go
neither to Hell below nor Heaven on high,
and Beeston was all of both I'd ever know.
He also taught music which he made me hate,
not quite as much as God, into my teens.
I'd never 've come to music even late
if that raid had blown me into smithereens.

I went to see the craters the bombs made
first thing in the morning and us lads
collected lumps of shrapnel from the raid
to prove we'd seen some war to absent dads.
There was a bobby there who didn't mind
craters being used by kids so soon for play
or hunting for shrapnel that he helped us find.
Clutching my twisted lump I heard him say:

'appen Gerry must 've been 'umane
or there'd 've been a bloodbath 'ere last neet.
They'd be flattened now would t' ouses in Lodge Lane,
Tempest Road, all t' 'arlechs, Stratford Street.
He dumped his bombs in t'park and damaged nowt
missing t'rows of 'ouses either side.
'umane! 'umane! And 'im a bloody Kraut!
And but for him, I thought, I could have died.

So now I celebrate my narrow squeak,
the unseen foe who spared our street in Leeds,
and I survived to go on to learn Greek
and find more truth in tragedy than creeds.
I stroke my shrapnel and I celebrate,
surviving without God until today,
where on my desk my shrapnel paperweight
stops this flapping poem being blown away.

A flicker of faith in man grew from that raid
where this shrapnel that I'm stroking now comes from,
when a German had strict orders but obeyed
some better, deeper instinct not to bomb
the houses down below and be humane.
Our house, thanks to that humane bombardier,
still stands; and those of Hasib mir Husain,
Mohammad Sidique Khan, Shehzad Tanweer.

INDEX OF FIRST LINES

So, Mister Moneybags, you're loaded? So? 84
So when she hears him clearing his throat 136
Solitaries? I wonder whether 95
Sorry they're shrivelled, your liberators' petals! 397
Sshhh! Ssshhh! though now shrapnel makes you shriek 398
Strawberries being bubbled in great vats 17

Thank God (the PM's pal) he's not resigned 401
Thanks for the haggis. Could you really spare 89
That summer it was Ibsen, Marx and Gide 152
That the *Peppered Moth* was white and now is dark 's 210
That they lasted only till the next high tide 169
The ambulance, the hearse, the auctioneers 155–6
The best wood to make chips with for our fire 181
The Blacksmith's quite a logical man 94
The Californians read the sky aloud 226–8
The Coast, the Coast, a hundred years ago! 34–7
The fire left to itself might smoulder weeks 196–7
The fireflies that women 108
The fire-patrol plane's tail-fins flash 237–42
The fosses where Caractacus fought Rome 207
The friendly fire from George Bush and his pards 398
The grace of Tullies eloquence doth excell 130
The heave and rattle of the freezer trucks 376
The hungry generations' new decree 57
The ignorant man does well to shut his trap 87
The judder of energy when I jump 175
The *Kourtaki* retsina that I buy 377–9
The mams pig-sick of oilstains in the wash 166
The 'miracle restore' you employ 102
The Ogling bottle cork with tasselled fez 149
The other day all thirty shillings' worth 15–16
The politician's elephantine conk's 88
The Pythia on her rock seat 428–36
The *shakuhachi*'s shattered, the *tatami*'s torn 387
The snake our cracker neighbour had to scotch 243–7
The struggle to preserve once spoken words 204
The tart passed round for sweet's so hot 100
The theft of fire, Man's worst bargain yet 91
The thing I drink 285–6
The two machines on Blackpool's Central Pier 157–9
The women all shout after me and mock 92

When you send out invitations, don't ask me 89
When you start sneering, it's not me 83
Where's the public good in what you write 88
Why is it, Lord, although I'm right 398–400
Why this desperation to move heaven and earth 80
Winter false dawns wake me: *thud! thud! thud!* 58
Winter's done his worst all round 418
With a son called Eros and a wife whose name 93
women all 90

Years later, with desperate need, I phone 385
Yes, I'm poor. What's wrong with that? 83
You brainless bastard! O you stupid runt! 87
You fat, failed ballet dancer's calves 53–4
You gave me your *Aurora* pen 349
You invite me out, but I can't attend 90
You might consider me more brazen if I diff 400–401
You serve me plonk, and you drink *reservé* 100
You swing past, a pong typhoon 101
You'd so brilliantly directed what I wrote 334
Your bed's got two wrong sides. Your life's all grouse 144–5
You're fucking Aufidia, your ex 101

Zeus isn't such a raving Casanova 92

INDEX OF TITLES